HUMAN RIGHTS AND COMMUNITY-LED DEVELOPMENT

This series publishes ground-breaking work on key topics in the area of global justice and human rights including democracy, gender, poverty, the environment, and just war. Books in the series are of broad interest to theorists working in politics, international relations, philosophy, and related disciplines.

Studies in Global Justice and Human Rights
Series Editor: Thom Brooks

Retheorising Statelessness
Kelly Staples
(July 2012)

Health Inequalities and Global Injustice
Patti Tamara Lenard and
Christine Straehle
(August 2012)

Rwanda and the Moral Obligation of Humanitarian Intervention
Joshua J. Kassner
(November 2012)

Institutions in Global Distributive Justice
András Miklós
(February 2013)

Human Rights from Community
Oche Onazi
(June 2013)

Immigration Justice
Peter W. Higgins
(August 2013)

The Morality of Peacekeeping
Daniel H. Levine
(December 2013)

International Development and Human Aid
Paulo Barcelos and Gabriele De Angelis
(September 2016)

www.edinburghuniversitypress.com/series/sgjhr

HUMAN RIGHTS AND COMMUNITY-LED DEVELOPMENT

LESSONS FROM TOSTAN

Ben Cislaghi

EDINBURGH
University Press

Edinburgh University Press is one of the leading university presses in the UK. We publish academic books and journals in our selected subject areas across the humanities and social sciences, combining cutting-edge scholarship with high editorial and production values to produce academic works of lasting importance. For more information visit our website: edinburghuniversitypress.com

Edinburgh University Press Ltd
The Tun – Holyrood Road,
12(2f) Jackson's Entry,
Edinburgh EH8 8PJ

Typeset in 11/13 Palatino LT Std by
IDSUK (DataConnection) Ltd

A CIP record for this book is available from the British Library

ISBN 978 1 4744 1979 6 (hardback)
ISBN 978 1 4744 1980 2 (webready PDF)
ISBN 978 1 4744 1981 9 (epub)

CONTENTS

ACKNOWLEDGEMENTS

Mi da yiɗno wiiɗee jarama sombonaaɓe sabu si wanaaŋo kaam ɓe ko
jewatmi toon waawaataŋo watde sabu ko kambe xolikam nguurnɗam
fulɓe kamɓe udditee kam bernɗe maɓɓe e natni kam nder suuɓe maɓe
nder saarende mi yiitoon besngu mawdo ele ko toon ŋjeyaami. Mi da
wiya jarama jom wuroŋgoo Abdulaay Ba e besngu muun sabu ko kambe
totikam suuɗu e gnaamɗe. Mi da wiya kadi jarama Aadama Kebe jan-
jinowoo toon sabu o tampi e liggede o naatŋi xeen judɗemum na feewi.
Si mi da gasŋa mi daa jarayoo Korka Soh Njaay saɓu kanko kaɗi ku
ŋeenam woono Senegal o xaaɗani tan xakunɗe ligoowoo e ligoonowoo
o natnikaam der besngumum ele ku mi biɗomako. Der dum ligeɗee na
wawno musɗe e miin esi na welno kam.

I owe many of the insights included in these pages to the fruitful dis-
cussions I had with many colleagues and co-authors. Diane Gillespie
(Emeritus, University of Washington Bothell), Lori Heise (LSHTM),
Gerry Mackie (University of California San Diego) and Fernando Ona
(Tufts University) have been an incredible source of inspiration. The
Tostan staff have been fantastic at all stages of my research; to them
goes all my gratitude. My brothers, Nicolò and Rocco, helped me find
the strength to put these pages together, albeit possibly unknowingly.
Julie has been an inspirational and caring partner, reading every page
and protecting me from the judgement of my most severe critic, myself.

My mother died as I was writing this book. I dedicate it to her living
memory, that shines warmly when I feel lost, and to my father, who
helped me in this time of sorrow.

ABBREVIATIONS

ACRWC	African Charter on the Rights and Welfare of the Child
CBA	cost–benefit analysis
CEDAW	Convention on the Elimination of All Forms of Discrimination against Women
CEP	Community Empowerment Program
CFM	child and forced marriage
CoP	community of practice
CRC	Convention on the Rights of the Child
DHRE	Decade for Human Rights Education
DHRET	Declaration on Human Rights Education and Training
FGC	female genital cutting
GII	Gender Inequality Index
HRE	human rights education
ICESCR	International Covenant on Economic, Social and Cultural Rights
ILO	International Labour Organization
IMF	International Monetary Fund
IPEC	International Programme on the Elimination of Child Labour
MDFD	Mouvement des Forces Démocratiques
NGO	non-governmental organisation
OHCHR	Office of the High Commissioner for Human Rights
UDHR	Universal Declaration of Human Rights
UN	United Nations
UNDP	United Nations Development Programme
UNECA	United Nations Economic Commission for Africa

UNESCO	United Nations Educational, Scientific and Cultural Organization
UNICEF	United Nations Children's Fund
WPHRE	World Programme for Human Rights Education

Chapter 1

INTRODUCTION

There is a way, it is argued here, to help people living in economically disadvantaged areas of Africa achieve together higher life standards; a way that empowers their self-help capacity and builds on their own cultural views of the world. Recent data show that the GDP of African countries is growing; they are managing to sell more of their resources and products. And yet, in spite of this outstanding economic performance, commodity-driven growth is not translating into social development (UNECA 2013). African countries might be getting richer, but their populations are not benefiting from it. Africa remains 'underdeveloped' and most of its people are not living better lives, they are not getting more educated, healthier or richer. The international economic system still expands, the world 'develops', but unevenly: the global economic growth enlarges the gap between rich and poor countries – rather than narrowing it (Bond 2006; Harvey 2005). Assuming – for now – that the richest human beings share a moral imperative of helping the poorest, what is to be done to help Africa?

Academics have argued in favour of foreign aid to fight African poverty (Banerjee and Duflo 2011; Sachs 2005) and against it (Easterly 2006; Moyo 2009). Scholars who write against aid (on the basis that aid overrides self-help capacity) have spoken in favour of increasing neo-liberal trade relations between African and non-African countries (Moyo 2009, for instance, saw in trading with China an opportunity for African development). Those who argue that aid is problematic are right. Part of the responsibility for the current living conditions of much of the African population is to be sought in the global institutions that guide world development. Since 1970, Bretton Woods institutions have fostered neo-liberal capitalistic economies aiming at stabilising macroeconomic conditions in the African countries. As noted by Ferguson (2005), this liberalisation process of African economies has instead resulted in the

1

opposite. Neo-liberal development has worsened governments' corruption and misbehaviour, and is stuck in a top-down approach where European and North American countries (over-represented within the organisations that lead the economic world order: the IMF, the World Bank and the UN Security Council) impose their perspectives on African development.

Development paradigms developed after World War II were based on a view of the world as striving towards the same direction: modernity. Modernity being a final goal, a holy land for everyone, some countries were considered in a higher position in the world rankings, more advanced than others. In this ranking, 'underdeveloped' countries (one could say, actively impoverishing countries) were not just below developed countries, they were behind, as if they were lying in some pre-modern state waiting to be promoted to the status of modern countries (once they had finally adopted, for instance, a free-trade system, solid infrastructure or an industry sector) (Ferguson 2005).

Westernisation, then, rather than development, where the underdeveloped countries – slowly – would join the club of the developed Western neo-liberal democracies to endorse Western values. Rather, modernity should be understood in terms of 'status', where all countries have the same recognition in the global social reality, without a ranking of some following others (Ferguson 2006; Sen 1999). In this book, I will show that the suggestion that there are many different, alternative possible 'modernities' unlocks a people-centred approach to development: from an approach to development that understands developing countries as 'not yet' countries, to one that helps people build the space to construct alternative characterisations of what is modern (Ferguson 2006). As Bond (2006) suggested, the global community needs a change in the relationship between Africa and richer countries and should change the way it understands development beyond simple statements of intention. As suggested at the end of this book, the understanding of development as Westernisation must leave room to one in which people are the protagonists, the subject of development programmes, rather than the objects of them. In this process, African civil societies should break the silence that gives consent to the capitalist dynamics keeping Africa in its dependency conditions and should challenge local ruling elites. As Bond (2006) recognised, however, to do so people in Africa must have space to raise their voice, to participate in the decision-making process.

In sum, if on the one hand aid is problematic because it can override people's self-help capacity, on the other hand, neo-liberal trade as such is not a viable alternative since neo-liberal reforms have aggravated (rather than improved) Africans' living standards. This book offers a possible alternative: a new understanding of development that gives to people the role of protagonists and the responsibility to lead the development process. You will find in this book, in particular, a development praxis based on human rights education (HRE), a praxis that neither undermines the capacity for self-help, nor rests on trade and neo-liberal policies all hopes for African development, but that empowers local actors to address issues of social justice that hinder their human development.

ORIGIN OF THIS BOOK AND RESEARCH METHODS

As I am writing this Introduction, a *Barbie in Africa* phenomenon is circulating on the internet: Barbie is ashamed of the poverty that ravages the entire African 'country' and wants to educate African children while taking selfies in the slums, dancing like a true 'native', and drinking coconut cocktails next to the swimming pool.[1] These satirical Barbie adventures (but why is not Ken also in them, I wonder?) are depicted in a set of provoking pictures and captions that mean to challenge the white saviour complex: the idea that Europeans and Americans should go on a mission to save Africa from the tragic conditions that poor Africans alone are obviously unable to improve. I do not intend to discuss here the extent to which this idea is narcissistic, imperialistic, unhelpful and also morally wrong – as essentially the entire book does that. But I have to confess that a little more than a decade ago I did feel that way; that is, motivated by the holy fire of the white saviour. An opportunity to reflect on the arrogance of similar approaches to development presented itself as I was working in Central and West Africa. There, it occurred to me that the programmes I was supervising were blind to people's cultures and needs; they seemed more concerned with addressing what donors wanted, than helping local populations address the problems that mattered to them. I thus began a quest to find culturally sensitive development implementations that helped people identify together their needs and collaborate to address them.

In 2009, I read about the work of the NGO Tostan. Since 1984, Tostan had been working on a human rights-based bottom-up approach to community empowerment that drew on existing local cultural values and that helped members of rural West African communities achieve their own goals together (www.tostan.org; Chapter 3). An impressive 99 per cent of Tostan's staff were from the same West African countries where they worked. It seemed a promising model worth investigating. That same year, I travelled to Senegal, where the NGO has its headquarters, and I talked to local staff members and previous participants in Tostan's three-year Community Empowerment Program (CEP). Most of the people I interviewed believed that the human rights education classes taking place in the first six months of the CEP were key to achieving the extraordinary community changes observed after the programme. My interest in Tostan grew exponentially: it seemed a perfect case to investigate how HRE could help people collaborate and lead their own human development.

In 2010, I started an ethnographic research in the small (200 people) Fulani village of *Galle Toubaaco* (the name is fictitious), in Central Senegal. At the time, the CEP was starting in the village. Between January and July 2010, I participated in Tostan's HRE classes as well as in the daily village life, taking notes of what I saw and heard. In addition to observing what happened in the classes and in the village at large, I interviewed about 20 men and women before, during and after the HRE classes. In this book, I call these 20 *informants* to distinguish them from the about 40 *participants* in the Tostan classes. Not all informants participated in the Tostan classes: among the 20 informants there were 10 men and 10 women, 10 under and 10 over age 25, 10 participating and 10 not participating in the HRE classes. I also interviewed local politicians, doctors, researchers and Tostan staff members. I analysed those data looking at what themes emerged from informants' descriptions of their experience and the changes they witnessed. I was particularly interested in the how the programme changed relations between men and women, public decision-making processes, and social practices that were inconsistent with international human rights standards. The next chapters reveal what informants said about their experience in the classes and their life in the village. Before that, I want to draw your attention to three useful things that this book provides and that are not commonly found in the literature.

THREE USEFUL THINGS THAT ARE IN THIS BOOK

1. A human development model tested over decades that has proven results.

Sen's 'development as freedom' was a Copernican revolution in the world of international development. Copernicus suggested scientists had the wrong belief about what was at the centre of the solar system, incidentally risking being burned alive for his ideas, as we know. Sen, meeting milder criticisms, suggested that development scholars and practitioners had the wrong beliefs about what should be at the centre of international development efforts. After his work, scholars and practitioners have become increasingly critical of measuring development by looking at national econometric indicators, and increasingly aware of the importance of exploring 'human' approaches to development. Sen (1999) – and Nussbaum (2011) after him – were especially influential in calling for development programmes that hold people's interests at their core; that is, programmes that aim at bettering people's lives in the direction these people want. Yet, a few questions on how this could be done remain. How can we help poor and disempowered people lead a life that is meaningful to them? How can we facilitate the conditions in which these people can voice out their aspirations for themselves and others in their community? How can we effectively support their collaboration to achieve those aspirations?

Sen (1999) and Nussbaum (2011) did not offer a practical model for their theoretical work, though they suggested that education has a central role to play in human development. Drawing on their theories, Appadurai (2004) specified that education should be part of human development programmes because it can foster poor and uneducated people's 'capacity to aspire', by engaging them in imagining alternative courses of action they would not experience in daily life. However, little to nothing is said in the work of these authors about the pedagogical processes in which participants should be engaged to unlock their capacity to aspire and further their human development (Walker and Unterhalter 2010). This book offers what is largely missing in the literature: a practical model of human development paired with an analysis of how and why this model works, grounded in an ethnographic exploration of the cultural understandings of the rural West African community in which the programme was carried out.

2. A theoretical and practical understanding of how human rights education can contribute to human development.

Tostan's programme makes great use of HRE. Scholars in the field of HRE have argued that HRE resulted in the past in social change and community empowerment. Various authors analysed HRE programmes as having had an impact on participants' behaviours and attitudes (Bajaj 2011; Bajaj et al. 2016; Claude and Andreopoulos 1997;

Koenig 2001; Tibbits 2002). However, little is offered in the relevant literature about what actually happens in the HRE classes that motivates change in the localities where those classes are implemented. In particular, nobody has, so far, offered rigorous ethnographic evidence revealing the causal pathways around HRE that lead to a change in how people think and act. This book fills the gap in HRE literature by explaining the class dynamics by which educational strategies and curriculum generate new behavioural possibilities for learners and their own community. In doing so, I also offer a model to explain how the critical learning of human rights can affect social change. By connecting social norm theory, human development theories, schema theory and situated learning theory, this book illustrates a conceptual framework where those models integrate with and uphold each other.

The book looks at the ways in which HRE can contribute to a process of social change and foster human development. In particular, it examines how HRE (1) increased people's participation in the decision-making process, (2) contributed to creating more equitable gender roles and relations, and (3) helped people renegotiate existing human rights-incoherent social practices.

3. A theory of how cultural understandings and social norms can hinder or accelerate social change for human development.

Social change is a phenomenon naturally occurring in all human societies. Think of the ways in which our grandparents used to dress, find a partner, travel, or work; while many social features might have remained stable, others have dramatically changed since then. In what ways can people living in rural Africa be protagonists of that change, deliberate democratically on it, and give it direction so that social practices that are unjust and hinder people's human development are identified, revised and possibly abandoned? Sen (1999) argued that democratic participation in the decision-making process of a community is a necessary precondition for community members to challenge and renegotiate practices and norms that hinder their human development. However, those social norms and practices can keep some people from participating in the decision-making process and thus limit the community's human development. Traditional social norms and practices can protect themselves from being changed by excluding from the decisional process those who have an interest in changing them. Imagine that by tradition, for instance, 'people taller than x' (Px) are excluded from the decision-making process of their community. The social change that *Px* might want to implement, when asked to envision one, could be a more equal participation in decision-making. *Px* cannot exercise their democratic power, though, due to the same norm they might aspire to change. Here is an example of how this works in practice: in November 2006, members of parliament in the Maldives had to vote on a proposal asking to introduce a female quota that would reduce gender disparity among them. In parliament there were 6 female MPs and 44 male MPs. The parliament rejected the proposal with about 44 votes against and 6 in favour (Fulu and Miedema 2015). In the Maldivian case, *Px* are women, and they cannot change local decision-making processes (to make them more egalitarian) as they do not have access to those processes in the first place. In other words, human development can be delayed or hindered by power processes that protect themselves from changing and that reproduce the social status quo. Thus, this book asks: *Who has access to and participates in the decision-making process of a given community (before and after an HRE programme)?*

Women have a strategic role to play in their communities as positive agents of social change (Nussbaum 2000; Sen 1999). Both the feminist literature recalled by human development theory and the relevant reports written by practitioners in the field suggest that different participation in decision-making has to be understood primarily in terms of gender (see, for instance, Kevane 2004; UNDP 2010). Gender roles and relations have significant impact on the way different community members participate in decision-making. This book explores if HRE impacts on the way participants understand gender roles and relations in their community and the effect that possible shifts in their understandings might have on their capability to participate in the decision-making process. Before we can understand how people make decisions together, we should ask: *How do participants in an HRE programme understand gender roles and relations in their community (before and after an HRE programme)?* For analytical purposes, I first looked at how community members made sense of gender roles and relations and how they impacted on decision-making.

The two questions given above take into account a change in community members' participation in decision-making and gender roles and relations. Human rights knowledge might impact on the way participants understand their daily life beyond these two aspects. If HRE is proven capable, for example, of creating a space to discuss local social practices and norms, then that space might be used to redraft local social behaviours, practices and norms more consistent with human rights. The book therefore analyses participants' understanding of certain local human rights-inconsistent practices (if any at all are in place) before and after the programme and their possible engagement in renegotiating them. Thus, a third question populates this study: *What other human rights-relevant social practices do participants in an HRE programme come to understand as harmful and how do participants promote their change in the community?*

As this book unfolds, it explores the possible links between human rights education and social change. In particular, it investigates if and how participants in an HRE programme come to challenge human rights-inconsistent local social norms and foster both their human development and the empowerment of their entire community.

PART I SOME USEFUL CONCEPTS TO RETHINK DEVELOPMENT PRACTICES

Research on human development and human rights education raises a series of issues around the cross-cultural legitimacy of human rights education programmes, and the cognitive and social processes that those programmes aim to facilitate. Chapter 2 starts by engaging with the argument that human rights are a tool for Western cultural imperialism. If human rights are a product of the Western culture (whatever that is), can human rights education programmes be legitimately implemented in the global south? Chapter 2 discusses how Freirian nonformal education strategies have the potential of translating human rights into a culturally relevant framework that people can use to critically look at their traditions and practices, helping them to visualise changes in the status quo. Those changes require new individual and collective understandings and actions. I use social norms theory to investigate the processes through which social practices are formed and change, and cognitivist schema theory to reveal how experience shapes individual beliefs and how new experiences can challenge those beliefs. Cognitivist schema theory helps understand how a community member can include new roles and behaviours that were considered exceptions within the conceptual horizon of what is 'normal', and social norms theory adds an understanding of the social dynamics through which community members can renegotiate together those public behaviours that they might support individually.

A social change process spurring out of the HRE classes, one would reasonably think, should start from class participants. To understand how class dynamics strengthened relations among participants and helped them act together as a group, I looked at the work of Lave and Wenger (1991), who studied the processes by which people coordinate their actions in a group, or what they called a Community of Practice (CoP). Their work seemed particularly relevant, as members in a CoP share the same domain of interest (achieving change in the village) and aim at gaining competences that distinguish them from other people (learning about human rights). This toolkit of useful concepts ends by reviewing concepts of gender and power relations as they might influence social change and the relations between class participants and the rest of the community.

In Chapter 3, the reader will find some important background information on the wider context of this research: the emergence of the human rights discourse in Senegal; the contextual factors characterising the Senegalese society (analysing gender roles and relations, decision-making processes and human rights challenges); the structure of NGO and its educational programme in Senegal; and the characteristics of the ethnic group that was studied by the research (the Fulɓe[2]), with its moral values and code of conduct.

PART II THE PROGRAMME IN ACTION

The second part of the book draws on the ethnographic evidence to explore the changes that took place in the community that participated in Tostan's HRE programme. In particular, Chapters 4, 5 and 6 show how informants made sense of gender roles and relations, access to decision-making and other human rights-inconsistent social practices before and after the HRE programme. Chapter 4 describes Galle Toubaaco before the Tostan programme, looking in particular at how community members understood gender, access to decision-making and other relevant social norms before the programme. I found gendered power relations that contributed to fostering traditional social norms hindering women's participation in decision-making processes. The same social norms, dialectically, locked access to those resources and reproduced a social status quo that reiterated a gender-uneven power structure. Amongst other social practices, two in particular had a negative impact on the life of community members in human rights terms: child and forced marriages and excessive child labour. These practices were held in place by the (limited) gain that members obtained in adhering to them. Informants could conceptualise the limited nature of that gain; however, they could not imagine different courses of action that would grant greater common gain.

Chapter 5 offers a critical understanding of the Tostan programme as carried out in Galle Toubaaco. The chapter explains in detail who delivered the classes and who participated in them and with what expectations. It also engages in detail with the curriculum of the classes, highlighting its different aspects and characteristics, linking human rights and Freirian problem-posing education. This includes an understanding of the different experiential learning strategies adopted and of how they allowed participants to ground the abstract human rights knowledge into their concrete daily life. The chapter offers an insight into the classes, giving an understanding of their dynamics and analysing how participating made sense of the participants' experience in class. It grounds in the empirical analysis of Tostan's pedagogy and curriculum the discussion of the shift in the way informants made sense of their community after the programme, as discussed in Chapter 6.

Chapter 6 engages critically with the analysis of the data collected during and after the programme, analysing a shift in informants' attitudes and behaviours towards gender roles and relations, participation in decision-making and other human rights-inconsistent social norms. Male and female informants' outlook towards women changed. Informants began to see women as capable of leadership and problem-solving skills. A new category emerged from informants' narratives, that of the *now-women* (a label grounded in participants' definitions): a new understanding of women that included a larger toolkit of freedoms and capabilities.

Access to decision-making also changed. Women started participating in village assemblies more than before the HRE programme. Young women, in particular, participated more. Finally, the large majority of the informants reported their intention of abandoning the practice of child and forced marriages. Due to the time constraints of the research, it was impossible to analyse how participants worked to gather consensus over the abandonment of those practices that they came to understand as harmful in class. However, there is evidence of a process of social change in action grounded in the data that showed a noticeable shift in participants' attitudes and knowledge, and some changes in their behaviour beyond simple statements of intentions.

PART III HELPFUL DEVELOPMENT

Chapter 7 analyses the role of the programme in creating a space where gender segregation could be overcome, where men and women could sit and talk together. Gender roles that limited contact between members of different genders were problematised in the class. Men and women were invited by the facilitator to discuss together how their daily behaviour could be understood in human rights terms. The chapter shows that participants developed new capabilities that allowed them to export their new understandings out of the class: they learnt to affiliate together to influence their social and political environment. They could frame new understandings of local social norms and invisible power relations (and share them with the rest of the community) because the experience of each other had in class diverged from their daily experience. Those new experiences influenced their perspective on local behaviours and, more widely, how they understood their community. The HRE programme helped them renegotiate local social norms that were limiting their empowerment, and made them protagonists of the life of their communities, where they could promote human rights-consistent social practices. In doing so, participants became protagonists of their human development.

Chapter 8, finally, looks at a few more promising interventions, offering a comparative analysis of their approach, field methods and results. This comparative analysis, paired with a deep understanding of the Tostan programme developed in the book, uncovers future action and research trajectories that can help economically disadvantaged populations achieve their goals in ways that respect their cultural shared understandings of the world.

Part I

Some Useful Concepts to Rethink Development Practices

Chapter 2

RETHINKING DEVELOPMENT INTERVENTIONS: POTENTIAL AND CHALLENGES OF HUMAN RIGHTS EDUCATION

INTRODUCTION

Exploring the role that human rights education might play in fostering community development presents four key challenges. The first relates to the applicability of HRE in non-Western contexts and takes into account the either universal or relative nature of human rights. If human rights have a Western (allow me to use the word for the moment) origin, and many think they do, how can they be used in non-Western contexts? I argue that there is a way of contextualising, 'vernacularising', human rights that justifies their use in the non-Western world. That leads to the second challenge (treated in the second section of this chapter): how can human rights be contextualised then? What processes can help people analyse human rights critically, and what role do those processes play in helping people collaborate for their collective development? I discuss how human rights education can help people use human rights critically to engage in a generative dialogue about the problems that matter to them, and how that can help them foster their collective 'development'. This raises a question about what development paradigm human rights education is contributing towards, the third challenge brought up in this chapter. I suggest that, while human development is an evident framework for transformative human rights education, 'indirect' human development is a more appropriate term for it, as human rights education enhances people's self-help capacity to achieve goals that matter to them, if necessary by challenging the socio-cultural status quo that hinders their success.

The last section gives an understanding of the forces contributing to sustaining an unjust social status quo. In particular, it looks at the role of social norms, cognitive schemas, gender roles and power relations. Social behaviours are regulated by social norms learnt by participation

15

in the life of the community. Alternative experiences can unlock diverging understandings of social relations that can in turn affect local social norms, thereby changing them. HRE then should support participants in the process of renegotiation of local social behaviours with their community by giving them the tools to transform new individual and social understandings into action. Community members can renegotiate social practices by participating in the decision-making processes available in the family and the community. The dynamics that grant different human beings with variable influence in decision-making processes are dynamics of power. However, those dynamics, as suggested by the literature reviewed in this chapter, are strongly shaped by the gender roles and relations that regulate behavioural expectations of 'normality'. The chapter, then, studies the role of gender in distributing to men and women different possibilities of social action by taking into consideration a feminist analysis of gender roles, division of labour and oppression. Finally, it frames a theory to guide the analysis of power relations within human beings that explains reasons for quiescence with social inequality and is compatible with the system of theories provided in this conceptual framework.

Conclusions engage with the argument brought forward throughout the chapter; that is, that nonformal human rights education can be used as a tool for human development in the non-Western world because it can help participants challenge local social norms and practices hindering their freedoms and the development of their capabilities. Developing new meanings of local actions and behaviours, community members develop the capacity to aspire, the ability to imagine a future that diverges from a repetition of the past.

BRINGING INTERNATIONAL HUMAN RIGHTS INTO LOCAL CONTEXTS

The debate on the universality of human rights is key for HRE. It undermines the rationale for the applicability of HRE programmes. The issue is not one with an easy solution, as the idea that human beings have personal entitlements emerged from the events of the last five centuries of European and North American history. In particular, the shift from objective rights to subjective natural rights took place in Europe during the 15th century and set the rational background for the emergence of individual human entitlements (Freeman 2002). Enlightenment's rationalism secularised the tradition of natural law, rendering human reason sovereign.

In the 18th century, key events such as the Reformation (with its violent consequences), the new social role of the emerging bourgeoisie and the related new social mobility (following the end of a static monarchic social order) moulded the principles of equality and dignity that laid the foundation of modern human rights (Beitz 2009; Dalacoura 1998; Donnelly 2003). In the years immediately before and after 1789, the European bourgeoisie began demanding equal social recognition from the aristocratic powers, claiming that human nature (and not census) was the only reasonable justification for social dignity. The same arguments were then used by members of other 'lower' social groups to request social recognition, economic consideration and political participation; in other words, the French Revolution created the conditions to demand equality (*egalité*) for all human beings (Freeman 2002).

Centuries later, when the idea of human natural equality had already been motivating revolutionary political movements throughout the Western world, the aftermath of World War II prioritised onto the international political agenda the urgency to ensure equal human dignity to all human beings. The newly created United Nations appointed Eleanor Roosevelt to preside over the commission that would draft the Universal Declaration of Human Rights (UDHR). The emergence of human rights has been understood by some authors as the product of 'the West' (see, for instance, Donnelly 2003). The contradictions of adopting a similar history of human rights in the wider framework of HRE have been studied by Spring (2000), who warned that it would result in fostering culturally imperialistic education. Spring (2000) argued that the risk of presenting the history of human rights as such is that it would influence students in the non-Western world, generating a sense of devotion and gratitude for 'the West' that strove to liberate human beings from fear and oppression. There is therefore a challenge in arguing – as I intend to do here – that although human rights emerged following particular events occurring mainly in Europe, they can be used universally as a tool for community empowerment in the 'non-Western' world.

One might be tempted to argue that human rights are not a Western product, but the result of a global deliberation. Some authors have highlighted, for instance, that many of the countries that existed in 1946 were invited to contribute to the drafting of the UDHR (Ramcharan 2000; Waltz 2001). Others have insisted on the fact that the commission that received the task of drafting the UDHR was composed of 17 members of different countries (including the Vice Chair Dr Chang from China and the Rapporteur Charles Malik from Lebanon) (McFarland 2008; United

Nations 2008). Scholars argued that the heterogeneity of this group contributed to a genuinely democratic and 'multi-cultural' drafting of the UDHR, that would be further demonstrated by its adoption by 20 Latin American States and 13 'non-Western' countries (Donnelly 2000; McFarland 2008; Ramcharan 2000; Waltz 2001). I do not think any of these is a strong argument. As Mutua (2007) suggested, when the UDHR was drafted right after World War II, the United Nations were culturally dominated by the USA and some other European countries that imposed their views on human rights on the rest of the world. Besides, when the General Assembly (GA) was asked to vote on the adoption of the UDHR, various African and Asian states were still European colonies and therefore acted as they were asked to (Mutua 1996). Even so, however, resistance to the adoption of human rights was reported during the drafting process, and recent history shows that certain non-Western states have kept that resistance active (Arslan 1999; Brown and Bjawi-Levine 2002; Franck 2001; Goodhart 2003; Manglapus 1978; Pollis and Schwab 1979).

One cannot argue for the universal applicability of human rights by dismissing the role played by Western countries in the human rights debate, both due to the historical background that sparked the momentum for their creation and to the 1946 socio-political world order. But then, what else is there to argue for the universal applicability of human rights? Some think that nothing remains, that is, that the human rights ideology should not be brought into non-Western countries. Similar doubts have been raised since the first draft of the UDHR. At the time when the UDHR was still being drafted, the American Anthropological Association (1947) condemned the attempt to find international norms regulating behaviour, due to the differences amongst human cultures on standards and values, and on ideas of what is right and wrong. Many other cultural relativists have claimed in the last 60 years that human rights embody a form of Western imperialism, arguing that cultures cannot be judged from the outside, that is, by members of another culture (Baxi 1998; Brown and Bjawi-Levine 2002; Goodhart 2003; Messer 1993; Pollis and Schwab 1979).

The cultural relativist position is not strong either. There are at least three arguments against cultural relativism that could be used to defend the universal applicability of human rights while acknowledging the impact of Europe and North America in drafting them. First, it is not very clear what 'culture' is: in the last two decades, anthropology scholars have elaborated culture as a contested, fluid and unbounded term, produced through hybridisation and creolisation (Abu-Lughod 1991; Appadurai 1986; Merry 2006; Preis 1996; Zechenter 1997). There are no pure unchangeable cultural values that have not been exposed to reconsideration through contamination with other traditions. Cultures, if something with this name exists at all, are not moral strongholds. They are markets or public squares where the leading values are continuously bargained. The term culture itself is a contested and ambiguous one. Terms such as social practices or behavioural expectations are more appropriate to define a dynamic set of local customs and values shaping personal beliefs and attitudes. For the same reason, the present research avoids using the term culture as much as possible when referring to local tenets and behaviours.

Second, it is a plain fact that ideas and norms can be used outside their context of origin. The concept of individual rights has a Roman origin; however, it is nowadays used everywhere indistinctly. It is incomprehensible why then the concept of *human* rights cannot be used in other places in the world as already happens, for instance, with Marxism, democracy or Christianity; or again with gun powder, coffee or mobile phones (Donnelly 1984, 2000, 2003; Nussbaum 1999, 2000). Nussbaum summarised this idea by using Aristotelian wit: 'in general, people seek not the way of their ancestors, but the good' (2000: 49).

Third, there is nothing inherently 'Western' in the values expressed by human rights; from ancient Greece to the crusades and World War II, the so-called West has given proof of being capable of inhuman actions and degrading treatments towards human beings; there is nothing exclusively European or North American in such values as tolerance and respect (Franck 2001). Rather, the values that are behind the UDHR and uphold those rights – the constituent elements of the concept of human rights – are found in different traditions, places and times of human history, although in various forms: being channelled within either religious commandments, local jurisprudence, ethical views or secular principles (Arab Institute for Human Rights 2002; Aziz 1999; Keown 1995; Kuschel and Küng 1993; Mahabal 2005; Murithi 2007; Nussbaum 2011; Sen 1999).

In the contemporary human rights debate, then, conflict and tensions over human rights mainly involve the political objectives of the actors opposing their applicability. Since human rights have become increasingly more important in defining what constitutes the modern statehood, international human rights norms have essentially put limits on national sovereignty. Concerns with human rights hence were mainly expressed by states and governments as duty bearers, rather than by the people entitled to those rights (Bierkester and Weber 1996; Risse et al. 1999).

There is a third position, in between the two extremes that human rights are universal because they are the result of a global awakening, and that they are relative because they are a Western product. This third position argues that human rights have applicability in non-Western contexts when the members of those communities are given the means to translate human rights within their own set of social values that regulate behaviour between human beings. The solution to the contradiction between their origin and their applicability lies in the use that is made of human rights. Human rights should not be understood solely as international norms to be enforced, then, but as paradigms resonating with traditional values that can be converted into social actions. When analysing the clash between global standards of social justice and local practices, human rights should be understood in daily life situations and in specific contexts, rather than in the abstract world of jurisprudence. International norms of human rights are general goals, while the values on which they are built are to be understood in situated contexts where the insiders, the local social actors, make sense of the meaning of those values (Cislaghi 2016; Preis 1996).

Human rights, thus, have the potential of being contextualised in a particular setting and translated into traditional values, local justice and social action. Namely, human rights can be 'vernacularised' (Merry 2006) by empowering social actors to explore the relevance of the human rights framework for their own lives, grounding it within local social behaviours and understandings. Human rights must be discussed and analysed at the grassroots level, to give people the opportunity to understand possible contacts between human rights and their local behavioural framework, to vernacularise the former on the latter. This vernacularisation does not include changing the fundamental meaning of human rights; rather, it adds a new interpretation of relationships and social structures that do not displace the existing ones. For domestic human rights conditions to be improved, domestic actors have to internalise human rights norms through a process of socialisation that packs human rights in familiar terms and links them with symbols or images (Merry 2006; Risse et al. 1999). When grounded in local understandings of the world, human rights can contribute to sparking new social behaviours and actions, by developing visions and aspirations that the local social status quo kept beyond the imaginative horizon (Appadurai 2004; Merry 2006). This process of vernacularisation, where members of local communities reframe human rights critically in local terms, is one of the tasks of human rights education and its success can be strongly conditioned by the educational approach adopted.

A NONFORMAL PROBLEM-POSING APPROACH TO HUMAN RIGHTS EDUCATION

Human rights education (HRE) offers practitioners a model to help people develop local understandings of international human rights. However, its nature is problematic. International human rights law has an authoritative potential that educators might impose over their students, without creating space for genuine dialogue that would facilitate a vernacularisation of those rights and a critical analysis of the local social reality. HRE becomes thus a challenging topic since educators must avoid implementing it by using authoritative educational models that might be as oppressive as the social reality that HRE can potentially help participants to unveil. Hence, it is fundamental to analyse which educational approach best suits the progressive nature of HRE.

The discussion about the best approach for HRE is linked to what definition of HRE one adopts. The history of HRE is connected to that of human rights from 1945 onwards. Both the UN Charter and the UDHR endorsed the necessity of HRE in the aftermath of World War II, when education came to be understood as a field of political action and research (Suárez and Ramirez 2004). However, historically there has been little consensus among scholars on the definition of HRE with regard to its content, approach and setting (Bajaj et al. 2016; Best 2002; Bigelow and Peterson 2002; Cardenas 2005; Flowers et al. 2007; Hornberg 2002; Lohrenscheit 2002; McQuoid-Mason et al. 1991; Morsink 1999; Osler and Starkey 1996; Ray 1994; Spring 2000; Starkey 1991a, 1991b; Suárez 2007; Tibbits 2002; Tomaševski 2001; UNESCO 1974; Weinbrenner and Fritzsche 1993). Yet, in the first human rights treaties, its definition is blurred and ambiguous. In the preamble to the UDHR, education is presented as a fundamental tool to promote respect for the rights of the Declaration, which would seem to suggest the need of HRE. Further on, Article 26(2) sets up the basis for HRE, stating that:

> Education should be directed to the full development of the human personality and to the strengthening of respect for human rights and fundamental freedoms. It shall promote understanding, tolerance and friendship among all nations, racial or religious groups [. . .] (United Nations 1948: Art. 26(2))

In more recent times, the United Nations has drafted two definitions of HRE, the first within the framework of the Decade for Human Rights Education (DHRE: 1995–2004) and the second for the World Programme for Human Rights Education (WPHRE: 2005–ongoing). Both are, however, quite open to debate since they define HRE quite generally as all efforts aimed at building a universal culture of human rights through *knowledge, skills* and *attitudes* (OHCHR 1998, 2006).

During the implementation phases of the DHRE (and then of the WPHRE, still ongoing), there has been a relatively abundant debate between different actors on the nature of HRE. In the last two decades, governments, academics and practitioners have come to very different understandings of what HRE is. In the framework of the DHRE, governments have claimed to mould local curricula with the learning of human rights and human rights conventions. Most countries that reported to the OHCHR on their activities in the framework of the DHRE associated HRE exclusively with students' gaining of knowledge on human rights (OHCHR 1998, 2003). While governments seem to have associated – at least in the past – HRE with teaching about human rights, academics, researchers and practitioners in the field have come to agree in the same years that HRE should not be limited to teaching but should at the same time aim to foster positive attitudes towards human rights (see, for instance, Amnesty International 1996; Lohrenscheit 2002; OHCHR 2003, 2006; Starkey 1991a; Tibbits 2002; UNESCO 2003). There are at least two possible explanations for this gap. The first is that policy-makers might have made the minimum uncritical efforts to guarantee an application of a limited interpretation of their citizens' rights (similarly to what happened for the application of the right to education in the analysis made by McCowan 2011). The other possibility is that there is (or there has been) a gap in the understanding of the governments and other actors that might undermine the role of HRE within national school curricula.

Possibly aware of this issue, the UN recently decided to draft a piece of international jurisprudence that could help different stakeholders make sense of what HRE is and how it should be implemented. In 2007, the Human Rights Council of the UN established an Advisory Committee to draft a Declaration on Human Rights Education and Training (DHRET), adopted by the General Assembly on 19 December 2011 (OHCHR 2011). The declaration understands HRE as encompassing education *about*, *through* and *for* human rights. HRE should thus aim at raising awareness on human rights principles, developing a universal culture of human rights, pursuing the effective realisation of all human rights, ensuring equal opportunities, and contributing to the prevention of human rights violations and abuses. The declaration emphasises that HRE should embrace, enrich and draw inspiration from 'the diversity of civilisations, religions, culture and traditions of different countries' (United Nations 2011b: Art. 5(3)). In spite of this view on the need to contextualise HRE, though, there is no mention in the declaration of the empowering and liberating effect that HRE can have at the grassroots level, beyond the creation of a universal culture of human rights. The declaration seems to suggest that HRE should aim at shaping a Human Rights world, where human rights overlap with other dominant cultures and become a globalised *doxa*.

Rather, HRE should aim at empowering people to become active members of a world where they can contribute to interpreting human rights. Namely, HRE should not foster a global cultural dictatorship of human rights; it should give to world citizens the means to challenge human rights through critical thinking and possibly (but not necessarily) accepting and interpreting them within local meanings and understandings. HRE should in sum be a liberating process; it should allow people to look critically at their world and the world (Bajaj 2011; Bajaj et al. 2016; Spring 2000). As analysed by Gerber (2011), the DHRET neither offers a path of implementation, nor does it suggest which educational approach would better suit the fulfilment of HRE goals. Therefore, the understanding of which pedagogical approach could better facilitate participants' consideration and negotiation of their local reality must be directed towards educational theories that have provided similar frameworks.

Historically, there has been a great debate on the relationship between students and teachers and on the role that the curriculum should play in that relationship. Two main paradigms (or metaphors) of this educational relationship exist: I call the first the authoritative model and the second the progressive model. In the authoritative model, the educational authority (the teacher) teaches passive students what the 'right' answers are. The process mostly happens in a credential-based setting where students' knowledge is examined by checking the appropriateness of their answer against what has been transmitted to them. In this model, some people, the *knows*, possess a knowledge that they share with some others through teaching, the *know-nots* (Sfard 1998). This model has been associated with a formal setting (the school) (Beckett and Hager 2002; Colley et al. 2002; Eraut 2000) and has been widely criticised for having limited potential to awaken students' creative imagination by those scholars (see below) who addressed the issue of how education should help students find their own answers to the problem posed.

The second, progressive model argues that knowledge is produced by the teachers and the students together. They engage in a dialogic participatory process in which the authority is in neither the curriculum nor the teacher, but is in the process that engages students and teachers in the investigatory dialogue. This model has its roots in the Socratic maieutics that engaged people in learning through dialogue, helping them to think for themselves, to find their own solutions (Ellerman 2006; Nussbaum 1997).

Socrates' pedagogy activated students' own energies in solving problems, rather than transmitting truth to them: Socrates was not interested in a process that would help fill a passive mind with store of knowledge; he wanted to facilitate the circumstances that would eventually help students realise what they could change, produce, create (Coburn 1968). Rousseau critiqued the authoritative model, arguing that transformative processes cannot be initiated by teaching students to respond as the teacher wants in order to escape punishment or extort reward (Rousseau [1762] 1979). Rousseau's Romantic reaction to the educational paradigms spurred during the Enlightenment period found a valid metaphor in Abrams's (1971) metaphor of the mirror and the lamp. The authoritative-mirror model is a narcissistic act of the teacher, an act of *amour-de-soi* in which the teacher has a precise idea of how the student should be and strives to change him or her. In the progressive-lamp model, the teacher's *amour-propre* allows an inversion of the educational process, with the teacher ready to learn from the students (Rousseau [1762] 1979).

More recently, two authors have widely contributed to an understanding of what meaning should be given to education in the framework of the progressive approach: John Dewey and Paulo Freire. Dewey ([1916] 1966) was very critical of the authoritative method because of its limited transformative potential. In Dewey's understanding of active learning, students would develop their own perspective on the world, owning the results of what they produced: the development of their personality. The role of the teacher, then, is to change the structural conditions where the educational relationship happens so that students have the opportunity to become able to independently help themselves. Even a benevolent teacher approaching education authoritatively would oppress students by forcing their liberation, by violating their autonomy, fundamental in their process of self-realisation (Dewey [1916] 1966; Dewey and Tufts 1908).

Amongst the various authors that dealt with the problems of progressive education, Freire (1970) is the one who most explicitly dealt with power relations, framing the work of the educator as facilitating a process of liberation from oppression of hegemonic social powers. Dewey also dealt with political issues, especially in discussing how education can contribute to the quality of democracy that people enjoy, but he did not provide an analysis of the power relations involved in the educational process as clearly and powerfully as Freire did. Freire (1970, 1973, 1995) engaged very critically with authoritative models (in his words, 'transmission models') of education that aim at making people fit in the world, rather than giving them the means to change it. His critique was driven by the idea that authoritative approaches serve the purpose of reproduction of the existing cultural hegemony. He argued that similar 'banking' approaches to education – that 'deposit' knowledge in the students' heads – create automatons rather than full human beings; they regulate the way students will see the world so that they will then fit into the system, after having been passively imposed upon with what they need to adapt themselves to the world. Rather than unleashing participants' potential to change their social reality, banking education contributes to the reproduction of both the status quo that generates it and its power structures, and serves the narcissistic purposes of the teachers (who, considering the students to be absolutely ignorant, justify their own existence in filling that void of knowledge) (Freire 1995).

Freire suggested that students should instead be confronted with the social problems that matter in their local reality. In 'problem-posing education' (as Freire called it), the teacher waives the narcissistic role of truth-provider and becomes an educator who both allows students to break taboos and name problems, and facilitates critical argumentation, debate and conversations. When the world appears to those who name it as a problem, Freire argued, it requires of them a new name, a solution. The educator and the students together challenge those 'limit-situations', as Freire (1970) calls them – obstacles to the realisation of full human beings that are suddenly understood by individuals as such – that emerge from a critical analysis of the social reality, and find in the world new ideas, concepts, values and hopes.

In this process, the role of the educator is critical. Educators must facilitate the discovery, targeting and reaching of internal aims, of participants' goals. To do so, they must accept their role of learners; to

Freire, humility and ability to listen are fundamental traits of a problem-posing educator and those are intrinsically linked to the facilitator understanding himself or herself as a learner in the interaction with the participants. The educator's task is challenging, because the oppressed tend to step back and ask the educator to give them answers; they feel that their role is that of listeners, waiting to be guided, to be told what to do to get rid of their oppression. The class generates a tension of power that might tempt the educator to seek self-realisation by instructing students, rather than engaging in a dialogue with them. Educators must resist that temptation, Freire argued, and facilitate the passage from naïve to critical thinking, increasing participants' ability to problematise the challenges of their times (Freire 1973). Critical thinking is immersed in temporality, in the actions that it generates in the community that produces it by perceiving reality as a process, as transformation, rather than as a static entity that cannot change. The process is liberating and revolutionary at the same time.

Liberating problem-posing education allows people to imagine new possible courses of action and new realities that diverge from the consolidated social status quo. Rather than being a process of accommodating the future to the past, education has the power to utilise the past as a resource to develop the future, reconstructing past experiences and conceiving them differently for the future. That critical experience of alternative courses of action is exactly the task of a liberating problem-posing education: it unites the people to cooperate against their oppression (which is not necessarily incarnated in one or more persons, but could be represented by structural socio-economic, political, essential or existential conditions) (Freire 1970).

Boal (1979, 1995) further developed Freire's work and structured a set of practical pedagogical techniques called the 'theatre of the oppressed'. His pedagogy has been widely used by development practitioners to foster community empowerment (Espskamp 2006). The purpose of Boal's theatre is to promote social change by questioning the current status quo. The theatre of the oppressed does so by overcoming the divide between actors and audience: the audience act and discuss what happens on the scene (Meisek 2004). Through theatre, in their quality of simple actors, participants are free of their daily social roles and can address responsibilities towards other community members without fear of any retaliation. In accusing men of domestic violence on the stage, for instance, an actress is asked to do so in the role she is playing but, at the same time, both opens up the floor to the discussion of that practice and shows to the community that she has the ability to name responsibilities. Other techniques of a Freirian pedagogy include debates in small groups, creative drawings, role-playing games where participants swap social roles, and others (see, for instance, Mayo 1999).

Problem-posing pedagogy allows participants to share with other class members feelings and individual perspectives that would not emerge publicly in normal life and that can give voice to silent oppressions: feelings and perspectives that participants have never come to understand as such or that are social taboos. Freire (1970, 1973), in sum, argued that problem-posing education has the potential to liberate people from the social oppression of the status quo that the current educational system – 'conservative education' – perpetuates by shaping oppressive relations of power. Conservative education merely replicates patterns of knowledge to protect the present status quo in the future. The future fades out of the horizon, disguised as a mere reappearance of a new past entrenched in the same relations of power (Freire 1970, 1973).

Cultural anthropology comes to the assistance of problem-posing education in giving a further understanding of the relation between existent cultural hegemonies and uneducated oppressed people's lack of capability to imagine different realities and work towards their implementation. Appadurai (2004) has called the capacity to bring the future back into its place the capacity to aspire. His theory resonates with Freire's in suggesting that education can challenge an oppressing social status quo. According to Appadurai, the 'poor', the economically disadvantaged, lack capacity to exercise their voice and debate. Thus, they strive to contribute to decisions affecting collective social life and cannot but subscribe to norms that exacerbate their inequality. Their voice is muted by cultural regimes, since they do not possess the educational background to exercise the capacity to engage social, political and economic issues in terms of norms, doctrines and ideologies. They struggle to strengthen their capacity to change the dynamics of consensus in their social worlds. The poor, in the terms of Appadurai (the oppressed, as Freire would call them), cannot aspire to an alternative life because they do not possess the capability to imagine it. While rich people enjoy a wider field of possible experiences and can more easily understand the links between a large range of means and ends, those who have less are in a worse position to explore different realities, since they lack the material goods and the immediate opportunities to learn how to produce 'justifications, narratives, metaphors, and pathways through which bundles of goods and services are actually tied to wider social scenes or context' (Appadurai 2004: 68).

In Appadurai's terms, poverty influences people's capacity to aspire, to imagine alternative courses of action. The poor lack capacities, voice and chances to exit the cycle of oppression that perpetuates itself. That capacity, however, can be developed through education. Appadurai did not detail a pedagogic approach on how education could do so, but Freirian education can provide a valid pedagogical framework. On the other hand, Appadurai helps make sense of the reasons for people's conforming behaviours with oppressive cultural hegemonies, and helps understand how problem-posing education can create the conditions for people to liberate themselves from that oppression. The Freirian approach to education, where facilitator and participants build the truth together and critically deconstruct the status quo, helps participants in conceptualising problems and issues of the current status quo and in challenging them. Problem-posing education can then give voice to participants by enlarging their horizon of opportunities and experiences, and by unleashing their capacity to aspire.

Freire's (1970) problem-posing approach offers an important framework for HRE for two reasons. First, it allows an understanding of the power relations involved in the educational process, analysing how a liberating process necessarily requires the educator to refuse the power that 'oppressed' students offer to her (or him) while asking her (or him) to liberate them (a process in which, Freire argued, they have to engage together) (Freire 1970). As seen earlier, awareness of a similar power relation is fundamental to avoid superimposing human rights values over local understandings of the world.

Second, problem-posing education allows participants to analyse social problems that matter for them and find possible moral-political solutions that can result in political actions of social change, realising the potential of HRE to challenge local social practices that threaten the respect of community members' human rights. HRE practitioners and scholars of international development have been calling for similar approaches to education in development that facilitate the conditions for the creation of internally driven motivation for social change (Ellerman 2006; Rodin 2012). Some commentators found in Freirian problem-posing education a valid educational framework (see, for instance, Claude 1999, 2000; Koenig 2001; Lohrenscheit 2002; Marks 1983; Print et al. 2008; Suárez 2007; Tibbits 2002).

However, not many scholars have addressed the issue of locating HRE within nonformal settings and focused on how HRE could integrate school curricula. The failure to recognise the potential that nonformal HRE can have in building a critical understanding of human rights knowledge, while participants explore the conditions that foster just or unjust social circumstances in their setting (Bajaj 2011; Meintjes 1997), represents a critical gap in HRE literature. HRE can (and I later argue must) engage the community as a whole – including adults who possibly never went to school, as may frequently happen in rural Africa – in the reconsideration of social practices that involve all members and not only those participating in a school programme. In addition to adopting a Freirian approach, HRE should have the flexibility of nonformal educational approaches.

Nonformal education is non-credential based, practical, learner centred and with a delivery system that is environment based and often associated with out-of-school activities (Fordham 1993). It usually presupposes a conscious educational effort (at least on the side of the educator); it is oriented to the development of the individual and/or the community; it is often voluntary and funded by a third party; and it makes use of various participative pedagogic techniques that allow the participants and the educator to construct critically the knowledge together (Bacquelaine and Raymaekers 1987). Nonformal pedagogy engages participants in active discussions, it is flexible both in the content and in the setting, based on listening to participants' needs, and admits detours from pre-existing planned structures following learners' needs and understandings. Nonformal pedagogy allows participants to critically engage together in the analysis of the topic, by unleashing creatively critical perspectives on it through the use of various techniques (e.g. drawing, theatre, games). It offers participants the means to investigate other participants' understandings of the topic and generates the opportunity for them to become aware of others' human emotional responses to a given problem. Due to its flexibility and its being centred on participants' needs and understandings of the world, nonformal education can help frame a human rights curriculum that incorporates the 'familiar' without preventing learners from imagining alternative social relationships (Allen 1992; Chanda 1999; Council of Europe 2007, 2009; d'Engelbronner-Kolff 1998; Flowers et al. 2007; Hudeki 2008; Kardam 2009; Mahruf et al. 2006; UNESCO 2006).

Nonformal problem-posing HRE can offer a valid pedagogical approach to help participants find connections to human rights, by allowing them to critique, discuss and debate those rights and their implications in the life of their community, dismissing them or recognising them as part of local understandings of the world. The purpose of nonformal problem-posing HRE should be to work with the pre-existing understandings that participants bring with them. If this is ignored, it may fail to grasp the new information that participants are exposed to (or they may learn it for the purpose of the class but revert to their preconceptions in their daily life). Its Freirian pedagogical approach should pose problems that matter to participants, offering them an opportunity to reconsider current social structures and reframe the future. Truth should be built together with participants, starting from participants' understanding of the world. HRE can thus be understood as a process that, critically presenting human rights to participants, solves participants' problems for participants' purposes, by questioning, thinking and testing new knowledge until the solution is part of participants' life.

Avoiding authoritative approaches that would make participants conform to a global cultural hegemony of human rights, problem-posing HRE offers participants a key to critique the social status quo, a perspective to analyse it. That perspective is the human rights framework that participants themselves translate into local terms and that they ground within their local understandings of the world. In offering participants the tools to visualise and problematise social change, problem-posing HRE has the potential to empower participants, making them protagonists of their own development. As the next section argues, nonformal problem-posing HRE is inscribed within a particular understanding of development.

A HUMAN DEVELOPMENT FRAMEWORK FOR HUMAN RIGHTS EDUCATION

Problem-posing HRE offers to the 'poor' and 'oppressed' the opportunity to develop the ability to raise publicly their concerns and to become protagonists of their social reality by participating in the construction of newly envisioned societies that HRE helped them conceptualise. Sen (1999) defined human development as the process through which human beings challenge their social reality by (and with the goal of) expanding their and others' capabilities and freedoms. He criticised other, 'narrower' views of development for mistaking so-called development (e.g. the growth in the gross national product or the level of industrialisation of a country) for one of the many means necessary to widen the freedoms and capabilities that members of a society enjoy. Material wealth, Sen argued, is a limited measure for development because it does not necessarily result in widening people's freedom and enabling them to live a life that is meaningful to them. Tradition and authority, for instance, can play a role in subjugating people's will (with brutal coercion in the case of authority or by impacting on people's inner motivations in the case of tradition), enforcing social behaviours that go against people's human rights and human development (Sen 1999).

Human development theory suggests that members of local communities should be given the opportunity to become full, active protagonists of the processes that shape their social, political and economic reality, rather than being simple recipients of banking development programmes that frame that future in a pre-made, imperialistic understanding of it (Sen 1999). Sen argued that education would play a key role in human development. In his work, he recognised that education should be about 'helping children to develop the ability to reason about new decisions any grown-up person will have to take' (Sen 2007: 160), but he did not offer in detail an understanding of what pedagogical approach could better serve this purpose. As seen earlier, problem-posing HRE can contribute to similar processes of reconsideration of local realities and create an opportunity for participants to widen the quality and quantity of freedoms they enjoy. The connection between HRE and human development is further tightened by Nussbaum's (2011) understanding of development.

Nussbaum's 'capabilities approach' is rooted in Sen's human development theory. She analysed in detail what capabilities are, how social forces can limit or create opportunities for people to attain them, and the connections between them and human rights. Nussbaum (2011) classified capabilities in three categories: basic capabilities (the innate equipment of individuals necessary to develop other capabilities: for instance, the imaginative potential); internal capabilities (sufficient conditions for exercising a function: for instance, the ability to use a language); and combined capabilities (the internal capabilities plus the external conditions that make the capability a real, existing life option). Public policies and development programmes should promote combined capabilities by supporting the development of internal capabilities and by making available the necessary institutions and material conditions needed for their development (Nussbaum 2011). Human rights represent a minimum threshold of external conditions granting human beings the combined capabilities they need to help orient their life. They set a logical unity that orientates the capabilities approach in framing a set of central, fundamental capabilities. Nussbaum (2011) identified 10 of those central capabilities. As a tool for human development, HRE should help participants develop the capabilities they need to actively challenge their social status quo. Amongst the central capabilities identified by Nussbaum, I suggest that three should be considered particularly relevant to this aim:

1. *Practical reason.* Being able to form a conception of the good and to engage in critical reflection about the planning of one's life.

2. *Affiliation.* (A) Being able to live with and toward others, to recognise and show concern for other human beings, to engage in various forms of social interaction; to be able to imagine the situation of another [. . .].
(B) Having the social bases of self-respect and nonhumiliation; being able to be treated as a dignified being whose worth is equal to that of others.

3. *Control over one's environment.* [. . .] Being able to participate effectively in political choices that govern one's life; having the right of political participation, protection of free speech and association.

(Nussbaum 2011: 33, 34)

The development of freedoms and capabilities is the main goal of human development. Problem-posing HRE education has the potential to engage participants in critically analysing their social status quo and helping them develop the capacity to reflect on their individual and social life (practical reason); understand each other's concerns and engage together towards a solution for those concerns that respects everyone's dignity (affiliation); and to change politically their social reality if they deem that necessary (control over environment). Both Sen and Nussbaum insisted on the role that education should have, without offering examples of praxis that could help practitioners in the field to implement human development programmes at the grassroots level. Due to its critical nature and its potential to help participants contextualise human rights within local understandings of them, HRE seems to offer a model of practical implementation of human development, a praxis that can help participants reconsider social practices that hinder their human development. HRE then connects human rights and human development by using the former (and their local interpretation) to attain the latter.

In this process, HRE can represent a revolutionary tool of human development because it leaves to community members the responsibility to decide together by themselves the direction of their own development. It creates the conditions for participants to generate inner motivations for change that Ellerman (2006) identified as critical for the long-lasting impact of development programmes. Ellerman (2006) explored transformative approaches to development, suggesting that 'indirect' approaches are the most viable solution because they allow people to be the protagonists of their own development, ensuring long-lasting motivations and sustainable goals. Direct approaches that substitute the goals of the development agencies for people's own goals resulted in 'unhelpful help'. For instance, people would do what they were told (e.g. use mosquito nets) because they were driven by external motivations (being paid for doing so). As the external motivation stopped, people would interrupt the externally motivated behaviour. This form of development is unhelpful because it overrides self-help capacity with social engineering or with benevolent aid, what Dewey ([1916] 1966) called oppressive benevolence.

An indirect approach to development offers people the means to become protagonists of their own development; 'helpers' willing to take on proper development programmes, Ellerman (2006) argued, should focus on the agency aspects of it: development should help self-help, should respect the subject's autonomy to take their own decisions about what is best for them. Benevolent aid programmes, in contrast, undercut self-help capacity by overcontrolling and manipulating the actions conducted by the subjects of development, the 'doers' (Ellerman 2006). Ellerman suggested that if the doers do something only to satisfy conditionalities and receive aid from the helpers, then the motive will falsify their actions: they will do something only to receive further assistance rather than having in mind the improvement of their local reality. The helpers should not replace the doers in the development process by providing motivations or teaching right answers; they should not solve the subjects' problems, either. Helpers, instead, should enable the doers to engage critically with their local reality, facilitating the doers' processes of exploration of local problems and possible answers by finding internal motivation for change and assuming responsibilities for the changes implemented. Autonomy-respecting help is indirect in its approach because it helps the doers to problematise the status quo and to find, implement, test and refine possible solutions.

Although Ellerman built his theory looking critically at those of many others (including Dewey and Freire), as Sen and Nussbaum did before, he did not provide a constructive understanding of how education can become a tool of indirect development. HRE draws on human development theory and Ellerman's indirect approach by giving to community members the tools to engage critically with their local reality while assigning to them the role of protagonists in the process. The indirect potential of HRE can result in the creation of inner motivations for change through the critical analysis of human rights and the analysis of their reality from the human rights perspective. Participants can discover human rights-consistent or inconsistent social behaviours and can act to change them, if necessary. Social behaviours, however, are fostered by social practices and norms regulating the existing social status quo. Changing those behaviours would then mean changing the social practices that regulate them and the social norms behind those practices.

COGNITIVE AND SOCIAL CONSTRUCTIONS OF THE STATUS QUO

Human development theory recognises 'tradition' as a possible source of unfreedom, but does not offer a critical understanding of how tradition is constructed and reproduced in human communities. Social norm theory and constructivism help fill this gap in that the former provides a framework to understand how behaviour is socially constructed and reproduced (and thus how it can be challenged); and the latter makes sense of how experience of the world influences the understanding individuals make of it (and thus how new experiences that come through HRE can change that understanding).

As seen earlier, problem-posing human rights education can create a space in which local communities might challenge that 'tradition' by problematising their social status quo. Social practices, and the norms that regulate them, are the expression of and contribute to reproducing that status quo. Challenging the status quo, then, means unveiling and challenging social behaviours replicating those norms and supporting the status quo. On the other hand, experience shapes how human beings understand the world. Capacity to aspire, to visualise a different social status quo, can be fostered by different experiences that change how participants understand their life. Cognitive processes of learning explain how experiences influence behaviour. Thus, as argued in this section, to be effective, an HRE programme must allow participants to generate new mental schemata that help them challenge local social norms and the process where those norms are learnt, namely, in their original community of practice.

Communities of Practice

Human communities make sense of reality by constructing meaning socially. Community members learn in their daily life how to behave and act according to the norms in place within the community. This learning is double layered: to be accepted and accorded full membership, young 'members' must yet learn how to behave. On the other hand, they must learn how to show to other members that they have learnt how to behave. This daily process of social learning in which newcomers learn from old members happens in what Lave and Wenger called a community of practice (CoP) (Lave and Wenger 1991; Wenger 1998). To become full members of a CoP, newcomers must be recognised by old members as able to behave like them, to speak in the same way and about the same things they speak. Amongst other case studies, Lave and Wenger analysed a community of photocopying machine repairers. While repairing a photocopying machine, the experienced worker talks about the epic wars he fought against terribly old photocopying machines. The apprentice, in that moment, is not only learning how to repair a photocopying machine, she is also learning how to talk and behave like an expert repairer so that, with time, she will be able to show to the old members of the community that she deserves to be considered a full member of that community.

Lave and Wenger defined a CoP as having three characteristics: first, members of a CoP share a domain of interest, implying a commitment to that domain and to the gaining of certain competences that differentiate members from non-members. Second, they share key resources (stories, tools, experiences, material resources) through time and, third, they enjoy sustained interaction in the community. Defining the locality of a CoP, Wenger (1998) argued that cities or entire offices cannot be considered as such: in doing so, one would overlook the disconnectedness that characterises the CoPs, due to the main practices that are involved in those communities. Viewing a nation as a CoP would 'miss crucial discontinuities among the various localities where relevant learning takes place' (Wenger 1998: 124). At the same time, however, Wenger argued that CoPs are above all about 'living meaningfully, developing a satisfying identity, and altogether being human' (1998: 134). However, I argue that Lave and Wenger's theory can be used to analyse behaviour-learning processes within small rural communities as CoPs. Small rural communities (like the one that was the object of this research) satisfy the criteria set by the theory as they fall into the midlevel category that characterises CoPs (neither a narrow group of people gathering with the purpose of carrying out a specific activity, nor a broad social group including millions of members). In small rural communities, members share, first, the same domain of interest (e.g. by living in the community, interacting with the others and defending the community from external aggression). Second, they share key resources: legends, family stories, anecdotes as tools through which community members frame their social identity and negotiate their roles as newcomers or old members. Third, they share sustained mutual relationships and ways of engaging in doing things together. In a small rural community, children (the newcomers) have to learn to behave like the old members (the adults) and hence they have to reproduce the social behaviours fostered by the adults. Newcomers learn by daily experience the social norms in place in a given CoP and how to put them into practice.

Social Norms

Social norms theory and schema theory together are useful for analysing individual and social transformative processes of Freirian problem-posing education. Social norm theory offers a framework where situated learning theory can be inscribed, helping make sense of the process through which old members, legitimating newcomers' full participation, protect the social status quo: only those who act in accordance with social norms and practices existing in the community are granted full membership, recognition of adulthood by the elders. The others might face exile or social derision: for instance, a child needs to learn that defecating cannot happen in public as he or she did when a baby; learning the behaviour will save him or her from social derision. However, this process can be problematic in human development terms because those social norms and practices in place might reproduce patterns of power that hinder certain members' participation in decision-making processes or that impact negatively on their human rights. Problem-posing HRE as a tool for human development should then give communities the means to challenge those norms and unleash their capacity to aspire to different social realities, empowering both newcomers and old members and engaging them in the critical discussion of the social norms in place.

Social norms are informal non-codified norms, beliefs about beliefs of others mainly formed by experience and very little by direct instruction. In the UK, social norms include, for instance: wearing black clothes at a funeral, not breaking into the queue, not having sexual intercourse with a sibling and shaking hands with people when meeting them (Elster 2007). Human beings follow a social norm because they believe that others will do so. A deliberative action makes us realise the reasons for what we are doing, but until that very moment we just follow a default rule learnt within a social context, without the need to understand it. A community punishes informally the transgression of social norms with a behaviour (shame, gossiping, isolation, exile) that generates a feeling of guilt in the transgressor and enforces adherence to the norm. A large part of social behaviour is built upon conformity with similar social norms (Bicchieri 2006). The way they are formed and enforced has very little to do with deliberation and much more through following behavioural rules. When we find relevant similarities between the current situation and others experienced in the past, we adopt cognitive shortcuts heuristically, that is, we follow default rules stored in our memory. When we are challenged by a new situation, instead we try to adopt an appropriate behaviour, acting according to those who possess our characteristics: we try to act 'normal' (Bicchieri 2006; Lamberts and Shanks 1997). The way we understand what is considered normal behaviour is by interpreting the world and transforming those interpretations in knowledge. Social norms and cognitivist theories help explain the cognitive and social factors that influence how people behave 'normally' and how they learn from others what normal behaviour is.

Schema Theory

Connectionist theory in cognitive science uses simple neural network models as a metaphor to explain the way knowledge is stored and activated when needed. The metaphor is as follows: interactive linkages between neurons form networks, schemata or mental structures that store knowledge and patterns of action. Those schemata can at the same time be habituated and open to novelty (Strauss and Quinn 1997). This cognitive interpretation of mental processes, called schema theory, is context sensitive in that mental structures and associations are connected through experience and the understanding of those experiences that a person makes of the world that surrounds him or her. Recent neurological research seems to confirm this model by suggesting that, although the genes encode the structure of the brain, neuronal connections are mainly determined by experience that an individual has in a determinate cognitive and social environment and are grouped together in 'semantic neighbourhoods' (Huth et al. 2012; Quartz and Sejnowski 2002). Social norms theory can adopt schema theory to show how shared normative beliefs influence daily behaviours and can be altered by making new experiences and knowledge or by re-evaluating past assumptions.

Schema theory of cognition has been adopted by anthropologists who argued in favour of the contextual dimension where the formation of those schemata happens. If we relocate the examples given above into a non-Western context, those social norms might not apply any more: in Japan people wear white clothes at funerals, in Saudi Arabia a man is not supposed to shake a woman's hand when they meet, and personal experience suggests that in Italy breaking into the queue is considered more or less doable. By interacting among each other and with the world that surrounds them, people come to share a common base for communication and action (Strauss and Quinn 1997). Of course, there can be divergent thinkers, due to the variations within any society in socially shared schemata. These variations are caused by the differences in how different pasts of different individuals weigh in rendering some inputs more significant than others. Connectionist models like the one described above, however, concede that schemata do not screen out any new knowledge but, instead, admit that new experiences can lead to noticing a schema-inconsistent behaviour (and therefore changing it) or to overriding old associations, creating new schemata that supersede the older ones (Bloch 1998; Strauss and Quinn 1997). Stable shared meanings, overarching mental schemata (Strauss and Quinn 1997), interact in the creation of a social norm. Cognitive schema theory, then, helps us understand why social norms are context dependent: preferences and beliefs are sensitive to situational cues and to one's interpretation of those cues offered by the specific given context. A person categorises those cues into scripts that – once activated – prompt belief and preferences that, in turn, activate behavioural rules and norms (Bicchieri 2006).

The way individuals make sense of their reality together has a profound effect on institutional performance (Chong 2000; Elster 2007). Structural effects of context-learnt social behaviours cannot be dismissed as temporary, since they have been shown to be remarkably persistent (Jennings and Niemi 1981) and change very slowly over generations (Nisbett et al. 2001; Putnam 1973). This is not to say that all people behave in the same way within a community: people covering different roles in the family or the community might behave very differently (Hofstede 2001). However, members of the same human community tend to have profound behavioural similarity and social conformity (Bednar et al. 2010; Bednar and Page 2007). Social behaviours might be slow to change because they play a central role in orienting the life of human beings in social communities. Within a community that shares a context there are certain social norms that must be learnt to become a full community member. Also, newcomers must be able to show they have learnt those social norms and are able to conform their behaviour accordingly. Rather than being deliberate or conscious, this process follows cognitive paths described by the schema theory, where norms and behavioural rules (often in place for the good of the community itself) are followed, seeking conformity rather than a rational choice. However, new mental schemata can be developed following new experiences. A new context or a different view of the same context (e.g. from a human rights perspective) can generate mental schemata that override or clash with the previous ones, raising awareness of the social norm. Where before there was a simple adherence to a social norm (wearing black clothes at a funeral), experiencing the existence of a different behaviour (wearing white clothes at a funeral) or the critical reflection on the norm (why are we wearing black clothes at a funeral?) transforms the previous unconscious adherence into a conscious behaviour.

The process through which individuals gain new perspective on social behaviours (and possibly include behavioural alternatives in their understanding of them) does not necessarily result in the adoption of a new behaviour or a new social norm. For new cognitive schemata to become social norms, a public discussion is required since the fact that a norm is needed (or perceived as such) does not bring it automatically into force; an intervention, a breakthrough is often necessary to change a social norm, that is, to connect new individual schemata into a public acknowledgement of those schemata (Elster 2007). For this reason, cognitive schema theory and social norm theory are both important in the understanding of how community members can renegotiate local social practices. Since it is society that shapes the sense individuals make of reality, society must legitimate a new understanding of the same reality. Within the social norms framework, unleashing capacity to aspire means giving people the opportunity to pay attention to new cues, to reconsider social norms in place through discussion, to question together the social status quo and possibly change it through deliberation. That is, to publicly reframe the social meaning of reality.

Social norms are built upon beliefs and expectations and represent a way in which a society makes sense of itself: in wearing black clothes at a funeral, people identify and recognise themselves as members of the same community, they appreciate being part of the same social group. They show that they know what is expected (or, better, what they believe is expected) from them and how to meet those expectations. Social norms then contribute to reproducing the status quo until they are challenged. They regulate social relations (shaking hands, saying 'bless you' after someone sneezes) as much as, for instance, social hierarchies ('hazing' and ritual abuse within army groups, gender gaps in average salaries). Social norms can contribute to reproducing or drafting power relations that have a strong impact on people's participation in the decision-making process (fundamental to human development).

Freire did not offer a model of how people come to reframe the world. He believed they did, and he highlighted the importance of the fact that people re-understand – rename – the world through education, although he did not explore the details behind processes of individual reconfiguration of the social reality (Freire 1970, 1973, 1995). Schema theory helps fill that gap in that it shows possible ways in which people cognitively come to include what is peripheral, exceptional or weird into the horizon of acceptable possible behaviours. What is exceptional is reformulated by experience into a new understanding of the same reality, into new schemata that condition what is considered 'normal' by individuals. However, cognitive schema theory does not explain how individuals frame social behaviours. Social norms theory helps in making sense of how an entire community negotiates new acceptable behaviours, integrating as such the social aspects of the diffusion of the new knowledge built through problem-posing education. Human rights education can offer to participants new perspectives from which they can challenge social norms that are protecting an unjust social status quo. Having vernacularised human rights in their local context and having gained the capabilities to act socially, participants have the potential to identify human rights-inconsistent practices and renegotiate them in class, first, and then at the community level. Through HRE, participants in class (and members in the community) together critically uncover dynamics and practices that limit or hinder human development of community members and renegotiate relations amongst them in terms, as suggested by relevant literature, of gender and power relations *in primis*.

GENDER ROLES AND SOCIAL CHANGE

Problem-posing HRE offers participants the opportunity to look critically at their social reality and act for change. Human development theory argues that for social change to happen, two processes must be in place. First, individuals have to explore what social practices or behaviours in place in their community they understand as unjust and desire to change. Second, they need to be actively able to participate in the political process where the discussion about changing those practices happens (Sen 1999). In a small rural community, men and women could raise their concerns in the existing decision-making processes in the family and the wider community. However, Sen and Nussbaum suggested that women's participation in the decision-making processes can be hindered by gender roles regulating what freedoms are accessible to them (Nussbaum 2000, 2011; Sen 1990, 1995, 1999). The nature of those roles must be examined, then, analysing if HRE can help participants shape new understandings of them that include wider freedoms and capabilities.

Feminist literature helped build a theory of gender roles as socially constructed. A similar perspective emerged particularly with de Beauvoir, whose work was symbolised by her declaration that 'One is not born, but rather becomes, a woman' (de Beauvoir 1973: 267). Feminist scholars analysed the pervasiveness of the (so-called) cultural influence on how babies are treated in accordance with their perceived gender, giving credit to theories of gender identity as socially constructed rather than biologically determined (for an experimental study see, for instance, Fausto-Sterling 1985, 1987). Nussbaum (2000) also argued in favour of the social construction of gender, taking up Mill's ([1869] 2008) point that the 'nature' of women is the artificial result of forced repression. It is because gender roles and relations are socially constructed that it is possible for community members to renegotiate them, addressing the issues of inequality that HRE might help them identify. By helping participants problematise their social reality from a human rights perspective, problem-posing HRE can help participants analyse what stands out to them as an important theme linked to gender roles in their community.

However, it is important to understand what structural factors play a key role in the social construction of gender roles, to make sense of how participants in an HRE programme might come to challenge them and against what possible structural counterforces. Engels (1902) suggested that men's desire to guarantee their family future access to their resources (land above all) impacts on the way they distribute those resources to their sons and their daughters, arguing that the latter will not receive any because they will leave the family of origin. Drawing on his and Marx's theories, Marxist anthropologists have looked at unequal bargaining power as influenced by relations of production that tie community members, shape uneven access to resources and impact on the different distribution of labour amongst men and women. The way labour is distributed amongst men ('productive' labour) and women ('reproductive' labour) shapes their different access to resources that are key for their bargaining power in the household and the community. Unequal access to resources in turn hinders women's political bargaining power, hence limiting their possibilities for challenging that distribution of labour (if they are willing to do so) (Benerìa 1979; Benerìa and Sen 1981; Boserup 1970; Meillassoux 1991; Nussbaum 2000).

Besteman (1995) identified two key factors through which women's independence was controlled in sub-Saharan Africa: access to land and marriage patterns. Access to land has a high gender component in sub-Saharan Africa (partly due to the effects of colonial land reforms) and dialectically influences and is influenced by distribution of labour. Especially in areas following Islamic inheritance laws (e.g. Senegal), women are likely to receive less land than their brothers (or even none) (Boserup 1970). The amount of land possessed impacts not only on the possibility of self-subsistence for a person (land means food) but also on the ownership of the highest revenue-generating asset (Agarwal 1995). Unequal access to land hence puts men in a strong bargaining position with their wives, who without their husbands would struggle for their (and possibly their children's) economic subsistence. Women, excluded from accessing key resources and from productive labour, are put in a role of subjugation to men that limits their political capability and freedom to challenge roles and relations (Cliff 1984; Sen and Grown 1987).

The second factor that fosters women's subjugation in sub-Saharan Africa is marriage patterns. While advanced industrial economies seem to experience a considerable reduction in the costs of living alone, poorer countries rely on marriage as a way to commit parties to a continuing economic relationship that is mutually beneficial (Kevane 2004). Households are efficient places to produce services, generate children and make investments (Weiss 1997). Marriage, however, is not always voluntary. Child and forced marriage (CFM) has been studied as a gender-based infringement of the fundamental human rights of girls and women. The practice has serious health and social implications for children and contributes to creating conditions of sexual abuse and violence in marriage. The phenomenon impacts on the lives of many women, the childhood of whom can be put at risk of being exposed to physical and psychological traumas (Ouattara et al. 1998). In being forced into child marriages, women are treated as assets needed for family reproduction in order to guarantee a productive labour force (Meillassoux 1991).

Limited bargaining power connected to gender distribution of labour is not only influenced by access to key resources. Different allocation of labour in one generation follows pre-existent social structures that shape the possible domain of choices limiting the freedoms of the people living in a given community. Gender distribution of labour is sustained by social norms enforced via their internalisation; since they are children, community members learn to conform with norms that assign to members of different genders different roles and places in the community (Kevane 2004). The social norms model helps make sense of why, in conditions of poverty, gender distribution of labour replicates itself even when being socially counterproductive. Take the example of a community in which men have little land and hope that their wives might go into the labour market and contribute to household income, or in which they would like to hire other men's wives to cultivate their land. Even if husbands individually found it preferable to withdraw from the norm regulating gender seclusion, they might fear the long-term social consequences of breaking the collusive equilibrium (Kevane 2004). Norms of gender labour therefore reproduce themselves generation after generation not only as a response to daily challenges, but also partly following patterns of pluralistic ignorance; that is, based on the lack of a place to express members' individual desire for change.

Gender roles are socially constructed and reflect the particular needs and views of the society where they are generated. This construction has a correlation with gender distribution of labour, can result in patters of domination and oppressions linked to different access to key resources, and is protected by a status quo that defends itself through role models, social expectations and what is referred to as 'culture' (Mukhopadhyay

1995; Sweetman 1995). HRE has the potential to challenge similar social constructions and activate members towards a more just status quo. However, the problem is who should be the social actors of that change (i.e. who should HRE empower): in the case of a women-driven liberation, that might generate men's resistance; in the case of a men-driven liberation, that liberation might be fictitious because it would be led by the oppressing powers that could then re-establish the social order on powerless women who are not aware of their political potential. Aware of this problem, practitioners in the field have suggested to 'men-stream' gender, that is, to include men within development programmes aiming at empowering the community as a whole (Chant and Gutmann 2002). Chant and Gutmann (2002) argued that, without men, the social impact of development projects aiming for women's empowerment would be hindered, a recommendation that still echoes often in more recent literature (ICRW and Instituto Promundo 2007; Jewkes et al. 2015). Approaches to development that only work with women might fail in their attempt to challenge traditional resistances at community level. In the worst scenarios, these approaches might aggravate the hostilities between men and women at community level and result in the sabotage of the actions aimed at improving women's life conditions. Also, 'women-only' approaches would not respond to the problems linked with a loss of men's social roles that would be linked to their insecurity and marginalisation. Freire (1970) also argued that for the *I* to emerge in an educational relationship, the *non-I* must be present to represent the different. The *non-I* directs the observation towards the self, towards phenomena that previously went unobserved or inconspicuous. In problem-posing education, what existed before (but was not perceived in its deeper implication) stands out with powerful strength. Development projects should, therefore, aim at empowering communities holistically, by including people of both genders amongst the beneficiaries of their work. HRE programmes should then help men and women look critically together at social practices in place in their communities that are influenced by gender roles. In doing so, HRE can unveil unbalanced relations of power in the household and the society that relegate women to the role of followers of male authority, meeting the priority of human development theory that identifies women as key figures for promoting social transformation and bettering the lives of both men and women (Nussbaum 2000, 2011; Sen 1995, 1999).

An analysis of the processes through which women can attain liberation through problem-posing education has been brought forward by Belenky et al. (1986), who developed a theory of women's silence as being framed by gender relations observed in the family and the community during their childhood and, dialectically, as shaping the way men's and women's biases over women's intellectual and social capacities are created. Women (uneducated women in particular) are kept from the talking because others do not consider them (and they do not consider themselves) capable of contributing to intellectual discussions. Women have no opportunities to develop public speaking skills and to demonstrate, to self and others, the erroneousness of those biases. Belenky et al. (1986) talked of women that felt deaf and dumb, unaware of the potential of their intellectual capacities. Silent women develop language but they do not cultivate the capacity of representational thought; that is, they do not experience the power that words have in developing thought. Silent women learn that they have a place to hold in the family and that maintaining that place is fundamental to their survival in the family. While experiencing the self as powerless, silent women see authorities as all-powerful. Following authority as such is a matter of survival; knowing the reasons for doing what they are told to do is not perceived as important (or, in certain cases, even possible). The women studied by Belenky et al. (1986) learnt to accept a subjugated role modelling the unequal gender relations between their mothers and their fathers. The same authority that subjugated their mothers had control over them: those women reported incest, abandonment, beatings and yet none of them mentioned rebellion. In the voice/silence metaphoric analysis of unbalanced household relations, men are the speakers, the subjects, the decision-makers, the unquestionable authority and women are the listeners, the objects, the decision-followers. Studying the processes through which women move from silence to speaking, Belenky et al. (1986) argued that problem-posing education can better help silent women to discover a talking self. Engaging them in the process of thinking and dialoguing, the teacher-midwife opens the thinking process to silent women and asks them to contribute. In discovering their talking capacity, silent women learn to discover themselves as thinkers, they recalibrate the potentialities of their self and enlarge the horizon of their possibilities (Belenky et al. 1986). Participating in problem-posing HRE programmes, silent women can develop a voice and join the men in their liberation and the empowerment of the entire community.

Programmes that empower women have been widely criticised by both cultural relativists and anti-feminists: the former argue that programmes of empowerment cannot appeal to universal norms of justice among gender, as such norms do not exist; the latter appeal to the argument that empowerment programmes can be disempowering in the long run because they can threaten men's role in the community. I respond to both concerns, showing how human rights has the potential to be used in the non-Western world and how the capability approach offers a framework to do so while empowering male and female community members together. HRE programmes should aim at empowering the community as a whole, inviting participants of both genders to make sense together of human rights in local terms and to contextualise an analysis of gender roles within that new perspective. They should challenge those power dynamics that relegate silent women to the role of listeners. Those power dynamics, fostered by existing social norms, are not necessarily visible or consciously shaped, as I have shown. In the last century, the contribution of those scholars that studied power dynamics led to conceptualising various models that help to explain why and how people conform to an unequal social status quo that keeps them subjugated to others, and why they might not problematise that status quo as unjust.

POWER DYNAMICS IN SOCIAL REPRODUCTION

HRE has revolutionary potential because it can help participants reconsider their social status quo, challenging gender roles that limit their human development. Sen was widely aware of the fact that human development processes (such as the one fostered by HRE) challenge existing social roles and relations; for that reason, he focused in his work on the importance that democratic participation plays in human development to challenge 'tradition' (Sen 1999). Both he and Nussbaum understood 'traditional' gender roles as potentially influencing what women understand as personal interest (Nussbaum 2000, 2011; Sen 1995, 1999). Women's misperception of their self-interest, Sen argued, combined with 'traditional' beliefs and concern for family welfare, might foster and sustain 'traditional' inequalities: 'the underdog comes to accept the legitimacy of the unequal order and becomes an implicit accomplice' (Sen 1990: 126). However, he did not offer an analysis of the conservative processes through which society protects and reproduces its inequalities from one generation to the other. He did not conceptualise the way in which 'tradition' influences people's perception of their self-interest. Sen offered a framework for development that would require connecting it with other theories approaching aspects on which he was not an expert, as in the case of educational theories (which I did earlier), or that he underestimated, as in the case of theories studying power and conflicts framing social relations (Walker and Unterhalter 2010). Social norm theory partly helps explain how 'traditional' harmful behaviours are kept in place by community members, but alone does not offer an adequate framework for understanding how people's interests clash or meet, influencing or constraining their behaviours reciprocally. In other words, to make sense of the role that HRE could play in challenging unjust social norms, we need a framework of power that can explain how unequal social dynamics protect and replicate those social norms.

In particular, a holistic understanding of the different forms in which power can be exercised is necessary to make sense of how tradition (or deeply entrenched social norms) can impact on gender roles so that community members comply with the status quo even in conditions of inequality. Gaventa (2006) developed a holistic understanding of power as having three dimensions – *visible, hidden* and *invisible* – drawing on the contributions of other less recent theories (including Freire's understanding of non-consciousness of deprived groups). There are countless theoretical explorations of what power is and how it works in the literature. I use Gaventa's framework because it offers a concrete, usable model to analyse how power influences the way in which people act, think and behave. His theory also allows combining discussion of power with the other theories I use: social norms theory, cognitive schema theory, problem-posing education, and human development theory.

Visible power relates to the dynamics involved in overt decision-making; that is, the power of A over B to make B do something that B would not have done without the intervention of A, who mobilises superior bargaining resources. This classical view of power draws on the literature that studied it as a vital feature in understanding how people accord their behaviour to other people's will and why: Rousseau, Hobbes and Machiavelli, to cite some, were mainly concerned with how issues of power influenced the social actions of individuals. In the second half of the 20th century, scholars who studied power became increasingly interested in the work of Weber (Weber et al. 1947) and later Dahl (1961), who looked at power as domination led by economic or authoritarian interests, as the capacity of an individual to influence the actions of another individual or many others so that they would act against their natural preference. In particular, Weber (1968) became interested in understanding the social legitimation of people's domination over other people and found it in three different forms of authority: legal, traditional and charismatic. The forms of authority Weber identified offer a good framework to analyse visible power, suggesting a consideration of how different authorities (legal, traditional and charismatic) in a community can intertwine to reproduce the status quo that HRE might challenge by constructing it overtly in the decision-making arena. In detail, obedience to legal authority is owed to an impersonal system, the dominance of which is grounded on a set of rules believed legal by society. The authority of the system extends to the persons that exercise an office by virtue of those rules, as in the case of a prime minister or a police officer. Obedience to traditional authority, instead, is owed to a person, the dominance of whom is grounded over ruled people's belief in the sanctity of immemorial traditions, as in the case of the elders of a community. Under traditional authority, subjugated groups do not challenge domination, even when it produces inequalities. Obedience to charismatic authority, finally, is owed to exceptionally charismatic leaders by virtue of personal trust in their revelation, as in the case of a prophet, a shaman or other figures possessing special powers (Weber 1968). Weber's work might offer a framework to understand how different authorities in a rural community exercise power over weak sectors of the population to reproduce the status quo. Similar forms of authority are part of the sphere of visible power as they justify the direct intervention of A over the behaviour of B. Visible power can be studied when access to the decision-making arena is relatively open (or considered accessible to all) so that power can be analysed by seeing who participates and who wins and loses within the political arenas (Gaventa 2006). The empowerment that might follow after a problem-posing HRE programme could hence impact on the relations amongst community members in the visible political arena, empowering weaker members in the decision-making process.

Hidden power is the power to exclude certain topics from the political agenda or participants from the decision-making arena. It is the power of A to construct barriers against the participation of B, through non-decisions or mobilising biases that hinder B's participation. Similar dynamics of 'non-decision-making' power emerged from the analysis of the critics of Weber's work, who suggested that power relations are not only about deciding, but also deciding what is acceptable to be decided. Bachrach and Baratz (1962), while agreeing on the existence of the first dimension of power analysed by Weber and Dahl, expanded the analysis of power to a second dimension: the capacity to create social and political values and institutional practices that limit agenda-setting to issues comparatively innocuous to the power holder. Under Bachrach and Baratz's work, power came to be understood as overt (decision-making) and covert (non-decision-making, agenda-setting). The covert dimension of power is exercised by the 'mobilisation of biases' (a term that Bachrach and Baratz took from Schattschneider 1960). Ruling elites mobilise bias to build game rules that play in their favour and reproduce an advantageous social and political status quo or by discrediting the legitimacy of the actors that threaten that status quo. Hidden forms of power can be analysed by looking at who controls the subjects for discussion brought within the political arena and who does not participate in various layers of the decision-making process. Forms of discontent outside of the political arena can also become a tool to analyse hidden power (Gaventa 2006). A problem-posing HRE programme has the potential to help participants raise their voices, bringing up topics and challenges that were previously excluded from the political agenda. HRE could thus give participants an opportunity to change the balance of hidden power built through mobilisation of gender biases. To do so, however, participants in HRE should first unveil those biases and the system that created them: invisible power dynamics.

Invisible power was studied by Gaventa (1980), drawing on the work of Lukes (1974), who took Bachrach and Baratz's analysis further, and has its roots in Marxist analysis of the pervasive power of ideologies and cultural hegemonies (on which Freire also drew in his approach to education) as, for instance, studied by Gramsci (1972).

In the work of Lukes that inspired Gaventa, invisible power was understood as the power of A to influence or shape the consciousness of B about inequalities, through control of information (Lukes 1974). Other than being decision and non-decision-making, Lukes argued that power includes the ability to insert in people's minds interests that are contrary to their good, contrary to their 'real' interests. Biases are not only mobilised, they are also created by the dynamics in place in this third dimension of power, are difficult to see and identify by those who try to do so, and at the same time are under the influence of those dynamics. Ruling elites, according to Lukes, possess the power to implant in people's minds interests contrary to their own good. Gaventa (1980) reviewed Lukes's understanding of power, studying the reasons for people's quiescence under glaring conditions of social inequality.

He found that the main purpose of power is to prevent certain sectors of the population from participating in decision-making and to obtain their passive agreement, their mute compliance, to the social status quo. In the initial work of Gaventa, invisible power was controlled through the processes of communication and information transfers. Those processes influence meanings and patterns of actions that make B believe and act her own good in a way that benefits A and that B would deem contrary to her own good if not subjugated by the social elite. As a PhD student, Gaventa (1980) developed his initial framework of power under Lukes's supervision, and his initial work is open to the same criticisms. Their tripartition is unsatisfactory in certain respects because it does not understand power as a dispositional concept but focuses only on the exercise of it; it concentrates simply on the exercise of power over someone (to force her to act against her will) as a coercive negative force, while power can also be productive and compatible with dignity, and it offered a binary understanding of power relations, while power is likely to be multifaceted. This last criticism seems the most solid to me. Gaventa and Lukes focused on power as agency, ignoring postmodern approaches that instead pointed in the direction of power as structure: oppression exists without oppressors, as in 'regimes of truth' dominated by unquestioned assumptions about the social reality (Bourdieu 1977; Foucault 1991). The most serious critique of this aspect of Gaventa's and Lukes's work was brought forward by Hayward (2000), who argued in favour of an understanding of power as social boundaries enabling or limiting the freedoms of social actors (an approach that links well to human development theory, social norms theory and Belenky's theory of silent women).

Reflecting on similar issues to those suggested by Hayward's work, Gaventa (2003, 2006) drafted a more comprehensive understanding of invisible power that includes both understandings, as structure and agency, and as such intertwines with social norms theory, Freire's understanding of oppression and Sen's analysis of tradition as a source of 'unfreedom'. In his more recent work, Gaventa also offered a solution to the issues coming from understanding invisible power as hindering people's *real* interests: what one's real interest is, is difficult (or even impossible) to say, even for the bearer of that interest. Gaventa (2006) instead conceptualised invisible power as shaping the 'socially acceptable': what people think that others expect from them (the link with social norms theory is evident), similarly to what Freire (1970) did when arguing the negative effect of the internalisation of oppression. For the purpose of the analysis brought forward, then, invisible power includes the dynamics by which people comply with the dominating hegemonic ideology and behave in accordance with unequal social norms that hinder their human development. To empower community members for their own development, HRE programmes should foster their political potential by challenging the forms of power that hinder that development. In challenging local norms of decision-making, participants in HRE might unveil invisible power relations regulating gender roles and relations that could keep certain segments of the society from accessing and exercising hidden and visible powers (thus protecting and reproducing the status quo).

Gaventa (1980, 2006) called this power-challenging dynamic of social change the process through which the powerless emerge from quiescence (or abandon false consciousness) and become participating political actors. Sen would look at it as a key process of human development, and Freire would define it as the dynamic of coscientisation (development of critical consciousness) and political mobilisation of the oppressed and the oppressors that together reframe the status quo.

The power framework analysed in this section helps understand two processes of social change. First, it contributes to making sense of the way in which human beings can join together in analysing their social reality from a human rights perspective to unveil invisible sources of unfreedoms that hinder their human development or threaten their human rights. Second, it helps understand the dynamics of their public mobilisation for change that might follow the initial process of coscientisation. HRE has the potential to empower local communities in challenging roles of silence constructed through structural invisible power dynamics and enhancing members' capacity to demand and obtain respect for their human rights in the political arena.

CONCLUSION

In this chapter, I suggested that human rights can be used as a tool for development in the non-Western world, given their relative universality and their potential for being contextualised in local understandings of the world by actors at the grassroots level. Problem-posing HRE can be the tool for this process of critical vernacularisation because it can unleash new participants' perspectives on themselves and their social setting. In doing so, problem-posing HRE becomes a tool for human development since it offers participants an opportunity to expand the capabilities they need to become politically active in reframing their status quo. To do so, they might have to challenge pre-existent social norms that act as sources of unfreedoms by isolating and segregating parts of the society. Problem-posing HRE, by expanding participants' sets of capabilities and unlocking their capacity to aspire, must offer them the means to renegotiate those social norms and the tools to reconfigure the social structure of the community. Through new experiences, participants develop new understandings of their local reality and the social norms regulating behaviours in it, which might in turn impact on the way participants adhere to the existing social practices and collaborate to review them publicly.

In this process, gender roles and relations play a key role, due to how they can limit or facilitate access and participation in the decision-making processes of a community, and should therefore be taken into consideration by HRE programmes. Those gender roles and relations can be structured by invisible power relations entrenched within social norms of non-participation in decision-making. Participants of both genders should then join the analysis of local norms and practices regulating, also, their gender roles and power relations. After the programme, the impact of HRE in unleashing social change processes should be analysed in all the three dimensions of power that intertwine in shaping and reproducing the social status quo of the community.

We have identified key characteristics of problem-posing HRE programmes aiming at human development by creating a system of theories for their application. In the next chapters, the reader will notice that I used this framework as a model to analyse social change dynamics linked to HRE classes and leading to human development of community members.

Chapter 3

MODERNISATION AT WORK: SENEGAL, TOSTAN AND THE FULƁE

INTRODUCTION

We could not try to understand the changes happening in Galle Toubaaco as it went through the CEP without an understanding of both the Senegalese context at large, and the ethnic group that people living in the community identified themselves with. I obviously also owe to the reader a critical description of the Tostan programme, with its strengths and limitations. This chapter analyses the emergence of the human rights discourse in Senegal, the current status of ratification of international human rights conventions, and the human rights violations in the country against which human rights activists advocate. The adoption of human rights law represents a jurisprudential legitimation for the HRE programme. On the other hand, the emergence of the human rights discourse in Senegal helps understand how participants might have made sense of human rights in their local reality (e.g. as something completely new or something heard before).

Second, the chapter looks at current Senegalese human development issues, with particular reference to gender issues, decision-making processes and other human rights-relevant practices in the country. The dynamics fostered by HRE are likely to intertwine with wider contextual factors: local gender roles and relations may, for instance, be influenced by wider traditional roles or, instead, by national processes of social change that challenge those traditional roles.

Third, the chapter examines Tostan's HRE approach in Senegal by looking at history, pedagogy and limitations of the programme. This analysis helps make sense of its intended structure as created by the NGO and its actual delivery in the rural community of Galle Toubaaco.

Finally, the last section gives an understanding of the traditional characteristics of the Fulƃe ethnic group in Senegal. In the process of vernacularisation, HRE interacts with the values in place that can be influenced by how a community understands and preserves those values on the basis of its (perceived) ethnic identity and the need to protect it. The section therefore analyses the threat posed to Fulɓe's ethnic identity by the 'Wolofisation' process coming into being and how the Fulɓe in Senegal respond to it by showing resistance to change and adherence to local traditional values that they deem contribute to defining their ethnic identity.

SENEGAL: GENDER, DECISION-MAKING AND HUMAN RIGHTS CHALLENGES

Scholars' interest in the country of Senegal has often focused on the role it played in the flows of slavery trade that started in the 15th century, when the Portuguese first, for a brief period, and then the French for a much longer time, controlled the region (Der Thiam and Gueye 2000; Ralph 2015; Sako 1998). Senegal became an independent republic and was politically structured following the French presidential model in 1960 (Ka 2001). Since its independence, four presidents succeeded in leading the country: Léopold Senghor (1960–81), Abdou Diouf (1981–2000), Abdoulaye Wade (2000–12). Elections in 2012 saw the victory of the current president Macky Sall.

A population of 12.7 million live in the Republic of Senegal, 52 per cent of them women. The population is relatively young: the average age is 22 years old, and about half of the population is under 15 years old (World Bank 2013). Many ethnic groups live in Senegal, who entered the region through different waves of migrations (Der Thiam and Gueye 2000; Ralph 2015). The Wolof are the biggest ethnic group; their language is used as the lingua franca amongst members of different ethnic groups. The Fulɓe are the largest ethnic minority. Peaceful relations amongst different ethnicities are reinforced by inter-ethnic marriages, peaceful coexistence of different religious communities and the tradition of 'friendly banter': 'poking fun at the names and physical characteristics of others' (CERD 2012: 3), a practice that contributes to reinforcing social cohesion and inter-ethnic harmony (Gellar 1995; Gueye et al. 1995; Sako 1998).

Senegal is a fairly politically stable country. Since its independence, no coups or mass-scale human rights abuses have been registered. However, there are a number of notable challenges to the government's stability and citizens' security. In 2007, people's food security was seriously compromised by a series of severe droughts that endangered the production and sale of basic nutrients. The crisis particularly hit those households prominently relying upon subsistence agriculture only. Riots were widespread in the country and menaced its stability. Wade, president at that time, blamed the UN and, in particular, the Food and Agriculture Organization, claiming it failed to control the soaring price of food (Boccanfuso and Savard 2008; Zounmenou 2008). At the beginning of 2012, more unrest hit Dakar in the weeks immediately before the presidential elections. Wade's government had banned demonstrations, in violation of the right to freedom of expression and assembly, and security forces used force against demonstrators, some of whom were killed. Tensions were eased after the victory of President Macky Sall.

Human Rights

International human rights norms are included within Senegalese national law (see Tables 4.1 and 4.2). Senegal both included the treaties as pieces of national law and made reference to them within its local jurisprudence (Heyns and Viljoen 2001). The 2001 Senegalese constitution, for instance, affirmed Senegal's adherence to the Universal Declaration of Human Rights (UDHR), the Convention on the Rights of the Child (CRC), the Convention on the Elimination of All Forms of Discrimination against Women (CEDAW) and other human rights treaties (Constitute 2012). A rule of interpretation included in Senegalese law requires that domestic jurisprudence must be interpreted as much as possible in conformity with human rights treaties (Heyns and Viljoen 2001). Tables 4.1 and 4.2 summarise, respectively, some of the international human rights instruments and the African legal instruments ratified by the Government of Senegal that are relevant for the research.

Table 4.1 Selected international human rights instruments ratified by the Republic of Senegal

International human rights instrument	Date of ratification
International Covenant on Civil and Political Rights	13 February 1978
International Covenant on Economic, Social and Cultural Rights	13 February 1978
Convention on the Elimination of All Forms of Discrimination against Women	5 February 1985
Convention on the Rights of the Child	31 July 1990
Convention concerning the Prohibition and Immediate Action for the Elimination of the Worst Forms of Child Labour	1 June 2000

Table 4.2 Selected African human rights instruments ratified by the Republic of Senegal

African human rights instrument	Date of ratification
African Charter on Human and Peoples' Rights	21 June 1981
African Charter on the Rights and the Welfare of the Child	29 September 1996
Protocol to the African Charter on Human and Peoples' Rights on the Establishment of an African Court on Human and Peoples' Rights	10 June 1998

The government established a Senegalese Human Rights Committee whose powers were extended in 1997 and that was asked to publicise human rights through advocacy. The committee was also requested to draw the attention of the authorities to human rights violations and, where appropriate, to propose measures to end them; to issue opinions or recommendations in all matters relating to human rights; and to submit an annual report to the president on the situation of human rights in Senegal (United Nations 2011a).

However, even if the Government of Senegal has ratified a fair number of human rights instruments and put in place an appropriate committee, human rights advocates insist that there are major abuses and challenges that need to be urgently addressed by the government. Activists claim that currently there are a few main human rights issues that the Government of Senegal should urgently address. The first is the threat to freedom of expression posed by pre-electoral State measures: Malick Noël Seck, for instance, was imprisoned after asking the Constitutional Council in writing to refuse Wade's candidacy for a third term. He was released shortly after, though, following ex-President Wade's pardon (Amnesty International 2012). The second concern is the use of torture in detention: police forces are said to have covered up cases of torture as prisoners' suicides. Third, the conflict in the southern region of Casamance – opposing the national army and the Mouvement des Forces Démocratiques (MDFD) – has been the theatre of many human rights violations and abuses. On top of those, the recent amnesty granted by erstwhile President Wade to all members of the MDFD deprived the victims of any hope of justice (Amnesty International 2012). The fourth reason of concern for human rights activists is the large-scale homophobic discrimination taking place in Senegal, which puts seriously at risk the physical and mental health of those engaging in same-sex relationships. Finally, activists are concerned with the exploitation and abuse of the young Talibé: students of the Qur'an aged 4–12 years who are forced to beg in the streets of Senegal, whose health is seriously compromised by the violence of their masters and the poor health conditions of their daily life (Amnesty International 2012; Human Rights Watch 2012).

Despite these challenges, however, Senegal is attaining good results in other areas of human development and human rights. There is widespread consensus, for instance, on the progress that the country has made in terms of good governance, development of infrastructure and gender equality (AFDB 2010; Mbow 2009; UN 2011).

Gender Roles and Relations

Women's roles in the family and the society in pre-colonial Senegal varied much and according to their ethnicity: while they had consistent political power in the Wolof society, they did not have equal access to public decision-making processes in the Fulɓe ethnic group (Creevey 1996; Diop 1989). It has been suggested that Islam impacted on women's role by granting them a higher level of freedom compared with the fundamentalist movement of the Arab world, although it relegated women to a position of second-class citizens (Creevey 1996; Gellar 2005). The economic transformations envisaged and driven by the French during their colonial rule increased work and responsibilities for women, while men could enjoy a new economic status, entering the newly created socio-economic hierarchy. These two historical events (the advent of Islam and the French colonisation) contributed in shaping an issue of social gender inequality: at the end of the colonial era, women had less access to education and fewer chances to be hired for a job, and they were unlikely to own land, to be politically represented and to be appointed to offices in government (Creevey 1996; Sow 2003).

Since independence, secular forces have promoted the idea of separating religion and laws as two distinct fields influencing citizens' life. First, in 1972, President Senghor passed a Family Code (strongly opposed by the Muslim orthodox brotherhoods) that provided a turning point for women's rights. The Code restricted some Islamic freedoms and was meant to improve the condition of women (e.g. divorce was introduced together with the option of legally declaring one's marriage as monogamist). On the other hand, the Code allowed citizens to choose whether to follow Qur'anic dispositions on certain matters – for instance, inheritance (which could be unevenly split) – fostering gender discrimination. Creevey (1996) noted that the Code legalised the status of women as 'second-class' citizens (e.g. according to the Code, the man was seen as the head of the family, having the right to decide where the family would live; and women could take a job only with the agreement of the husband). The adoption of the Code caused angry reactions both between the marabouts (local religious authorities), who declared the Code contrary to the Qur'anic principles regulating family relations, and the feminist groups, who claimed that it relegated women to an inferior status (Creevey 1996).

In 2007, Wade's government reviewed the Civil Law and passed a specific law on gender equality for electoral lists (approved some months before the 2007 legislative elections). Mbow (2008) has argued that this action was an effort to destabilise any coalition that could threaten Wade's parliamentary majority. Whatever the reasons, though, the 2007 Civil Law represented a milestone in the struggle for gender equality. The 2007 Civil Law, other than emphasising, in various places, gender equality and women's rights to purchase land and personally manage their properties, granted to women the right to seek a job without needing their husband's written consent (United Nations 2011a). In the last 10 years, the ratio of the female to male working age population actively engaged in the labour market grew and became higher than in many high-income countries, including Spain, Greece and Italy. Compared with the first years of the Republic, the political representation of women rose significantly, reaching levels of political representation that are not yet met by some developed countries (Kassé 2003).

Yet, gender inequality is still a major issue in Senegal. The Gender Inequality Index (GII) is one of the indicators adopted by the United Nations Development Programme (UNDP) to measure levels of human development in different countries. The GII is determined mainly by three factors: health (maternal mortality ratio and adolescent fertility rate); empowerment (female and male population with at least secondary education, and female and male shares of parliamentary seats); and labour (level of female and male labour force participation) (UNDP 2010). Senegal's GII (0.521 in 2015) is relatively low, especially due to gender differences in access to education (UNDP 2016; UNESCO 2001; UNICEF 2009b). Although in recent decades women living in urban areas have become more and more present in the liberal professions (Gellar 2005), men still outnumber women in those professions, such as in media-related jobs and in the high echelons of administration. In rural areas, work is strongly gendered, with women taking responsibility for more and harder tasks (Seck 2007). In the urbanised areas (espe-cially in Dakar), the ratio of girls to boys accessing secondary educa-tion has grown exponentially (91.8 per cent in 2012) in favour of the girls. Women can aspire to higher professional opportunities (compared with to 20 years ago) and challenge traditional roles that tied women in to relations of economic dependence on their husbands. On the other hand, however, a wide segment of the population (especially in the rural areas) still does not enjoy access to school; less-educated women are seemingly more attached to family roles that keep the man as undis-puted head of the household (Gellar 2005; World Bank 2013).

In spite of these persisting traditional roles, Gellar (2005) suggested that both education and modernisation are contributing to challeng-ing norms regulating gender roles and relations. When he returned to Senegal 40 years after his first fieldwork, he observed the change in the villages he visited the first time: in 1962, the meeting was dominated by the eldest male (the village chief) and the young men sat quietly at the back; women were absent from the meeting. In a later trip, in 2004, women were present and spoke up and were not afraid of contradicting the men when they disagreed (Gellar 2005).

Tostan nonformal HRE targets rural areas, where access to formal education is low and where gender inequality is higher (World Bank 2013). HRE programmes in rural Senegal should take into account the fact that, although traditional gender roles are being relatively chal-lenged by wider access to education and processes of 'modernisation', they might still represent a source of social injustice in terms of access to labour and to decision-making processes. In other words, in present-ing participants with a set of problems that might help them challenge their local status quo, deliverers of HRE should take into account both the process of change in gender equality happening in certain areas of the country (that might help women participate in decision-making processes) and the persistence of gender roles that reproduce gender inequality in others.

New understandings of possible gender roles are emerging in Sene-gal, especially (but not exclusively) in the urban areas. HRE programmes can look at how citizens in those areas are negotiating socially those new roles to understand the way in which members of rural commu-nities might make sense of new, emerging roles in their local context, challenging gender relations that hinder or limit women's access to local decision-making processes.

Decision-Making and Political Structures

Rural community members' access to local decision-making processes can be influenced by both Senegal's administrative structure (which shapes people's opportunities to participate in the decision-making process) and the way in which the democratic discourse is conveyed by national and local politicians (which might encourage or discourage community members from participating in local politics). Here, I look briefly at both the administrative structure and the way in which politicians embody the democratic discourse, arguing that the latter is more harmful to people's freedoms and development than the former. If I am right, that is, if the problem is in how people make sense of what is 'democratic' rather than the actual administrative structure in itself, an HRE programme would be a promising solution as it would help participants change local collective beliefs of who can participate and how, that is, existing norms regulating access to decision-making. Let me discuss this a little more.

The Senegalese constitution guarantees the participation of all citizens in public life, with no discrimination of any sort. All citizens have the right freely to set up associations, economic, cultural or social groupings, and companies, provided that they comply with the formalities laid down in laws and regulations (Constitute 2012; United Nations 2011a). Between 1970 and 1980, Senegal established a multiparty system and democratic institutions. The 2001 constitution established a semi-presidential system. The amendments of 2007 and 2008 established a Senate. Legislative power is exercised by a parliament formed by the Senate and the National Assembly (United Nations 2011a).

Being a republic with only four presidents in about 60 years, some have argued that Senegal is similar to an absolute kingdom rather than a constitutional republic (Mbow 2008). In spite of this, for many years Senegal has been considered a model of African democracy (Fatton 1987; Gellar 1995) and some journalists still describe it as such (BBC 2017). Recently, scholars have instead spoken of Senegal as a democracy in crisis: it is politically and administratively dependent on France's will, its rulers generally favour corruption rather than the country's economic development, and votes are often sold and bought, especially at the rural level (Diouf 1992; Gellar 2005; Mbow 2008). In 2011 and 2012, the population marched against Abdoulaye Wade's intention to change the article in the constitution that stopped him from running for a third mandate (BBC 2012b; Loomis 2012). Although Wade tried to be re-elected by any means, including undemocratic or violent ones (he threatened the constitutional judges, repressed marches with the use of force, declared unlawful Youssou Ndour's intention to be a presidential candidate, to cite some), he lost the elections against Macky Sall.

It is difficult to assess whether the results of the elections represent a democratic victory of the civil society (as 'hailed' by the US Secretary of State, Hillary Clinton: BBC 2012c) or simply a shift in who controls the most politically influential clientelist power factions. Shortly after his election, however, Macky Sall gave proof of not holding democratic institutions as the highest priority of his political agenda; for instance, suggesting the abolition of the Senate to fund flood relief actions in Dakar, a Senate that incidentally hosts a political majority hostile to President Sall (BBC 2012a).[3] Caution in 'hailing' democracy is suggested by the long record of failures in the post-colonial African attempts to build democratic political systems (failures exacerbated by neo-liberal economies that favoured corruption and clientelism) (Allen 1995; Allen et al. 1992; Szeftel 2000). In looking at Macky Sall's government as a shift towards a more democratic state, one should at least acknowledge the different interpretations that democracy can have and its relations with neo-patrimonialist dynamics that play an important role in strengthening 'weak' post-colonial African governments (Chabal and Daloz 1999; Englebert 2009).

At the local level, Senegalese educated elites and the rural population translated and made use of the concept of democracy in very different ways. The Western-educated elites adapted the colonial democratic language, creating meanings and concepts that made little to no sense for the majority of the population (especially at the rural level). Few Senegalese during the colonial rule had exposure to modern democratic institutions or to free civic education (Hesseling 1985). Educated elites (especially those of the opposition) spoke of *démocratie*, mainly referring to free elections and political *alternance* (change in power). The Senegalese population at the grassroots level instead coined the term *demokaraasi* incorporating notions of civil liberties within traditional values such as collective consensus in decision-making, solidarity and mutual reciprocity in how resources are shared, and equality in the way family members are treated. One of the most distinctive features of *demokaraasi*, for instance, is that rural communities come to a consensus on a party of choice and vote united for that party, rather than leaving political choice to individuals (Gellar 2005). Collective voting, however, does not pose a problem in democratic terms in itself: individuals might have an effective interest in conforming to collective voting practices. Village chiefs have higher bargaining power with local administrators when they represent the vote of an entire village and this can help them in obtaining support for their local communities (e.g. in terms of resources, infrastructure and policies). Hoffman and Gibson (2005) demonstrated that, in Africa, gatekeeping and patrimonialist governments where local authorities have higher powers of taxation resulted in a more effective implementation of local public services, and they suggested that this might be due to the bargaining relations that exist between collective voters and local administrators. When the administration of local public services is in the hands of the national government, local rural communities receive minimal services due to the little accountability of the central government and complaint capacities of local rural communities. From a human development perspective, the problem is not with the voting procedure itself but rather that nobody should be forced to vote in a way that limits his or her freedom and coerces his or her will; *demokaraasi*, then, does not seem to pose a challenge to the life of the members of a rural community.

Social hierarchies in Senegal are largely based on age. In pre-colonial Senegal, elders dominated family and village structures, with the eldest male descendant of the founder of the village inheriting the post of village chief. They maintained control over key resources, such as land, livestock, women and children. This control enabled them to ensure a social order dominated by limited youth participation in decision-making (Allen 1995; Gellar 2005). Recently, however, elders' traditional roles have started to be challenged. Perry (2009) argued that, due to the recent neo-liberal reforms that allowed young people to have greater economic independence, young Senegalese Wolof citizens were respecting less and less the elders' traditional authority in the urban areas. In response to these 'revolutionary' dynamics, the elders in rural Senegal tried to preserve social order and traditional power roles, sometimes even requesting the intervention of the State and the police (Perry 2009). Decision-making is not only influenced by age factors: women also enjoy limited access to decision-making processes dominated by male members of rural communities (Talla 1999). Although Senegal grants by constitution the right to vote and to participate in the political life of the Republic to all citizens, the way in which national and local politicians have embodied the democratic discourse as well as traditional patriarchal norms or respect for male elders have alienated most marginalised citizens (particularly children and women) from active participation in the political life of their communities.

An effective HRE programme in Senegal should include different gender and age groups of local communities to guarantee an effective empowerment of the community and foster participation in local decision-making places. It should also help participants engage critically with the national and local political discourse, looking at the way in which they both make decisions in their villages and demand accountability of local elected administrators.

Other Human Rights-Inconsistent Social Practices

According to human rights activists, there are three widespread social practices in Senegal that are inconsistent with human rights norms: female genital cutting, child labour, and child and forced marriages (Amnesty International 2012). The government is working towards their abandonment; nonetheless, those practices persist.

The first, female genital cutting (FGC), is a widespread practice that was declared illegal by the Government of Senegal in 1999 (Rahman and Toubia 2000). It can seriously harm the girls that undergo it and it produces life-long pain that can be persistent or appear while having sexual intercourse. The practice is still followed mainly because of the much higher marriageability of cut girls compared with the very low chances of getting married that uncut girls have (Shell-Duncan 2008; UNICEF 2008a).

The second challenge, child labour, affects thousands of children in Senegal. The Government of Senegal also participates in the International Labour Organization (ILO) programmes that target child labour, and has promoted a jurisprudence setting the minimum age for work at 15 years old (and 18 years old for hazardous works). However, many children still work in agriculture using dangerous machinery and tools. Others work in cattle herding and are exposed to injury or diseases. Also, many children are enslaved and used as beggars (as in the case of the Talibé children analysed earlier) (Human Rights Watch 2010; UNICEF 2009a).

Finally, CFMs are still widely practised despite the Senegalese legislation aimed at ending them. Law enforcement is unsatisfactory and, especially in the rural areas, there can be a high incidence of domestic violence. Marriages are conducted when girls are very young and, although they are often given the option of refusing the marriage, social expectations play against their rejection of the future husband. However, the age of marriage is slowly rising in Senegal, which might suggest a possible gradual abandonment over the long term (UNICEF 2001).

Freire (1970) argued that educators that want to engage participants in problem-posing processes of liberation should be aware of
the possible themes that might emerge in the class, and be ready to ask
participants to express their opinions on those themes as they emerge.
The human rights challenges that Senegal currently faces could represent, for a deliverer of HRE in a rural community, a possible agenda of
themes that might emerge in class and that the educator (or facilitator,
in the case of Tostan) should be ready to grasp as soon as participants
make reference to them.

THE NGO TOSTAN: APPROACH, CURRICULUM AND LIMITATIONS

The NGO Tostan has been working in Senegal since 1982, implementing development programmes aimed at empowering local communities.
Tostan's initial mission was to tackle illiteracy through education programmes within rural communities, particularly targeting unschooled
rural women (Gillespie and Melching 2010). With time, Tostan's mission changed and came to include community empowerment through
wider education programmes (see Box 4.1).

Box 4.1 Tostan mission statement (source: www.tostan.org)

Tostan is a US 501(c)(3) nongovernmental organization whose mission is to empower
African communities to bring about sustainable development and positive social
transformation based on respect for human rights. Working primarily in remote
regions, we provide holistic, participatory education to adults and adolescents who
have not had access to formal schooling.

The original literacy-based curriculum was created by a cross-cultural
team that included the founding director of the NGO and local practitioners in the field of education. The team who produced the curriculum
did not start from any specific pedagogic theory. Rather, they worked by
reframing the curriculum following success stories. The team interacted
with the participants in the early stages of the programme to meet the
needs and expectations of the local population. In the period between
1980 and 1990, Tostan paid particular attention to participatory programme development, involving rural Senegalese women in the process
of revising curricula and programme activities. Curriculum development
grew out of respect for local women's perceptions of salient community

problems and learning styles. Tostan's programme came to integrate interactive facilitation and an education offering composed of problem solving, health, literacy and management (Easton et al. 2003; Gillespie and Melching 2010).

In the decade between 1990 and 2000, academic research interest in Tostan's history and methodology grew and the NGO revised its curriculum following participants' feedback. Engaging local facilitators and educators and responding to local demand, the NGO developed new interactive modules on democracy, human rights and women's health (Gillespie and Melching 2010). According to scholars who researched Tostan's history, the modules on human rights and women's health raised a lot of interest in participants, who would link what they learnt in the programme to community organisation and social action (Cislaghi et al. 2016; Easton et al. 2003, 2009; Gillespie and Melching 2010). In 1997, as a result of the pressure coming from participants in the HRE programme for social reorganisation, a rural community publicly declared for the first time the abandonment of FGC amidst neighbouring communities, media and local officials through a public event (Easton et al. 2003; Gillespie and Melching 2010; Johnson 2003; Koenig 2001; Mackie 2000; Tostan 2009b; UNICEF 2005). After the precedent set by this first rural community, other communities began critically examining their adherence to the practice. Following the impetus generated by the first public declaration on the abandonment of FGC, Tostan began addressing the practice from new perspectives, exploring how HRE as presented in its programme might lead to retaking into consideration traditional social practices (Mackie and LeJeune 2009; UNICEF 2008a).

The above chronology – other than framing the key events in the curricular reform – gives an understanding of how Tostan came to give to participants the tools to challenge local social norms, creating the framework for improving life in their communities together. The programme was not created against the social practices that it claims to challenge. However, the step-by-step curricular reforms undertaken by the programme shaped the context in which a community could discuss social practices. Following the review of the events analysed above, Tostan emerged as an interesting case study to research on the possible connections between human rights education and social change.

Human Rights Education Curriculum in the CEP

Tostan's Community Empowerment Program lasts three years and is split into three different phases. The second and third phases address issues such as hygiene, health, literacy, maths and project management. The first phase of the programme (called Kobi 1) introduces democracy, human rights and problem-solving techniques. Kobi 1 is the object of my research.

Tostan's curriculum has been defined as participative, learner centred and built on the local 'cultural' features of the communities that participate in it (Cislaghi et al. 2016, 2017; Easton et al. 2003; Gillespie and Melching 2010; Welch 1995). The NGO claims that its curriculum is structured as such to ground its offerings in the local context; is designed through participatory research with participants; cultivates positive relationships with religious and traditional authorities (so as to demonstrate respect for existing values and customs); comprehends issues of participants' interest; and gives participants the task of running the programmes and the follow-up activities (Easton et al. 2009).

The classes are delivered by a facilitator trained by Tostan, who lives in the rural community for the duration of the programme and receives a monthly salary granted by the NGO. The rural community provides the facilitator with food and shelter (Easton et al. 2009). Tostan trains facilitators before the beginning of the Kobi 1 in a one-week training course and gives them a manual that guides them through the programme session by session. From the first session of the Kobi 1, participants are asked to express hope and desires for the future of their villages; through these discussions they discover shared goals and begin to realise the transformative potential of their community (Tostan 2009c). In the first session, participants are introduced to the programme and get to discuss their expectations of it. This session asks participants to imagine how they would like their village to be in the future and will serve for future reference to motivate participants' collaboration and participation.

Then, in the second session, participants express their vision for the future of their community; they identify community goals and draw them on flip chart paper. In the third session, participants discuss everyone's place in the world: in their family, in the community, as well as in the nation and in the entire world. In this session, participants are invited to discuss the importance of each human being in a community that works for common goals. They discuss the importance of every-one's work in the community and link this to prevailing values through the use of local proverbs (e.g. *Conflict does not exist; only a lack of dialogue exists*, or *It is useless to prepare lots of rice if no one likes rice*).

In the following sessions, participants discuss the organisation of soci-ety (laws, governments and constitutions) and the purpose of democracy. Then, they are introduced to human rights. This set of sessions presents, for instance, the human right to life, the human right to be protected against all forms of violence and discrimination, the human right to health and the human right to education (Tostan 2009a). Every session starts with a drawing depicting a situation. Participants are then asked to comment on that drawing. They are often split into small groups to deepen the aspect examined at the beginning of the session. Classes usu-ally follow a structured pattern, presented in Box 4.2.

Box 4.2 Standard structure of Kobi 1 classes

1. Warm-up through a dance or a game.
2. Review of last session.
3. Showing a drawing representing a human right (for instance, a draw depicting different people at the beginning of the session on discrimination).
4. Large group discussion on the human right led by questions such as 'What do you see in this drawing?'; 'What unites all people in this drawing, despite their different colours, hairs, clothes, religion, etc.?'
5. Small group discussion/game/preparation of a sketch following a discussion.
6. End of the session with a dance or a game.

The facilitator triggers the participation of everyone through small games and active skits. The programme as described in the manual makes use of a series of different pedagogical techniques (see Table 4.3), aimed at enhancing participants' interaction, debate and participation.

The manual asks the facilitator to invite participants to be critical about what the facilitator is saying. Participants are always invited to engage in the first person with the human rights content under discus-sion. These suggestions are in line with Freire's critical pedagogy that underlines the importance of generating critical dialogue in the class, coinvestigating with participants the themes that emerge and matter to them (Freire 1970). Also, the use of the skits resonates with Boal's (1979, 1995) understanding of theatre as an educational tool for development,

Table 4.3 Pedagogical techniques suggested in Tostan's facilitator manual (Kobi 1) (drawing reproduced with permission of Tostan)

Pictures of human rights	'Show participants Drawing 2 (a woman and man sitting among members of the community)' (Tostan 2009a: 46).

Learning grounded within participants' life experiences	'Have participants discuss what constitutes violations of this human right, giving concrete examples from their community' (Tostan 2009a: 44)
Small groups discussion and group reports	'Have the participants divide into four groups. Explain: We will work often in small discussion groups in order to give everyone a chance to speak out and participate actively. Before starting any group activities, it's important for each group to choose a spokesperson who can summarize their group's ideas and results' (Tostan 2009a: 2)
Class discussions moderated/ encouraged by the facilitator and with direct questions	'Ask: In your opinion is this human right generally respected in your family, community, and country? Why or why not? (Conduct a discussion and encourage participants to give concrete examples)' (Tostan 2009a: 47)
Expression through arts	'Put an empty sheet of flip chart paper in front of the group. Take out several markers. Ask **each** participant to come one by one, take a marker, and draw a representation of what will be found in the community 5 years from now' (Tostan 2009a: 11)
Games	'Explain: We are going to review the previous sessions with the"The Democracy Game." Here are the rules of the game: Each participant chooses a partner [. . .]' (Tostan 2009a: 32)

Role-playing	'Ask a participant to play the role of Mrs Irresponsible and defend herself before the People's Council. She should explain her point of view without being interrupted' (Tostan 2009a: 67)
Songs and poetry	'Ask each group to create a short song or to make up a poem addressing the question [. . .]. Allow them sufficient time, and then ask for a volunteer from each of the four groups to present the song or poem to the larger group. Help them to write down the songs or poems after class and post them on the wall' (Tostan 2009a: 16)
Theatre	'Have the volunteers perform the skit they prepared before the class. When the participants have finished performing their skit, ask them to discuss it' (Tostan 2009a: 52)

seen earlier. Participants are invited to bring the abstract knowledge into their daily life, by linking human rights to the social behaviours in practice in their rural community. By doing so, HRE offers the class the opportunity to re-understand those social behaviours through a human rights perspective. Avoiding a banking approach to human rights, where participants' knowledge would be evaluated as right or wrong through exams or tests, the HRE approach described in the Kobi 1 manual allows participants to deconstruct local realities from the human rights perspective that is presented to them with an interactive pedagogy. In being asked to imagine a different village, as the manual recommends doing in one of the first sessions, participants are encouraged to develop alternative views of their life. Throughout the human rights sessions, the facilitator is requested to make reference to that ideal village, linking the positive behaviours that participants identify with that common goal. The class, then, is invited to share with the rest of the village their findings and the new knowledge they have acquired. They are invited by the facilitator to adopt a learner and to share their ideas with the neighbouring villages.

Organised Diffusion of the Results

Tostan believes that the CEP facilitates social change through a six-phase process (Diop et al. 2004). In the first phase, a village committee is created to manage and adapt the programme. In the second phase, a part of the rural community participates in the educational programme. In the third phase, each participant 'adopts' a person who does not participate in the programme with whom he or she shares the acquired knowledge. In the fourth phase, those who took part in the programme initiate a process of social mobilisation: discussion leaders ask for community support in denouncing harmful practices. Then, in phase five and if the community expresses support, the community leaders start gathering support from other villages during village meetings and using family ties; the result is the diffusion of the new knowledge. Finally, in phase six, a group of villages organise a public declaration to manifest their intent to abandon harmful practices (such as FGC or CFM) (Diop et al. 2004).

Phase one takes place before the beginning of the classes. A village committee is created, sharing responsibilities and tasks on different areas (amongst the different roles are a secretary, a person in charge of environmental cleanliness, a person in charge of health issues and a person in charge of education). This committee will be responsible for the adoption of the programme in its different aspects. Phase two is the object of this research. Participants attend a common programme and develop new visions. They discuss human rights and link the new knowledge to daily norms and practices. Phase three is meant to multiply the effect of the programme within the rural community while the programme is still running.

UNICEF has analysed phases four, five and six – the 'organised diffusion strategy'. Here, information diffuses out from the community that enjoyed the programme to new communities with whom they are in contact. The shift in social norms gains new consensus through discussions, and the diffusion process spreads from communities to bigger intra-marrying groups throughout the social network and the ethnic group (UNICEF 2008a).

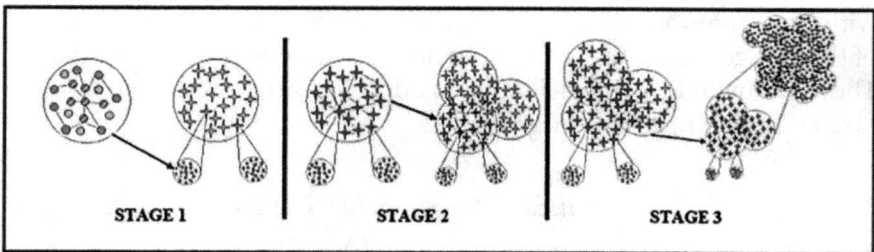

Figure 4.1 Three stages of organised diffusion (adapted from UNICEF 2008a: 20)

Figure 4.1 shows three key stages of the organised diffusion. In the first stage (on the left in the figure), participants and the adopted learners seek consensus among much of the community (not necessarily amongst all families, though). This community then seeks the approval of those being in the same larger group of communities (defined by family ties and intra-marriageability).

In the second stage (in the middle in the figure), two communities (in the smaller circles) have successfully created a consensus through discussion in the group of communities. The group moves towards a public declaration of abandonment of a harmful social practice: the change is collective and simultaneous. Certain communities of this last group, however, are also part of other groups: family ties and intra-marrying groups overlap.

In the third stage (on the right), the diffusion process spreads to other groups, which again must reach consensus and then acknowledge the change publicly. Finally, the diffusion process can extend beyond the initial community (and even state) boundaries and influence other groups throughout the social networks and the wider ethnic group (UNICEF 2008a).

Potential Limitations and Pitfalls of the Tostan Programme

There are at least four potential limitations that might threaten the impact (or the understanding of the impact) of the Tostan programme and that informed the analysis of the programme in the field. The first one is related to the indicators chosen to measure its success. According to the NGO staff, UNICEF is one of Tostan's most important donors. To evaluate the impact of the Tostan programme, UNICEF has for a long time adopted village declarations of abandonment of 'harmful' social practices (as for instance FGC and CFM) as the key indicator. However, the very idea that indicators of impact should by chosen by others than community members could be contested. Ellerman (2006) suggested that international development agencies have the tendency to override people's self-help capacity with social engineering programmes (the greatest example being the structural adjustment programmes). In other words, that development agencies have an idea of how the world 'should be' and try to make it as such. As I said before, though, development programmes should not make 'developing' communities conform to the imaginary of international agencies in the 'developed' world.

Rather, they should create conditions for community members to participate together in reflection on their social reality and decide if they want to change it and, if so, how. Since I began this research, Tostan has expanded its monitoring and evaluation framework to include a wide range of indicators, now including measures for improvement in communities' governance, education, health, environment, and economic conditions. Even in the face of Tostan's efforts to capture more meaningful data on community empowerment, though, I wonder what the place in the development business is for NGOs that – on the one hand – are trying to help communities drive their own development, while – on the other hand – having to report to donors on a set of expected outcomes. This is a major problem in international development. The place for similar NGOs is unavoidably uncomfortable, struggling to find donors who are ready to finance projects that cannot commit to specific results beforehand, and trying to help communities achieve together what matters to them.

The second limitation of the Tostan programme is linked to its potential for people empowerment and creation of aspirations. Developing capacity to aspire might be dangerous as it might raise people's hopes and expectations over certain outcomes without providing them the means to meet them. The Tostan programme might raise expectations of future professional careers, for instance; or, it might create aspirations in human development terms (e.g. one of equal dignity of all human beings) that cannot find immediate satisfaction in the community and might thus lead the 'newly empowered' to frustration. Within a non-problem-posing education framework, capacity to aspire can potentially gather various sectors of the community in a dialogue over individual or communal aspirations. It is to be understood how the awakening of similar new aspirations fits or clashes with existing power relations. Potentially, the Tostan programme might unleash hopes and expectations that disrupt those power relations and generate normative reactions of power holders (threatening the immediate well-being of the powerless or of the entire community). Deep divisions and differences are likely to exist in the rural communities where Tostan operates, and achievement of new status quo of certain community members might produce heterogeneity in ideation. This heterogeneity might in turn provide the circumstances for contradiction, contestation and conflict. Studying Tostan's programmatic strategies hence becomes important as it can offer insights into how HRE can possibly connect together people from different 'sectors' (castes, genders, economic classes, ethnic groups) of the community and engage them in a conciliatory dialogue over collaborative improvement of everyone's life.

Finally, the NGO might have gathered over time sufficient authority in Senegal so that its facilitators could be seen by participants as dispensing truth, rather than building it up with them. If that was the case, then, community members would do what Tostan facilitators suggest only because they have seen (or heard of) the advantages of the Tostan programme in other communities. Freire (1970) noted that similar tensions are typical in all educational programmes: the oppressed expect to 'be liberated' because they initially deprecate the self as powerless. The role of the deliverer of the programme is to convert this tension (potentially as oppressive as the conditions that problem-posing education wants to challenge) to a constructive one. To explore the extent of this possible pitfall, what must be analysed is what happens in class, the way in which facilitators understand their role and how participants make sense of it in their relation with the facilitator. No research has so far studied what happens within the human rights education classes that can motivate social change or the abandonment of certain practices.

Addressing these limitations, I offer in this book an analysis of Tostan's HRE programme in the field. I studied what actually happens both in the classes and in the community that motivates change, and I looked at the features of that change: externally superimposed and conflictual, internally driven and harmonious or anything in between.

THE FULƁE IDENTITY: VALUES AND CHARACTERISTICS

The Fulɓe are a very large nomadic ethnic group spread throughout Central and West Africa. Thus, they often represent the largest minority in the country where they settle (for short or longer periods). Botte et al. (1999) reported that, as a minority, they often declared feeling at risk of losing their ethnic identity under the cultural homogenisation processes driven by the ethnic majorities and reacted to that by reaffirming what they understand as their traditional values. The complexities that arose while trying to define the characteristics of the Fulɓe, their language or moral code, challenged all researchers on the Fulɓe, shaping a multi-faceted Fulɓe question that makes problematic the reification of a Fulɓe category (Azarya et al. 1999; Botte 1999; Burnham 1999; Krause 1883; Monteil 1950). In Senegal, the Fulɓe (also called Peul in the French literature) live in the central part of the country and are often considered as forming a single ethnic group with the Tukuloor (Toucouleur in the

French literature) who live in the basin of the Senegal River, in the northern part of the country (Clark 1997; Hrbek 1992). However, these two groups of Haalpulaar'en (literally in Fulfulde:'people who speak Pulaar', Pulaar being the name used in Senegal for Fula/Fulfulde, the language spoken by Fulɓe), although being united by the common language, differ much in values and social customs (Boutrais 1994; McLaughlin 1995). While the Tukuloor are traditionally a sedentary people, the Fulɓe are traditionally semi-nomadic pastoralists (McLaughlin 1995).

The Fulɓe of Senegal claim that their uncorrupted traditional values and the related behaviours distinguish them from a spurious and Westernised Wolof majority (McLaughlin 1995). However, scholars in the field found some inconsistencies in what those values are throughout the various Fulɓe groups that live in the continent. This might be due to the large dispersion of the Fulɓe in the continent, on the one hand; and on the other, because in the past the Fulɓe identity has been negotiated with the colonial powers to ensure their support in maintaining a high position in the colonial hierarchy (Bierschenk 1999; Leblon 2006; Salamone 1985, 1997). Also, it has been argued that various populations might have adopted Fulɓe values and customs to ascend to the rank of the colonial elite (Salamone 1985). As Weber (1968) has observed already, what defines an ethnic group is not common descent, but it is the belief in that common descent, reified within customs and social behaviours, even when an objective blood relation does not exist. Being a Pullo (singular for Fulɓe) is not a question of direct genealogy, but it is related to meeting a set of social expectations and behaviours. Being a Pullo means being capable of behaving accordingly to the Fulɓe code of conduct; it means being able to show to both members and non-members of the Fulɓe community adherence to the Fulɓe code of values (Djedje 2008; Haffanden 1930; Riesman 1992; Salamone 1997). The Fulɓe in Senegal face the challenges of defending their identity threatened by the process of Wolofisation and, at the same time, making sense of that identity through a set of local social behaviours.

There is general agreement amongst scholars on some of the characteristics composing that set of norms and behaviours today. In particular, researchers have identified four: speaking the Fulɓe language (Fulfulde); leading a pastoral and nomadic life; following Islam while believing in black magic; and showing adherence to a moral behavioural code called *pulaaku* (Azarya et al. 1999; Botte et al. 1999; Dupire 1996; Issa and Labatut 1974; Leblon 2006).

The Fulɓe consider their language a sacred ensemble of unique concepts and views of the world (Breedveld and De Bruijn 1996). McLaughlin (1995) analysed the relationship between language and identity in Senegal, arguing that Tukuloor and Fulɓe create a single ethnic identity based on their common language. Given the role of Fulfulde as 'watermark' of ethnic identity, the Fulɓe (and all Fulfulde-speaking Senegalese people in general) feel threatened by a process of linguistic Wolofisation as they fear it might result in an ethnic homogenisation. Fulɓe and Tukuloor react with a proud return to (what they understand as being) their original (linguistic and ethnic) identity (McLaughlin 1995). Language, then, is intrinsically related to the way Fulɓe see and make sense of the world and their social relations and behaviours. The significance that Fulɓe attach to the Fulfulde language shows the relevance of carrying out an HRE programme in that language, allowing participants to renegotiate the world for what it is in their original understanding of it, and not in foreign cultural meanings.

In spite of recent changes in practices caused by the severe drought of the last 20 years, pastoral activity is still a strong mark of identity for the Fulɓe, and the association between Fulɓe and herding is strong and immediate for many Africans living in Western and Central Africa (Davidheiser and Luna 2008). The ethnographic studies by Botte et al. (1999) described the Fulɓe as characterised by a nomadic spirit, either effective in their actual movement or potential in keeping life conditions that would allow a possible migration. Their nomadic nature is related to the daily basic needs of their herds: pastoral resources are non-static and animals need movement to access them. Avoiding insects, weather, thieves and a hostile social environment are only some of the many factors linking mobility and herding (Awogbade 1983; Benoit 1975, 1988; Davidheiser and Luna 2008; Salzman 1980). The *ngaynaaku* (shepherding) is a fundamental character of the Fulɓe identity, and is strongly interrelated to the concept of *ndimaaku* (nobility and dignity). The other ethnic groups that come into contact with them in all sub-Saharan Africa have traditionally valued the Fulɓe's herding skills, which grants them a certain level of respect within social hierarchies (Botte et al. 1999). In certain areas of Senegal, due to the climate conditions of the last 30 years and to government policies discouraging nomadism, the Fulɓe have preserved their nomadic trait only as potential capacity, and some have adopted a more sedentary lifestyle while other Fulɓe still subordinate agricultural practices to herding (De Bruijn and Van Dijk

1994; Riesman 1992; Santoir 1994). Human rights practices, within this framework, might have to deal with the challenges of a pastoral life in terms of, for instance, work distribution, health and hygiene conditions or village structural improvement.

Islam has taken in the last century a more and more important role in the daily life of Fulɓe communities. While in the past knowledge, of Islam was reserved to the political centre and the nobility, in the course of history it has become a 'folk-religion [that] has by now become one of the most important ideological forces [...] of Fulɓe society as a whole' (De Bruijn and Van Dijk 1994: 104). Religion shapes values and social behaviours of the Fulɓe as much as their – effective or potential – nomadism. In Senegal, however, where the belief in the black magic powers of the marabouts mixes with more classical approaches to Islam, the Fulɓe integrate Islam with paganism and animism (Houtsma et al. 1993; Monteil 1950; Ogawa 1993; Salamone 1997).

The Fulɓe society is strongly hierarchical, in both internal and external relations. A belief in their superiority (as being the top rank of the social hierarchy) regulates uneven ethnic relationships between the Fulɓe and other ethnic groups. Such a superior identity is explained by their respect of the *pulaaku* conduct (Sall 1999). Fulɓe see themselves as opposed to the *Haaɓe* – a word that alone designates all the other sub-Saharan Africans who are not Fulɓe (Azarya and Eguchi 1993; Leblon 2006). With the term *pulaaku* the Fulɓe identify their common identity, despite their great diversity throughout Africa. The ambiguity of the concept is linked to the various interpretations that the different Fulɓe themselves make of it; however, almost all scholars agree in making reference to it as 'the Fulɓe way': an ensemble of Fulɓe qualities and a Fulɓe behavioural code of conduct (Botte et al. 1999; Leblon 2006; Ogawa 1994). Reframing social norms necessarily challenges such a traditional behavioural model (social and moral code), unless new norms are built within and respecting that specific model – hence the importance of understanding the meaning of this behavioural model.

According to the literature on the *pulaaku,* there are three qualities that any good Pullo should be able to demonstrate: *seemtende* (modesty and self-control), *munyal* (patience and fortitude) and *hakkillo* (care and forethought) (Botte et al. 1999; Stenning 1959). *Pulaaku* regulates relationships between Fulɓe of different social categories and between Fulɓe and other ethnic groups. To do so, the *pulaaku* includes *seemtende*: the responsibility to avoid shame, and to safeguard honour and self-control. For example, during assemblies the adults should not sit close to the elders; young people have to avoid integration with the group of adults while working or going to the market and have to show respect to the elders. Due to *seemtende*, amongst the Ful6e of Nigeria and Burkina Faso women avoid contact with men and do not talk in front of them to avoid the shame of doing so, and in general people of different social classes avoid eating together: men and women, young people and elders, strangers and members of the indigenous community (Leblon 2006). Self-mastery is the fundamental character of Ful6e identity. Consider the proverb *'pornde wootere hantataa fuudo kaa na semtina dimo* (One fart does no harm to the asshole but it still shames the gentleman)', cited by Riesman (1992: 24). Farting, lying, stealing and defecating are acts that Ful6e children must learn to control early on to avoid social shame. To be a Pullo, then, is to master the self, the world and even the others by showing adherence to a code of conduct. *Seemtende* can thus have an impact in human rights term by influencing, for instance, how young people participate in decision-making processes within a Ful6e rural community. Also, it can influence gender segregation practices that can hinder (or challenge) the human rights knowledge brought by the HRE programme by keeping women from talking in public when they think they might risk being judged as stupid or uneducated (Botte et al. 1999).

The Ful6e system of values and behaviours is said to be extremely dynamic (Djedje 2008). The fact that *pulaaku* is a fairly flexible ethos, where a certain degree of change can be bargained within a community, suggests that participants in HRE can reframe that set of moral norms by making it consistent with a critical re-understanding of their social relations. HRE might then offer a new understanding of the *hakkillo* concept from a human rights stance and invite participants to explore its application within their community. In so doing, participants would not be assimilating human rights within their set of values. Rather, they would be rediscovering local values from new perspectives and, based on them, renegotiating social norms and associated practices.

CONCLUSION

HRE in Senegal can be grounded on the wide amount of human rights law that the government has integrated within local jurisprudence, by committing both to human rights principles within the constitution and to all laws recently drafted. Brought to a rural context, there are certain key themes that participants in HRE might generate through their discussion. The first one is linked to the issues of gender equality: the Government of Senegal has striven to improve women's representation at the high levels of the national administration. However, the human development-based gender equality index shows that equality is still far from being reached, with women enjoying fewer job opportunities, poorer access to health services and a narrower amount of freedoms (especially in the rural areas of the country). On the other hand, however, deliverers of HRE should be aware that the social situation has changed extensively in the last 40 years and women are obtaining more and more recognition of their equal status, and that participants might have seen diverging roles for women in the reality that surrounds (or includes) their local rural community. There is a potential tension that deliverers of HRE must take into consideration: that of new gender roles being available for educated women to which uneducated women might aspire, and men's desire to preserve current roles in the family.

A similar tension might emerge with regard to the norms that regulate decision-making in a rural community. The democratic dynamics that HRE brings to the class might challenge pre-existing norms of hierarchy in the decision-making process. In Senegal, decision-making in the family and the society is largely male dominated; in particular, the elders enjoy a traditionally higher status. However, their role is threatened by modern views on the social position of youth; and, especially in the urban areas, alternative approaches to the decision-making process have emerged, with young people acting independently and questioning the elders' authority. Within rural areas, the elders try to maintain the local status quo unaltered. Deliverers of HRE should therefore be aware of the possible tensions that might occur in the classes, exposing divergent ideas about who should participate in or lead the decision-making processes. By avoiding conflict, the classes should help participants make sense of reciprocal needs and aspirations, offering elders and young community members an opportunity to express reciprocal feelings and concerns about existing norms of decision-making. Also, in Senegal a number of social practices may be the cause of concern from a human rights perspective. Those practices include FGC, CFM and excessive or hazardous child labour. HRE might be brought into communities where those practices exist and it should therefore give participants the opportunity to discuss and debate their appropriateness.

There is also evidence of fast-progressing forces of social change in Senegal. Should HRE impact on local social change processes, this impact should be inscribed within the wider social change dynamics existing in the country. HRE has the potential to positively impact on harmful social practices that the government is trying to fight (although law enforcement is seriously hindered by various factors, including the lack of resources needed to implement laws in the remote rural areas of the country); that potential should therefore be explored and linked to those major human rights issues. Tostan does so by framing human rights within the first part of the programme (Kobi 1) through the problem-posing pedagogy discussed by the NGO in the facilitator's manual. However, due to the differences in behavioural and moral codes of different ethnic groups, its implementation might differ from how Tostan envisaged it. The most critical challenge to the vernacularisation of human rights within a Fulɓe community, in particular, seems to be the process of Wolofisation that exists in Senegal. The HRE programme in Galle Toubaaco, as in other Fulɓe communities, should be aware of possible resistance to changes in local social practices and the relative norms, based on the understanding that the local community might have of its ethnic identity.

Part II

The Programme in Action

Chapter 4

GALLE TOUBAACO BEFORE THE PROGRAMME

INTRODUCTION

By drawing on the empirical data, this chapter offers an understanding of how community members in Galle Toubaaco described their community before the HRE programme. The first part of the chapter presents the village of Galle Toubaaco, exploring the structural characteristics that help make sense of members' relations that will be examined later.

In the second part I discuss gender roles and relations, decision-making processes and social practices that are inconsistent with human rights in place in the rural community. Gender norms in Galle Toubaaco granted men authority over women both in the family and in the village. As I looked in the data to understand the reasons for this gendered unequal distribution of power, two sets of resources seemed to be particularly important. I examine those two 'resource sets' (that I call labour and marriage resources) and their impact on women's human rights and human development. I then look at the political structure of Galle Toubaaco and the decision-making processes. I examine the relations of power that tied community members, and suggest that 'invisible' power dynamics (hegemonic ideology) shaped women's access to visible and hidden forms of power; that is, that gender roles and relations impacted on women's capability to access decision-making and agenda-setting processes. I found that unequal capabilities to participate in the decision-making process (with women and young members being excluded from it) contributed to fostering (and reproducing) an uneven social and political status quo.

The last section analyses two human rights-inconsistent social practices in place in the community: CFM and child labour. I do so to explore whether participants came to understand those practices as harmful during or after the HRE programme.

GALLE TOUBAACO

The village of Galle Toubaaco is located in the recently created administrative region of Kaffrine, in the rural community of Touba Mbella (Ministère de l'Intérieur 2008). The village is about 400 km from the capital Dakar and about 60 km from the urban centre of Kaolack, where major services (like hospitals or trade centres) are located. Distances are, however, difficult to cover due to the lack of roads and means of transportation (mainly horse carts) that can link the village with the closest urban centre.

The area surrounding the village is mostly desertified for nine months a year (i.e. always except during the rainy season), with some sporadic trees or other minor vegetation completing an arid landscape. The village is in a relatively isolated part of the region, in terms of both human settlements and natural resources. Families gather in households (*wuro*) of three or four houses that are relatively distant from each other.

Wolof villages resemble a dense agglomerate of houses, while Fulɓe villages look more like archipelagos of households, meeting animals' needs to move and reach grazing fields. Grazing fields begin 4 km away from the village, while closer fields are used for cultivating subsistence crops (millet and peanuts). The French colonisation introduced single-crop cultivation systems and the newly independent Governments of Senegal incentivised the cultivation of peanuts, confident in privileged economic relations with France (White 2000). To maximise their profit, the community of Galle Toubaaco invested in peanut cultivation of the surrounding fields (which, since the colonial land reform, they could legally own: Faye 2008) and adapted their life to new sedentary circumstances: since 1930, the village has remained in the same place. Bambara and Serere male 'slaves' (as informants called them, most likely prisoners condemned to public works) sent by the colonial State cultivated the land until 1949. Mandinka male sharecroppers, employed by the community members, did it afterwards. The fact that the community could employ sharecroppers is an indicator of the wealth they enjoyed after World War II and until the end of the 1960s. The big drought of the beginning of the 1970s and the end of government's incentives for peanut production in 1996 that followed the fall of international demand, instead seriously affected the community's living conditions and considerably slowed its economic development. The series of severe droughts further compromised the entire country's agricultural production and brought about a widespread famine (White 2000).

This international economic juncture impacted on the life of the small community of Galle Toubaaco. Informants said that, from 1970, community members started to eat the product of their crops (with the health implications that a low-nutrition diet based just on millet and peanuts implies), rather than selling them (and buying with the money a wider range of food: rice, vegetables and meat, for instance). The village's economy shifted from one of accumulation, where the surplus value generated by sharecroppers could be reinvested, to one of subsistence, where the family farmers cultivated their own (and sole) source of nutrition.

When this economic juncture required Galle Toubaaco to stop exporting peanuts, men – according to informants – withdrew from agriculture (or from managing cultivation) and dedicated themselves to other practices, mostly (as discussed later) looking for jobs in the weekly markets. Women, instead, continued to take care of subsistence cropping even though, often, they did not own the land they worked. As in Boserup's (1970) analysis, in Galle Toubaaco the colonial rule had an impact on women's role in farming, benefiting the men. Men – considered by colonial powers to be the ones meant to farm – were given the means to cultivate the land to generate capital, while women were relegated to subsistence crop production. The international economic juncture, in other words, indirectly contributed to fostering the gender distribution of labour analysed later in this chapter.

Every family in the village possesses a variable portion of land following lines of descent and past inheritances. Land is inherited from (or given by) parents and is owned in large percentage by men. There are no facilities of any kind (e.g. educational, religious, health or labour) in the village. At the time of the research, the building of a mosque had begun, but the project had then been abandoned due to lack of funds. The closest health post is about 15 km away, three hours by horse cart (the only transportation available in the village) in the desert. As a consequence, community members cannot visit the health post as much as their health status, according to the nurse at the local health post, would recommend. In the village there are two public water facilities and three private taps in the household (installed before the public ones). Therefore, not all women gather at the well tap (three families out of six have private water facilities), which might impact on the quality of social relations they enjoy in their household.

Due to the village's location, the contact that non-travelling community members have with the outside world is seriously challenged by the lack of electricity (and might in turn influence the speed of processes of social change compared with more urban areas). Battery radios are the only media present in the village. Cell phones are charged at weekly markets. Isolation is problematic because it can limit community members' ability to envision alternatives to local daily life.

The Fulɓe living in Galle Toubaaco identified themselves as a Fulɓe ethnic sub-group, the Haaboɓe (literally: those who get angry easily). Family relations link all community members of the rural community. At the time of fieldwork, in Galle Toubaaco there were 318 community members, 182 males and 136 females.

GENDER ROLES AND RELATIONS: INVISIBLE POWER

The relations between human beings in the production of goods to meet their material needs contribute to constructing human societies differently in distinctive geographical and historical contexts, which, in turn, gives shape to different social interactions between categories of individuals. Rural communities in particular are socially structured according to the relationships amongst community members caused by (and in turn regulating) relations of production (Meillassoux 1991). In sub-Saharan Africa, the power relations involved in the gender distribution of labour and property can limit women's bargaining power and force them to acquiesce to the unequal status quo (Folbre 1982). Unequal access to resources and gender segregation, then, contributes to the shaping of uneven distributions of power in the household (as analysed in this section) and in the community (as analysed in the next section). Gender roles, in particular, shape (and are shaped by) invisible power dynamics: the creation of biases, the process that gives form to psychological and ideological boundaries of participation (see Chapter 2; Gaventa 2006).

In Galle Toubaaco, community and family roles are socially constructed around the allocation of daily work; the gendered distribution of labour in the village and, more generally, a gendered life impacts on the access women and men enjoy to two different sets of key resources (i.e. labour and marriage resources). Unequal access to those key resources fosters the social status quo and limits women's (and hence the community's) human development. Findings show that resistance to men's power was reported, but in episodic and isolated form.

I will discuss these findings in greater detail below, as I intend to suggest that a change in social practices that regulate gender roles and relations might then spark and structure an alternative access to some (or all) of those resources. Rather than at a normative level (e.g. granting women's legal access to land), it is at a cognitive level that human development programmes must operate, allowing participants to unveil different social roles for each other, by sharing the struggles and challenges that the current social status quo poses to both genders.

Access to Labour Resources

In Galle Toubaaco everyone is called to contribute to the development of the village according to social and family roles. Men and women play different parts in the community and in the family and engage in different activities. Labour distribution in Galle Toubaaco mainly assigns productive tasks to men and reproductive ones to women, although some exceptions (analysed later) exist (Benerìa 1979, 2003; Benerìa and Sen 1981; Boserup 1970).

Men's roles in Galle Toubaaco are linked to economic production and the associated social value. To be a man in Galle Toubaaco means having the responsibility for generating revenue and providing for the family's subsistence. Amadou, a 27-year-old man who recently got married, explained to me that: 'a man should be working in his farm, herding cattle or doing some kind of business to generate money so he can provide for the family' [S2I9AB].[4] Fatou Diallo, a mature woman who described gender roles drawing on her experience in two marriages, said that: 'The men are the ones who go out and work, the women do not have the means to go out [of the village] and work' [S3I11FD]; a man in Galle Toubaaco:

> after having prayed, goes and checks out the cows, milks the cows, eats breakfast and goes off to business [then] he gets [back] home around 6 p.m. and then goes and checks to see if the kids are back from herding the cattle and makes sure everything is OK. Then he eats dinner, enjoys the family and goes to bed. [S1I14ABY]

One night, Samba Diallo, having returned from a hard day of work with his cattle, told me what it means to be a man in Galle Toubaaco: 'respecting and taking care of your parents, working hard, building a house, starting a family and taking care of [them]' [S3I6SD]; that is, make a family and provide the basic goods that women will use to respond to the family's basic needs. Men take care of the animals and, during the rainy season, prepare the land that is then farmed by women and children during the rest of the year. Most of the men in Galle Toubaaco also buy and sell animals in the weekly markets in the region. There are no markets held nearby, so men who work as sellers or middlemen travel to bigger town centres, where they meet people from the surrounding areas and access facilities they do not have in their village (e.g. electricity, media, hot and clean water, hospitals or banks).

Being a woman in Galle Toubaaco means taking care of the house and the family through various activities, including food production (some women farm in the fields) and preparation. Talking about what his mother does in her typical day, the 'young' Amadou (aged 19) said that she:

> wakes up in the morning, prays, sweeps the house, makes break-
> fast, fetches drinking water, makes lunch, after lunch she rests for
> a while, after her rest she makes dinner, after dinner she gets the
> chickens in, sits around and talks for a bit and then goes to bed.
> [S1I14ABY]

Penda, the third wife of Ndene (one of the elders of the village), described her day by saying:

> Once I wake up in the morning, I take a bath, make breakfast for
> the family, after that I go get water and then go out and fetch fire-
> wood for cooking lunch. In the evening I make dinner and after
> dinner my work is over so I rest and go to bed. [S1I9PS]

Ami, when asked about women's role in the community, said: 'the most important things a woman should do are praying every day, keeping clean and being polite and greeting everyone, doing laundry, dishes, and cooking and cleaning the house' [S1I6AS]. In summary, then, as Mas said:

> [Both] men and women are important to this village's future;
> everyone does their best to make sure the village evolves [...]
> It has always been organised this way [...] men farm and herd
> cattle and women stay at home cook, clean and take care of the
> kids. [S1I4MD]

African farming has been understood as a female agricultural system where easy access to land, together with low population density and little class differentiation, resulted in men preparing land for farming during the rainy season and women cultivating subsistence crops (all year long) (Boserup 1970). Fatou Diallo, in her first interview, spoke of the work women do in the fields:

> To contribute to the development of the village the women farm millet and peanuts [. . .] The men also contribute to the development of the village by farming on a larger scale. They are much stronger and use horses to help them plough the fields but the women do everything by hand so that is why men have much bigger fields. [S1I11FDY]

In Galle Toubaaco, while men are dedicated to revenue-generating activities, women's work mainly includes a number of reproductive functions: taking care of the children, gathering and preparing their food and farming subsistence crops. Deviance from this distribution exists. Fatou, in the same interview cited above, said that after having harvested the field, women 'will sell the peanuts' [S1I11FDY] but neither the observational data nor any other informant confirmed that women would sell the products of their work in the field. The fact that Fatou was a widow (with both higher revenue-generating responsibilities and freedoms) and that she had a little commerce in the village might explain her view on the potential for women to sell the products of their work in the fields. Generally speaking, informants included little deviance in their understanding of gender division of labour. Mas, the village *griot* – the entertainer, the 'master of the word' (Leymarie 1978; Mbaye 2007) – said that if in a house a wife is sick, 'I call for another woman to come and cook for us [. . .] the work is shared, the men have their work and the women have theirs [. . .] [if] men [were] cooking [there] would be a problem' [S3I4MD]. When I asked Djombo, a young man, what he would think of a woman who works and generates revenue (e.g. selling bread), he said:

> If you have work then it's not good to sell bread. If you are supposed to fetch water, you have to cook, wash the kids and do other housework, it's not good to try and take on selling something like bread because it will take away from your other work. [S2I7DS]

The 'old' Amadou also confirmed that:

> It's not good [for a girl to leave the house], if she gets out too
> much her parents-in-law won't respect her and they will start
> disliking her. She can get herself into trouble; she might go to
> the wrong place or say the wrong thing to someone. [. . .] When
> a man goes out he is looking to find a living for the family but
> when a woman goes out it's to entertain herself. [S2I9AB]

It can be hypothesised that, as suggested by Boserup (1970), following the
creation of a neo-liberal economic order in post-colonial Senegal, men of
Galle Toubaaco abandoned the fields for the markets, leaving to women
the roles of subsistence farmers, caretakers and housekeepers (Benería
and Sen 1981; Boserup 1970). It is possible that, following dynamics similar to those analysed by Kevane (2004), a similar distribution of labour
then contributed to building a social equilibrium where labour and identity strongly intertwined, with the former contributing to defining the
latter. As suggested by Mas's quote above, in Galle Toubaaco labour distribution plays a key role in defining gender norms (women have their
tasks, men have theirs). In taking care of what they are expected to, men
and women hold a social role and fulfil the social expectations for their
gender that they learnt to comply with when they were children. That
social role, then, in turn reproduces the existing gendered distribution of
labour and fosters the social norms that regulate it.

From a human rights and human development perspective, a gendered distribution of labour does not pose any problem in itself, as long
as this distribution respects people's freedoms, offers equal opportunities
for development of capabilities, and protects their human rights. Issues
come with the fact that, as seen later, women's work is considerably
harder and unhealthier, hinders women's freedoms and development of
capabilities and limits women's access to key resources, which, in turn,
restrains their power within the family and the rural community. In particular, the division of labour discussed above gives men privileged access
to money, information and services. Access to these three resources is
granted by the work and travel a person does outside the village, money
mostly resulting from work in the market, information and services being
accessed in bigger urban centres or villages where they are available. I
therefore call these three resources 'labour' resources.

The first labour resource is the revenue that work can generate. Men,
in Galle Toubaaco's families, are the breadwinners. They generate revenue through their work and control how much money goes to other

family members and how they spend it. The entire family, and women in particular, are considered to be under the eldest male's responsibility. Amadou Ba Mbaring, who at the time of the interview had been married to his first wife for three months, made sense of his responsibility for his wife by saying: 'It can be hard [to manage a woman] because you are responsible for her. You brought her into your home and if you are not able to support her it can be very difficult' [S1I16ABM].

Having control over economic resources means deciding how much money a wife will receive, as the young Djombo exemplified: 'men here give to women 20,000 FCFA[5] at Tabaski,[6] the rest they give them is to buy what they need to cook' [S1I5DS]. An entry in my diary contributes to this analysis:

> Today I saw Abdoulaye taking 1,000 FCFA from his bum bag and I realised he has a lot of money. However, I have never seen him give any to his wife; when she asks, he often says he doesn't have any. Korka (interpreter) heard men talking about this as a behaviour men share around here, motivated by the idea that 'women spend their money on futile things'. [Diary, 07.05.2010]

The father/husband's control over economic resources makes the entire family dependent upon him. Men's privileged access to revenue generation grants them a strong source of bargaining power they can use to reproduce the social and familiar status quo.

Next, men in Galle Toubaaco enjoy wider access to another labour resource: information. When travelling to urban centres or bigger villages, they can talk to people who often come from different backgrounds and areas of the country (or even from other countries). Besides, in the urban centres the amount of information available is obviously much larger than in Galle Toubaaco. Mas, for instance, said he would: 'watch TV some times when I go to a different village' [S1I4MD]. Almost all female informants instead never watched television.

In his interview, Moudi Sow showed some knowledge of international politics and alternative social roles (to the ones in Galle Toubaaco). Asked about where he learnt such things, Moudi told me without any hesitation:

> You know I have travelled a lot, I lived in the Gambia for five years, I have been to Kaolack and Dakar so I have experienced a lot. I have never been to school but I know a lot because of the exposure I got from travelling and talking to different people. [S2I13MS]

Women instead have little to no opportunity to travel. The 77-year-old Hawa, for instance, said: 'I didn't get the chance to travel anywhere; I have been here since the day I got married' [S1I12HB] and the 20-year-old Fatou said: 'I haven't left the village yet' [S3I8FDY]. Mobile phones are also a source of information; every male informant possessed a mobile phone, while not a single female informant had one. Knowledge is an important resource because it grants the power to shape the social truth, the *doxa*, and the biases that reproduce the status quo (Bourdieu 1977; Dewey [1916] 1966; Gaventa 1980, 2003, 2006). Limited access to knowledge means limited opportunity to develop capacity to aspire and to question the status quo (Appadurai 2004).

The third labour resource that men enjoy when travelling is the access to services that are not available in Galle Toubaaco. In big villages and urban centres, there are health posts, electricity and water facilities, and means of transportation. Access to services means the ability to control, for instance, the recharging of cell phones (strategic communication tools) and the chance to multiply access to the first two resources (e.g. by taking a bus and reaching bigger centres). Also, access to services means more opportunities to visit a doctor and enjoy clean water and a wider variety of foods, that is, access to better health conditions. After my first month in the village, Korka (my interpreter) told me that she overheard men talking of 'historic food performances outside Galle Toubaaco':

> Men around here are all bandits [*laughs*] they practise alimentary banditry!
> *What do you mean?*
> I mean that they don't like the food they get at home so as soon as they can they go to a village and eat in a little restaurant. Then they go home and pretend nothing has happened, because otherwise they should take some back home. It's normal though, all Peul [Fulɓe] do that. [Diary, 22.03.2010]

Some variation in the distribution of labour discussed above is reported. In the village, there are three women who sell a few products. Two of these three women are widows, though, that is, they are independent from the control of a male elder, and, due to their age, they cannot exit the village to gather the products they need. Rather, they send their sons to the closest weekly market. The third woman instead would sell bread on behalf of her husband; a male cousin would bring the bread from a neighbouring village. Access to money, knowledge and services granted men in Galle Toubaaco a position of power within the household. Men possessed authority on choices regarding both the family as a whole and its members individually and, as seen later, influenced women's outlook on themselves and on social hierarchies.

A second set of resources contributes to shaping family and social power relations between men and women: land and the network of relationships. I called these 'marriage' resources because they are influenced by members' marriage patterns. Those resources differ from labour resources in that, while women's access to labour resources is hampered by a social understanding of male adults as family breadwinners, uneven access to marriage resources is shaped by male and female children's different marriage patterns. That difference is still built upon an instrumental understanding of women and, as demonstrated below, contributes in structuring uneven access to arable land and to a wide local network of relationships.

Access to Marriage Resources

In Galle Toubaaco, endogamous marriages (with husband and wife both from Galle Toubaaco) are very rare and the husbands generally bring their future women to their family house from other communities. Aisata Ba, who abandoned her home village and arrived in Galle Toubaaco at the age of 14, explained to me that her daughter (aged 13) also left her village of origin (Galle Toubaaco) to get married because 'when a couple get married it's always the woman from another village that goes to the man's house, never the other way around. This is our tradition and it has always been done like this' [S1I10AIB]. I reconstructed the family tree of the village with the help of a large group of male members, taking note of the village of origin of all community members. The near totality of the women living in Galle Toubaaco were born elsewhere, while almost all men were originally from Galle Toubaaco. Similar paths of 'gyneco-mobility' (the fact that wives relocate from their villages of origin to their husbands' villages) are a strategic response to the structural productive and reproductive needs of the community. Gyneco-mobility expands the reproductive capacity of the community over its original capacity (constrained by the number of women born in the community) to the bargaining capacity of the single families. In other words, and in line with the perspective suggested by Meillassoux (1973, 1991), the families of Galle Toubaaco need women from other villages to expand their community beyond the limits imposed by the limited number of possible marriage combinations within the community. At the same time, men are needed in productive labour, away from the village, so they cannot defend their families in case of kidnapping or attack. As a result, there is social pressure for non-violent regulation of marriage patterns amongst communities (conciliatory – finding marriage agreements – rather than predatory – for instance, kidnapping women). To meet productive and reproductive needs, families in Galle Toubaaco engage in a multilateral exchange of women that to be functional cannot include women's possibility to refuse a marriage. Galle Toubaaco's need for exogenous marriages (with the subsequent practice of wife eradication from the community of origin) contributed to shaping uneven gender access to land and network of relationships (marriage resources) that in turn impacted on visible and hidden power structures in the community and the family.

According to informants, marriage represented a rite of passage towards full membership; it was considered the official threshold between infancy and adulthood for both genders, consistent with Fulɓe customs observed elsewhere (Riesman 1992): 'To be a complete person a man has to get married' [S2I12ABM]; 'you are not allowed to sit with the grown-ups until you are married' [S1I5DS]; 'I realised my daughter was grown up when she was getting married, she was 15 years old' [S1I4MD]; 'My friends are still not married and I think once we get married then we will consider ourselves grown-ups' [S1I13SB].

Often, although not always, marriage is used as a means to strengthen geographically distant intra-familiar relations. Mas, for instance, said: 'My wife is a relative and it's our parents that united us, my dad went to ask my wife's parents for me. [. . .] I didn't choose my wife but I was lucky that my parents chose somebody I actually liked' [S1I4MD]. Sidi Ba (a 38-year-old man who had been married to his wife for 21 years) said: 'My wife is my cousin' [S1I3SB]. Ami explained that: 'My parents chose him [the husband] because he was a good person; he was a relative and a hard worker' [S1I5AS], and Penda, talking of her wedding with Ndene, said: 'My parents talked about him [the husband] before because he was a relative but we never saw each other' [S1I9PS].

Various male informants, asked about the qualities that a woman has to possess for them to marry her, made reference to the help she could guarantee through her physiological reproductive functioning (giving birth) or material reproductive working ability (managing the house, preparing food), rather than to the characteristics of her personality:

If you are looking for a good woman to marry what would you look for?
I would look for a woman who is hard working and someone who is into her religion. [S2I1SB]
Why did he [the husband] divorce the other women?
He married but she couldn't have kids so he divorced her. [S2I2DS]
What characters should a woman have for you to marry her?
Someone who doesn't cause trouble and takes care of the family. [S2I9MB]
Why does a man get married?
You get married to have a woman at your side to have kids with you. [S3I4MD]
To me the best [the most important thing in my marriage] is that my mum is finally able to rest a little from housework. Now she has someone who can take over cooking and cleaning and give her a break, she was getting really tired from doing all of the work. [S1I8AB]

From the sample, one case only stood out for expressing a different view about his wife, that of Sidi Ba, who said: 'My wife is the most important person in my life. She knows me very well and takes care of me and I trust her with my life' [S1I3SB]. The way other men talked of the qualities to be sought in a wife suggests that they value their contribution to family work for social reproduction.

Local dowry practices also support a similar understanding. When asked about his marriage, Sidi Ba said: 'I gave the dowry when she was only 8 and I just really liked her and I didn't want someone else to come and marry her off' [S1I3SB]. The dowry for the first wife is usually paid by the elders (the parents in Sidi Ba's case above), since young people are excluded from the reproductive organisation of the community. Ami, for instance, talked about her son's marriage in these terms:

My son chose his wife while she was very young [. . .]. Since my son's wife was too young, he asked for us to save her for him. We the parents agreed with his request and saved the girl until she was old enough to marry. [. . .] once she turned 15 she agreed and we brought her to our family home. [S1I6AS]

The dowry is a form of credit that binds in a contract the family that gives it and the family that receives it; as such, it ties the two families within the same conceptual *aire matrimoniale* (marriage area), an alliance for the reciprocal help in absolving reproductive functions (Meillassoux 1960, 1991). The dowry is often shown to possible competitors and allies with a concrete object. In the case of Galle Toubaaco, as Ami said, continuing her narration above, it is a necklace: 'Once a girl is promised to someone, she wears a promise necklace so everyone knows she is engaged' [S1I6AS].

Finally, I would like for the reader to consider the verbs commonly used for 'to marry' in Fulfulde by members of Galle Toubaaco: *hoowude* (to copulate, from a man's perspective) and *ɓaŋude* (to bring the bride to the husband's village). I am not suggesting that men and women in Galle Toubaaco were not capable of mutual love and respect, as I observed the opposite to be true. Rather, what I am saying is that people's shared narrative used to describe women's and men's roles and relations (including marriage) – that is, the choice of words that people used to talk about those – conveyed a sense of superiority and dominance over men that partially contributed to sustaining gender inequality in the village.

Marriage patterns unveil a structure of the family and the society where women were unlikely to gain the full status of social and political equals. Women in Galle Toubaaco were caretakers and cooks that would live in other communities, rather than revenue generators, breadwinners or political leaders. It is unlikely that men would change their view of women before being challenged with the task of acknowledging their human dignity – this process being, inter alia, the task of problemposing education (Mergner 2004). As has already been suggested over a century ago by Stuart Mill, if men are raised in the idea of being superior to women, it is implausible that this will not impact on their social behaviour or that they will not shape a society that raises children in the same belief (Mill [1869] 2008).

These power relations, where women had little chances of being socially empowered, were also shaped by (and in turn contributed to regulating) access to marriage resources: land and network of relationships. Informants helped make sense of the reasons for a patriarchal lineage in access to ownership of land. They reported that in Galle Toubaaco, parents give the land to male children so that they can farm crops on it and provide for their families. Their female children instead will leave the village, so there is no point in giving them land. Women would get a 'mobile' dowry when they get married: bed sheets, some

goats and maybe one or two cows. These are still valuable assets in absolute terms, but offer less sustainable economic stability (animals can die,
be eaten or sold). Talking of heritage rules, Sidi Ba, for instance, said:

Which one of your kids is going to inherit your land?
The boys are going to inherit the land; they are going to share
the land.
What about the animals?
The same thing for the animals.
What about the house?
It will be their house just like everything else.
What about the women, do they inherit anything?
Women can only inherit animals but not land. Women get mar-
ried and go off to different places and can own land where they
are married at but not their fathers' land. [S2I1SB]

Informants reported that married women would work small parcels
of land in the village of destination; land would not be theirs, though,
since if their marriage ended after divorce, 'my husband would take
back the field in which I used to farm' [S1I11FDY]. Often women did
not own land in their village of origin either, due to the same social
norms regulating dowry practices linked to traditional marriage patterns, as in Sidi Ba's case above. Their access to land was then always
conditioned by working for the patriarch in producing subsistence
food for the family.

Land is a crucial form of power; arable land is an important form of
private property, and access to it is a vital factor influencing the gender
gap in economic well-being, empowerment and social status (Amanor-
Wilks 2009; Kevane and Gray 1999). Access to land, then, represented
a challenge both in human rights terms and from a human development perspective for the community of Galle Toubaaco. The need to
increase women's land access in sub-Saharan Africa has been defined
as vital, especially at times where food security is compromised (as in
recent years in Senegal) (Kuiper and Sap 1995; Pearson and Sweetman 2011; Toulmin 2007; Tsikata 2009). Another study on Fulɓe customs has evidenced that women do not own land due to other factors
as well; they are also ashamed of doing so because of social norms
regulating what women are expected to possess or the way in which
labour is expected to be distributed between genders (Buhl 1999). Due

to the resistance of similar customary traditions, supported by power relations amongst community members, State normative intervention and law enforcement in this direction has been proved weak in the past (Amanor 2007). Structural power relations influence access to land and, dialectically, access to land grants men that power. It is at the level of power relations, then, that development programmes can foster women's empowerment in realities like the one in Galle Toubaaco. Later, therefore, it will be seen whether Tostan's programme impacted on those relations.

The second key marriage resource is the network of relationships. Most of the married women in Galle Toubaaco left their village of origin, where they were part of a relational network built during childhood. They arrived in Galle Toubaaco as their husbands' wives to take on house-caring responsibilities and with fewer opportunities (in terms of time) to build deep friendship relationships with other women in the community of destination. With marriage, girls exit the relational network built during childhood and face the challenge of developing a new one in the village of destination. Kardiata, a 70-year-old woman, said with regret during her first interview:'I haven't seen my childhood friends for a long time, they all have gotten married and gone to different villages. I have one friend who is still here with me, her name is Diallo' [S1I7KS]. Most female informants told me they found it difficult to'open their heart'with each other. Dembaye Sow, another female elder of the village, at the end of the first interview murmured: 'Alas! The things I think about I can't talk about at all. I don't talk about things I think about with others' [S1I1DS].

The men of Galle Toubaaco, instead, are still part of their childhood relational network. Asked to list their friends, male informants could easily name many people still living in Galle Toubaaco and with whom they still spent time. Take, for instance, what 27-year-old Amadou Ba said: 'My childhood male friends are still here, my best friend is a Abdoulaye Sow [. . .] Back when we were little kids there weren't many young girls in the village' [S1I8AB].

A weak network of relationships affects people's opportunities to affiliate and overcome a group social inequality. If the oppressed social sectors have fewer opportunities to structure individual concerns into a programme of action than the social sectors who are oppressing them, the former cannot coordinate to challenge the social status quo fostered by the latter. People's associative and decisional liberties are strongly connected: limiting the former means hindering the latter (Nussbaum 2000).

Internal and External Segregation

Some forms of gender seclusion and segregation conflict with human development when they limit the development of members' full human functionings, with particular reference to the capabilities of imagination and affiliation, framed conceptually earlier in the book (see Chapter 2; Nussbaum 2000). Data from Galle Toubaaco suggest that gender internal and external segregation contributes to fostering unequal power dynamics within the household and the rural community that hindered a reconsideration of the unequal gender access to strategic resources. A gendered life, with little or no opportunity for sharing mutual concerns over social norms in place in the village, contributes to protecting the social status quo by hindering women's opportunities to renegotiate their status by challenging men's outlook. In similar conditions of segregation, isolated and episodic resistance, such as that reported in the village, struggles to challenge the status quo: information about sharing the same conditions, the same fate, is fundamental to renegotiating relations of power amongst different social groups (Clegg 1989; Mann 1986). To challenge social power structures influenced by (and at the same time regulating) access to key resources, community members had to overcome gender segregation, if not in their daily life, at least in new places structured for this purpose (e.g. the HRE class).

Gender segregation in Galle Toubaaco has a double facet: it is amongst people of different gender (men/women) – *external* segregation – and amongst people of the same gender but of different age (young men/old men and young women/old women) – *internal* segregation. The differences in patterns of internal segregation have social causes and consequences; causes are to be sought in how children experience their parents' authority and in the different relational networks men and women enjoy. Consequences are in the relations of power amongst and within gender-homogenous groups of men and women. In Galle Toubaaco, relations of power shape different hierarchies within the group of men and the group of women that had an influence on the different way young women's and men's participation in decision-making changed after the HRE programme.

Male and female members do not have many occasions for meeting up and sharing time together. A gendered division of labour limits the opportunities they have to interact. Their social roles within the family narrow down those interactions further by structuring a network of relationships where men and women are limited to no opportunities of sharing ideas or opinions. Ami Sow, for instance, when asked about her motivation to go to classes, reported that this was her only opportunity to talk with other members: 'If I stay home I have nobody to talk to, all of my kids are boys' [S2I11AS]. Asked to give more detail, Ami explained that boys and men are not interested in talking with women and vice versa, while if she had at least one daughter, they could spend some time together talking. Talking of relations between men and women, Samba Diallo said: 'I don't go to the women's meetings [. . .] The only time I see everybody is during events like baptisms or weddings' [S2I15SD]. Confirming the limited opportunities for men and women to talk and interact, Mas identified the reason for little contact between men and women in terms of a natural predisposition to share time with people of the same gender: 'It has always been organised this way, the women have their group and the men have theirs. I think this is how things are because women feel more comfortable amongst women and men feel comfortable amongst each other' [S1I4MD].

Gender segregation is rarely perceived as problematic (as in Mas's case above); rather, people believed that it is natural, fostering a higher moral order, and they do not see it as the result of social biases that force men and women into assuming social behaviours and roles (Saltzman Chafetz 2006). Adolescent and young men also reported limited or no contact with women. Djombo, a 22-year-old man, was (and probably still is) the strongest player of *chokki* (a game similar to chequers) in the community. When I asked him if he ever played *chokki* with a woman, he answered that could never happen: 'we [the men] have never tried to play with women. The only time we play with the women is when there is an event and we play the drums and the women clap and dance' [S1I5DS]. Although recent research conducted with American adolescents suggests that gender segregation during adolescence might be physiological to a certain extent (at least in certain societies) (Mehta and Strough 2010), in Galle Toubaaco that segregation is aggravated by the different social roles that girls are called to cover after their wedding, when they reach puberty.

Child marriages contribute to fostering gender segregation. This is because they limit young girls' interactions with their brothers or local friends by segregating them within the household where they take up the role of wife and comply with their husband's authority. Different marriage patterns might impact on members' social behaviour when they reach adulthood: it has been argued that the gender segregation that boys and girls experience during their childhood influences their adult relations by fostering the same segregation (Maccoby 1995). This seems to be the case in Galle Toubaaco, where men and women have opportunities to share the same space: marriages, baptisms or assemblies are just some examples of those opportunities. Even then, though, members do not behave differently from the social order they are used to: women and men are not used to talking together, and during social events they replicate the external segregation they experience in other moments:

> Today Mamadou Sow is getting married for the second time and has prepared a great celebration. We have been dancing and playing all night. Mas, the *griot*, has shouted for hours entertaining all the public. When I first arrived I couldn't see any women around. Ndene tells me they are taking care of cooking the food after the men killed the cow. Other women are preparing the bride and the house (Dembaye is burning some plants in the house to keep out evil spirits). The men are playing cards with the groom and are making fun of Mamadou. [Diary, 04.05.2010]

Also during baptisms men and women are separated from each other: the women take care of the baby and congratulate the wife, while the men choose the goat to slaughter or drink tea:

> Today I was invited to a baptism. I have been told the baby will be called Ben after me although Korka says it's a lie – he will be called Djombo. I entered the baby's room, where the mother and other women gathered. It's Fatou Diallo's grandchild who will be baptised. I feel weird for being the only man in the hut (apart from Abdoulaye who brought me in) and I see the mother of the baby is not completely at ease with me (and possibly Abdoulaye) being there. But Fatou is very welcoming and gives me the baby to hold. She is very happy today. Abdoulaye insists on taking a picture of me holding the baby. When we go out of the hut, the men are slaughtering the goat and making tea. Amadou Sow shouted, 'Ben come here with the men, where your place belongs,' and laughed. [Diary, 12.05.2010]

Other village gatherings reproduced gender segregation: Figure 5.1 offers an example of gender distribution during a village meeting and Figure 5.2 shows participants' distribution during two of the first HRE classes.

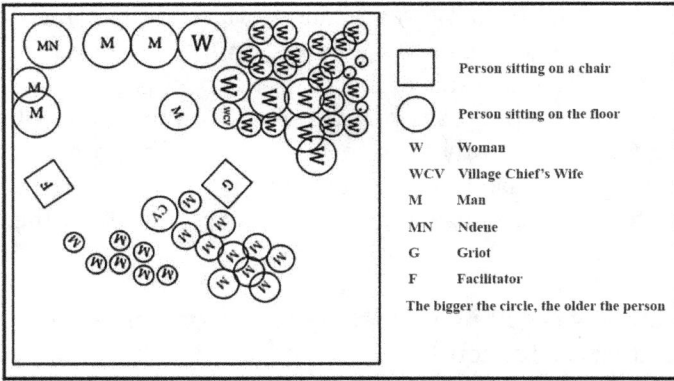

Figure 5.1 Distribution of community members in a village meeting held on
10 April 2010

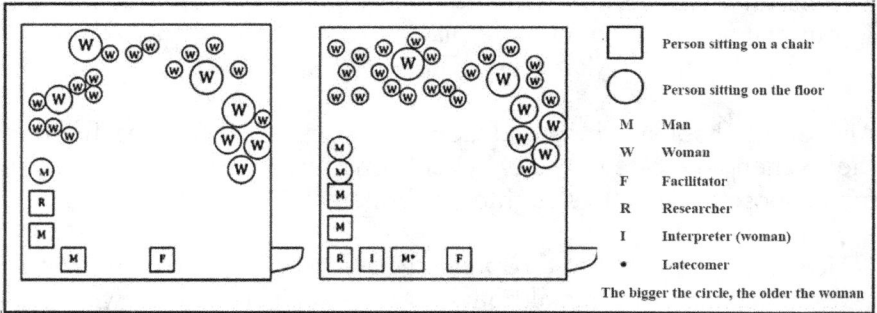

Figure 5.2 Distribution of participants during two HRE classes held on 26 April 2010
and 30 April 2010

Both figures show that there is a strong tendency to sit beside people of
the same gender, following gender segregation practices as described
above. Gender segregation seems to be a normal practice in the other
villages around Galle Toubaaco:

> Abdoulaye, Amadou and I went to Mbos today for the weekly
> market. There is a ceremony of the socialist party, there must be
> around 3,000 people and I am the only white person. All women
> are sat on one side of the square and all men on another side. I
> asked Abdoulaye and Amadou why men and women sit segre-
> gated. They answered, embarrassed: 'that's the way it has to be'.

They asked me if in Italy 'it's different'. I said yes, we can sit close together and nothing happens. They replied that in Senegal if men and women sit one beside the other they would kiss, and laughed vigorously. [Diary, 08.05.2010]

In addition to these forms of external segregation, in Galle Toubaaco there are also practices of internal segregation within gender-homogenous groups. Internal segregation, however, impacts differently in women's and men's groups. Men are split into age segments with limited interactions among them. Women have more interaction with other women of different ages. In Galle Toubaaco, young women and men question the elders differently: Omar Ba (one of the intellectuals of the village) and Fatou Diallo, for instance, reported that 'in the men's meetings the older men speak the most and make all of the decisions and the young men respect the decisions, it's not the same in the women's meetings' [S2IS2OB]; and that 'The men respect their elders much more than the women do' [S2I8FD].

According to informants, relations between young and older women are more informal and frequent than between young and older men. Data analysis suggests that the causes of this difference are to be found in child and polygamous marriages. Young first wives need older women's advice on how to deal with a wife's tasks. Young Fatoumata Diallo (who had the same name as the older Fatou), for instance, told me that all her friends would visit an older woman to ask for advice, and that: 'There is an old lady here named Metta that I go to every time I need to talk to someone' [S2IF5DY]. Young girls have much contact with older women while men (as seen later) tended to stick to men of their age when seeking advice. When they are not first wives, rather, young girls have to defend the legitimacy of their role with other co-wives – usually older women. Or, vice versa, older women might feel threatened by younger wives. They might be afraid that the higher reproductive capacity of the young girls might threaten their source of power in the relation with the husband (Meillassoux 1991). The relation between young and old women, then, becomes problematic by virtue of the renegotiation of the power equilibrium into which the presence of a younger (and supposedly more attractive and fertile) woman engages older women:

I see it [discrimination] all the time, I see some men for example marry several women and he will start favouring one woman over the others. [. . .]

Can you give me an example of discrimination that has happened here before?
For example you have a first wife and then you marry a second wife and after that stop taking care of your first wife, it happens here all the time. [S2I2DS]

[. . .] the first wives are discriminated against when the husband marries a second wife. In some cases, he starts treating his first wife badly and doesn't talk to her much. [S2I3OB]

The changing power dynamics in the household, following the arrival of a new wife, frequently generate jealousy and tension amongst co-wives. Fatou and Dembaye, for instance, said: 'I fought against my husband's first wife because of our kids [. . .] She is jealous that my husband married me and we started having kids' [S1I2FD]; 'I had several fights with my co-wife, especially when we were younger, even over little things' [S2I2DS]. Similar fights are usually settled by the husband: 'my husband came and decided for us' [S1I2FD]; when this happens, women experience both the higher authority of their husband (acting as a judge in the fight) and their equal conditions in terms of the resources they can mobilise to gain power. In gaining their husband's approval, young women can count on the power that comes from their reproductive capacity and older women can use age and experience.

Women, then, experience fluid relations of power within their gender group. Young girls – possibly strengthened by their higher fertility that gives them a position of advantage in the family – can question the authority of the female elders, hoping to be backed up by their husband's support by virtue of their higher reproductive capacity rate. Women see young women fighting – or fight themselves – against older women and, possibly, see the young woman winning the conflict (obtaining her husband's favour). In other words, women learn to challenge same-gender elders.

Men, instead, experience more hierarchical power dynamics within their group. Young men learn that everyone in the family recognises the eldest male as embodying the highest authority. In Galle Toubaaco, respect for the male elders is likely to be derived from a patriarchal structure of the family, shaped by capitalist relations of production. Young men learn that the family works and produces for the patriarch, family members work for him, and he, in turn, grants them protection (Meillassoux 1991). It is made even stronger by the fact that the patriarchal structure is embodied in the ethnic tradition of the Fulɓe

(Buhl 1999) that, in Senegal, contributes to defining their identity against the cultural imperialism of the ethnic majority (see Chapter 2; McLaughlin 1995; Riesman 1992).

Data suggest that women in Galle Toubaaco have limited freedoms and decision-making power within the family. This lack of power is evident in family and society because of the limited access women have to 'travel' and 'marriage' resources (which, in turn, replicates and fosters unequal access to these resources). In addition, gender segregation in place in Galle Toubaaco contributes to reproducing an unequal social status quo, where women's human development and human rights are not fully protected. Gender segregation limits social interactions between genders that are essential for men and women to problematise that status quo and change it together. Women do have a space of autonomy: they enjoy time together while gathering water, cooking during marriages or baptisms, and possibly in other moments inaccessible to a male researcher (or to Korka, who visited the village sporadically for the interviews) and that therefore cannot be documented. However, women lacked both moments of full social interaction with the men and the capacity to problematise social behaviours as a changeable status quo.

Women would need to problematise their social reality together with the men, overcoming gender segregation and collaborating with them in renegotiating gender roles and relations. The different components analysed above (access to travel and marriage resources, and gender external and internal segregation) intertwined, affecting the distribution of power among men and women within the household.

Power Distribution in the Household

In Galle Toubaaco, gender segregation and access to labour and marriage resources contributed in shaping power as domination. Gaventa (1980) argued that power holders make use of available social mechanisms to obtain passive agreement of subjugated groups to the social status quo they want to reproduce. In Galle Toubaaco, power distribution among genders does not only impact on overt processes of decision-making and covert processes of definition of the political agenda (as analysed in the next section on decision-making); it also influences members' perceptions of men's and women's social status and roles. The fact that women in the first set of interviews described their position within the household as defined by tradition or culture (that it'has always been like this' [S1I10AIB]) helps to explain why women tended to comply with unequal distribution of freedoms and uneven access to resources.

Unequal access to labour and marriage resources contributes to structuring the power that men in Galle Toubaaco exercise in the family. In the interviews, many informants referred to the fact that the husband could choose, for instance, how much money the wife received for her personal needs, could decide whether she could try to find a job, could influence her vote during election periods, could engage her in duties (such as the Tostan classes) without having asked her opinion before, and could have control over her religious practices and sexual inter-course. Some informants depicted the situation of the women as with-out any power to make decisions. For example, the 'young' Fatou, who wanted to join Tostan classes, said: 'My husband didn't permit me to take the class' [S1I11FDY] and in a later interview said: 'if my husband tells me to stop doing something I will stop [. . .] if I make a decision I make sure my husband will accept it, because he brought me here so I have to respect him' [S3I8FDY]. Amadou Ba Mbaring, talking about his wife participating in the classes, said: 'If I wasn't happy she would not be taking the class' and added: '[A woman's role is] to respect her husband and do as he says' [S1I16ABM]. The 'young' Amadou also said:

[if a mother asks something of a child and a father asks him to do something else] He should do what the father sent him to do. The father is the man of the house and has priority over everyone in the house. [S2I14ABY]

However, resistance to men's authority was reported. For example, informants recalled some arguments in married couples, mostly because of women refusing to have sexual intercourse with their spouses. That refusal generated male normative counter-resistance actions and domestic violence: 'if you see a husband beat his wife it's maybe because she refused to sleep with him' [S1I12HB] 'The worst thing a wife could do is refuse to sleep with her husband' [S1I16ABM]. According to infor-mants, such forms of behaviour challenging men's authority (such as an argument between co-wives, contradicting the husband's prescription of a peaceful family setting) could lead to domestic violence, with the husband beating up his wife. The nurse at the local health post reported that domestic violence was widespread in the area: '[There are] a lot [of women that come to the health post with signs of violence] and even women that are pregnant [...] when they arrive they always say it's their husbands that beat them' [S3IS1HP]. Penda, talking of her sister who lived in another village, said:

After getting back home from the hospital the husband started beating her. [...] He beat her because he was stronger and she was just a kid. She was still healing so she was in bed resting a lot and he would always ask her to do things she could not. There were certain things the doctors had told my sister she could not do but the husband didn't care and he insisted that she had to do all of the work. [S1I9PS]

This does not mean that women in Galle Toubaaco are totally power-less. Although rarely, it happened that at night some wives and husbands argued so loudly that they could be heard from the other side of the village. Also, during a human rights class, women revealed having tried various times (before the programme) to convince the men of their need to practise family planning. Data show resistance in the village to men's power in the form of women refusing to sleep with their husbands; however, female informants considered this as dangerous due to the violent consequences that might follow that refusal. In the data, there is little evidence of diverging trajectories from the public roles that men and women covered and claimed to cover; a reason for this could likely be, for instance, that informants in their first interviews could have been reluctant to declare their divergence from behavioural norms, especially to an outsider. Alternatively, the high value which the Fulɓe place on respecting the role they are expected to play within their society might have impacted on their capacity to conform with behavioural norms in public spaces where I could observe their behaviour (Botte et al. 1999; Riesman 1992). However, there seems to be little doubt that the social norms regulating power between men and women gave men authority over women, and not vice versa; that authority had its foundation in power coming from privileged access to labour and marriage resources.

Those power relations were not completely static and, since they were influenced by structural conditions that had changed over time, were open to change again. I spent two hours with Hawa Ba, the oldest woman in the village, talking about the difference between what life was like in the 1950s and today. She saw in the modernisation processes of the last 50 years (and the related technology) the cause for women having more time to get together, having more public speaking skills and a changing (more flexible) role:

> Women have more free time to do whatever they want, they have a lot more clothing and the women communicate better and are more organised. It's not much about more time but maybe a little bit more flexibility to do more. Women still work just like I did before, they still go work in the farms and come home, cook and clean. But there is always time for other stuff. [S1I12HB]

Kardiatou, Fatou and Dembaye also confirmed that life had changed for the women in Galle Toubaaco in the last 50 years. Thus, the power equilibrium that influences gender roles in Galle Toubaaco seems to be dynamic and likely to follow the variations in the structural factors that contribute towards shaping it. HRE's potential to challenge those roles might therefore be based on the fact that those roles are not static and that change happened over the years, only very slowly.

So far, I have argued that unequal access to labour and marriage resources in Galle Toubaaco structured uneven power relations that in turn created domestic violence, unequal healthcare and unequal educational opportunities. Similar power relations have been understood as limiting women's human development and hindering their access to basic freedoms and human rights (Nussbaum 2000). Nussbaum (2000) saw in the family a social construct that has been the major site of women's oppression. The social relation built within the family and the report that informants gave of it suggest that in their control over (or struggle to control) their wives' lives, husbands saw in them a tool for social reproduction, not a human being having freedoms and capabilities that deserved recognition of their dignity and expansion.

Reasons for lack of 'revolutionary' social change may vary. A revolutionary power renegotiation, with a woman demanding, for instance, the right to work against her husband's will, was possibly hampered by the interrelation of three factors. First, women lacked capacity to conceptualise a social alternative. Gaventa (1980, 2006) called 'dynamic of invisible power' the processes that construct people's understanding of the reality as the only one possible. In exercising their daily roles, men and women of Galle Toubaaco reproduce the social norms that both regulate access to power in the household and foster mental schemata and biases that uphold that status quo. To break the reproduction of power (and powerlessness) relations, members of Galle Toubaaco had to affiliate together and develop the capacity to aspire to a different distribution of power within the household by having the experience of alternative possible courses of action.

Second, if women possessed the capacity to aspire, their limited access to key resources might give reasons to fear isolation from the family anyway. A wife might fear that challenging male authority could result in her husband divorcing her, and she might want to avoid the social humiliation and the economic disadvantages of that (a woman had no land or revenue). As Folbre (1986) argued, poorer women are more likely to behave in their husbands' interest, fearing the welfare reduction that might occur with divorce (or cooperation breakdown). While the social situation analysed before the programme put women in a disadvantaged condition (limited power in the household for economic safety), breaking up with that situation might have led to even worse conditions (excessive economic burden and social isolation). Women need to comply with a position of limited gain because they cannot exit that condition, at least not individually. Only if all women in the community challenged that social condition, would men then need to renegotiate their role (Bicchieri 2006; Nash 1952; Osborne 2000). A woman's reproductive function is replaceable with that of another woman (Meillassoux 1991), but that function would become inalienable if all women stood on the same ideological position: one of equality, for instance. A woman alone cannot, however, refuse to abide by household dynamics (when they do not exit from the socially accepted), the risk passing from a limited disadvantage and gain, to a totally disadvantaged condition.

Third, when women tried to renegotiate certain behaviours (as in the case of family planning or sexual intercourse), men showed resistance to change and implicitly refused to renegotiate the power relations that ultimately granted them the authority to deny women's requests. Men could not be forced to change power dynamics, since they could use violence and authority to reinforce them.

Room for change existed, though. The way informants justified different gender roles admitted different trajectories for the future. Informants did not refer to biological or religious reasons to justify differences in gender roles and responsibilities. Instead, they mostly referred to the fact that 'the things have always been like this amongst the Fulɓe [S2I13MS]. The words of the 'young' Amadou Ba Mbaring are paradigmatic: '[A woman's role is] to respect her husband and do as he says. We found things this way in our culture' [S1I16ABM]. The way participants explained gender differences is of paramount importance for analysing possible room for social change within the rural community. The low resistance to men's authority helps understand women's difficulty when it comes to enhancing their bargaining power in the household within the limits of existing social norms (Kevane 2004). The renegotiation process of gender identity was possible because participants did not understand gender differences as based on immutable circumstances (say, for instance, religious will or 'nature'). Beliefs that societal roles follow processes beyond natural human influence would threaten the relationship between political action and change in the collective future status quo (Kashima et al. 2011). An appeal to biology or theology, external forces or 'authorities' would lead to determinism, and perhaps to the impossibility of renegotiating relationships. In contrast, in the HRE programme, social practices could be re-examined and reconsidered for their fairness, practicality or long-term well-being of the community.

POLITICAL STRUCTURE AND DECISION-MAKING: VISIBLE AND HIDDEN POWER

The idea of *demokaraasi* that in Galle Toubaaco gives form to the political structure in place in the village perpetuates uneven access to visible and hidden power and, as such, limits the community's empowerment and members' human development. It reproduces the patriarchal relations of power-regulating gender dynamics analysed above. Male elders control agenda-setting and decision-making in the political arena. They hold a traditional form of authority which, being built upon tacit norms of power, cannot be questioned without the conceptualisation of it as unjust and changeable.

Political Structure

In Galle Toubaaco, the political decision-making process is structured over three different layers accessible to a variable number of people: a governing level accessible to three men only, a consultative level open to an elite of male elders and a direct-democratic level open to the entire village. The 'triumvirate' includes Abdoulaye Ba, the village chief, Sidi Sow, the Imam and Ndene Ba, the self-appointed 'respon-sible for political activities', a role that does not exist in Senegalese law: 'Ndene and Abdoulaye make decisions for the village. They are both very important for the village' [S1I10AIB]; 'Apart from the Chief and the Imam, Ndene is the only other influential person [*decision-maker*] in the village [. . .]' [S1I3SB].

According to Senegalese law, the village chief must be democratically elected since he represents the Government of Senegal in the village and is the sole legally recognised local administrative authority. The vil-lage chief is responsible for the respect and the execution of the law in the village; controls the application of State measures; takes care of the village census; collects all taxes; and promotes the economic, social, cul-tural, environmental and health development of the village (République du Sénégal 1996). In Galle Toubaaco, Abdoulaye Ba had been designated village chief through line of descent at his father's death when he was 32 years old. Due to his young age, he was considered unfit for leading by many informants. Informants reported respect for him due to the 'legal' authority he embodied, rather than the charisma they instead found in other elders or *intellectuels*.

Ndene, uncle of Abdoulaye Ba and 'responsible for political activi-ties', also plays a key role in the decision-making of the community. According to informants (including the village chief himself), Abdou-laye consults Ndene on every political decision to be taken. Ndene did not have a pre-defined role (either administrative or religious); how-ever, he built his power through age, experience and knowledge. At the death of the former village chief (Geladjo, Abdoulaye's father), Ndene tried to embody the charismatic authority held by the previous chief, delegating the legal-traditional authority to Abdoulaye (who became village chief). He did not succeed; rather, community members' respect for him was based on his 'dangerous' knowledge and attitude. Omar, who brought forward his candidature after Geladjo's death, explained:

Why did Ndene want Abdoulaye to be chief?
When the elections for chief occurred I went to the government officials four times because I was against Ndene's decision but eventually the rest of the village backed Ndene on his decision because they were afraid of him [. . .] Whenever you talk with Ndene he talks about the law, he likes the law too much but the people here are afraid of the law. [S2IS2OB]

Sidi Sow, the Imam, represents a key political figure and is taken into consideration by Abdoulaye and Ndene for most of the political decisions taken. His authority is directly derived from his religious role. Before becoming the village's Imam, he was one of the marabouts of the community. He took on the role on the death of the previous Imam (his father).

At the second level of decision-making stand the elders and wealthy married men. Less often, and only in certain circumstances (either dictated by contingency or rational deliberation), the three men described above consult a wider group of male community members, either because of their positions of elders, *intellectuels*, rich members, or due to the nature of the decisions to be taken (which, for instance, might regard a particular family):

> I finally have made sense of what happened the other day. Ndene was coming back from Mbirkilane and started talking with some young people. Two of them, who took *iassi* (a talisman that causes those who drink it to faint – if they become angry – so that they avoid hurting other people), lost consciousness (and who knows though, they might have been just drunk). A third one, Aliou, insulted Ndene. Ndene's son (Moussa) was about to fight with Aliou, but Kebe (the Tostan facilitator) calmed him down. The following day, Aliou went to Ndene's house and cut the leaves of the trees there, as a form of offence. Ndene was about to hit him, but Omar intervened. Ndene then called the forest rangers who took Aliou to prison. Abdoulaye then summoned a meeting with Ndene, Sidi Sow, Omar, and other *intellectuels* to settle the dispute. The following day, Aliou went to Mbirkilane and paid a bail of 25,000 CFA. [Diary, 02.05.2010]

At the third level of decision-making are village assemblies, in which every community member (with no limitations of age or gender) is free to participate. The assemblies observed during fieldwork took place in Abdoulaye's courtyard. In all the assemblies observed before the HRE programme, Ndene spoke for the largest amount of time (compared with other members individually). Other interventions, in equal measure, were made by Abdoulaye and the elders. Dembaye (the female elder) also spoke once. No other women or young male members ever took the floor.

The spatial distribution of people during village meetings also helps us understand the roles that community members held during those

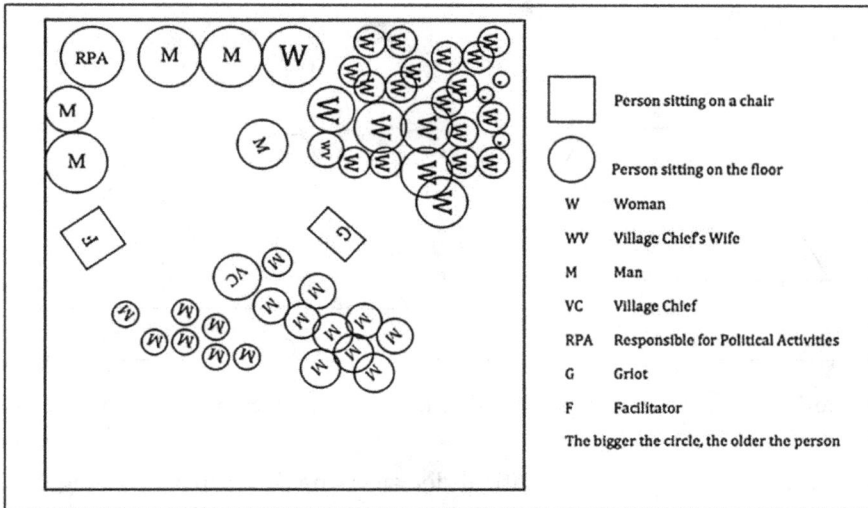

Figure 5.3 Distribution of community members during a meeting held on 10 April 2010

assemblies. It is common sense that the direction in which people look depends on whom they are listening to and/or whom they expect to talk, that is, who leads the meeting. In Galle Toubaaco, the seating order represented in Figure 5.3 remained the same during all village assemblies.

On a mat at the centre of the meeting, the male elders sat together with, at the edge of the mat, Dembaye. Ndene sat in the middle of the group of elders. Abdoulaye (the village chief) sat amongst the *young* married men of the village. The women sat on the right, men on the left. Mas – the *griot* – sat on a plastic canister, between men and women. Kebe, the Tostan facilitator, sat on a chair. The distance from the centre of the meeting seems to reflect members' age: the older, the closer. Members' distribution suggests a meeting held by the people sitting on the mat: Ndene in particular. Abdoulaye's position was consistent with data about members' perception of his role related to his age.

Figure 5.4 offers a representation of power distribution and participation in the decision-making process among population clusters that emerged during data analysis and shows the demographic distribution of community members within the same population clusters.

In human rights and human development terms, this political configuration does not pose problems in itself: modern liberal democracies

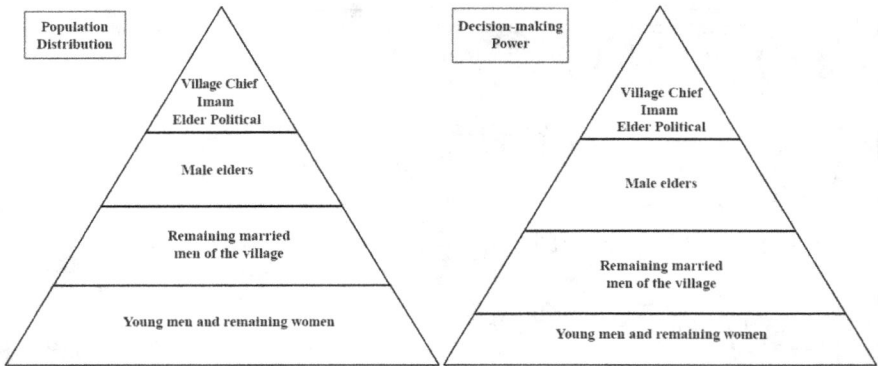

Figure 5.4 Population distribution and decision-making power in Galle Toubaaco

are built on the idea that political decision-making must be delegated to elected representatives (see, for instance, the referential work of Dahl 1971). Issues come both with the democratic capacity of the system and with the power distribution in the processes of decision-making and setting the political agenda. It is hence necessary to understand how community members succeed in making use of that political structure to exercise their visible and hidden power and to contribute to the human development of their community.

As seen earlier, instead of being elected through a democratic procedure, Abdoulaye was designated by line of descent at the death of his father. At that time, Omar put his name forward for the position. He did so by claiming that the line of descent had been erroneously interpreted, rather than demanding a fair democratic election. Ndene, however, convinced community members that Abdoulaye was the one to be supported: 'Ndene is the one who installed Abdoulaye as chief and has decided Abdoulaye will be chief for as long as he is alive' [S3I2PS]. Once the decision was taken, Ndene requested community members to vote accordingly and votes were then taken to the local urban prefecture to be validated. Rather than being democratically elected, then, the political authorities in the village governed following an arbitrary justification of their authority. This use of democracy as a tool for the formal justification of political power recalls national election customs in place in the village: in the year 2007, the village voted united for Wade, under pressure from Ndene. The decision was taken through a village assembly held to decide (or communicate) who the village should vote for at the forthcoming elections:'we hold a meeting to decide who to vote for and whoever the elders decide on, that is the person we will vote for' [S2I12ABM]:

> I realised today Ndene's influence over members' votes. Abdou-laye yesterday, in front of Ndene, openly praised Wade's government. Today we went to Mbos, where the Socialist party opposing Wade is holding a public ceremony. When I asked him again what he thought of Wade, Abdoulaye told me *'oo co . . . fou'* – he's crazy. [Diary, 08.05.2010]

Although collective voting in itself is not necessarily problematic (I mentioned this in Chapter 2), *demokaraasi* in Galle Toubaaco did have implications for members' lives from a human rights and human development perspective. Sen (1999) considered the existence of a fair democratic political system to be an essential component of the development process: it is *intrinsically* important because it is associated with certain basic capabilities; it is *instrumentally* important because it enhances the opportunities for people's concerns to be heard; and it is *constructively* important because it helps the conceptualisation of local needs and priorities. In human rights terms, also, democracy is considered the natural environment for the realisation of human rights, without which basic entitlements can be seriously threatened (United Nations 1948: Art. 21(3)). The problem lies not in the local interpretation of democratic principles: it lies in the fact that such interpretation limits access to the political arena for certain segments of the society and does not grant them the opportunity to influence the political life of their community.

Furthermore, it is important to analyse how community members participate in their local political system. An understanding of that interaction is important for analysing possible shifts in community members' behaviours after the HRE programme. Since village assemblies are formally accessible by every member, room for all community members to exercise visible decision-making power exists. Also, members can theoretically be influential in setting the political agenda by calling a meeting or intervening during a meeting with a new topic to be discussed. However, as discussed in the next two sections, invisible power dynamics and social norms in place in the village hinder access to the remaining two faces of power for all community members, except male elders.

Gender Factor in Decision-Making and Agenda-Setting

In Galle Toubaaco, women exercise very limited visible power in all three layers of the decision-making processes and have no say in setting the political agenda. As Penda said very clearly: 'the men are the ones who make the decisions' [S2I4PS]; Amadou reiterated:

> *Do you think a woman can be a chief?*
> I only see a man be a chief. It's always a man who commands a woman here so I just don't see a woman being a chief; [. . .] it's not easy to *develop a woman* without the help of a man. Everything a woman decides has to be accepted by a man first otherwise it should not be done. A man should always be the head of the decision-making, not a woman. [S1I14ABY]

The first level of decision-making is closed to women's access: traditional customs require the village chief to be chosen via patriarchal lines of descent and the Imam's gender is dictated by the Qur'an. The second level of decision-making includes a group of male elders and Dembaye (the female elder). According to Dembaye's description of it, she did not have an active role. In the meetings, Ndene and Abdoulaye also confirmed that Dembaye would only be consulted on specific topics rather than invited to contribute to the political agenda or the making of key decisions. When interviewed about her role in the decision-making of the community, Dembaye declared: 'the fact that the men take all decisions is the way we have done things for many years and it works for us' [S1I1DS]; 'we [the women] are still not involved in the decision-making process' [S2I2DS]. Her power in setting the political agenda, then, is related to what the ruling authorities grant her: she can suggest issues to be discussed, but only when requested to do so. The direct-democratic third level of the political structure (the village assembly) offers community members the most accessible opportunity to participate in the decision-making process. In those meetings, though, the agenda (usually including just one topic) is not discussed with the floor and can be influenced only by those actively participating in the assembly. All members of the community are granted access to village meetings and are allowed to speak: 'If we [the women] have something to say we will say something, there is nothing that says women can't talk in meetings' [S1I6AS]; 'When meetings are held men and women are free to talk, anyone who has something to say can say it' [S1I5DS]. However, data from interviews and observations reported little or no women's participation in village assemblies before the HRE programme. When asked about the reasons for this, informants referred to customs and habits, that is, those prejudices that Gaventa (2006) included within the dynamics of invisible power:

> The thing is we grew up like this and saw that women don't talk in meetings [. . .] Women are not going to speak at meetings with men. [S1I6AS]

> Men tend to make most of the decisions because women are too shy and don't speak up and sometimes they are afraid to speak because they are women. [S1I5DS]

Informants said women do not speak out in the meetings because they are shy, not used to talking in public and because they are used to men taking decisions. Asked about the possibility of this situation changing, female informants could not imagine any variation, as in the case of Hawa: 'Men will always make decisions instead of women' [S1I12HB] Alternatively, they could only imagine being empowered by the men, rather than claiming their own social and political dignity. The old Kardiata, discussing opportunities for women's empowerment, said:

> I think it's possible for us to make a change so women can be part of the decision-making process in our village. Change is very hard in our culture but we will try. We will ask the men to work hard and allow everyone to have a voice. [S1I7KS]

Kardiata's capacity to imagine a different social alternative was limited by the invisible power of the social status quo that fostered her quiescence with male authority. She could not imagine a different self. She did not possess the capacity to aspire to a diverging future social reality, where the women themselves would stand up and talk in the meetings, getting the social empowerment they deserve as human beings, rather than having to ask men's permission to do so.

Women's power in decision-making and in setting the political agenda is hindered by the same norms that relegated them to the role of second-class family member, of tools for social reproduction. Gender roles and relations in Galle Toubaaco are socially biased, the result of socially constructed norms built on the reproduction of an unequal status quo influenced by (and replicating) unequal access to key resources. Those biases that influenced power distribution in the family also went beyond the household to enter the political admin- istration of the community. Relations of power among gender in the family were thus reproduced in the society by following dynamics also observed in other contexts (Kevane 2004; Kevane and Gray 1999; Mill [1869] 2008; Nussbaum 2000). As they did when talking of gender roles, informants reported on women's lack of participation as a social construct, rather than as the result of a religious or biological differ- ence. As per gender roles, then, this shared belief indicates that room for change exists and resides in how members challenge together those social constructs.

Age Factor in Decision-Making and Agenda-Setting

According to anthropologists who studied the Fulɓe customs, members of Fulɓe communities hold knowledge in the highest regard. The elders obtain social prestige mainly from the belief that their life experiences granted them knowledge and wisdom (Azarya and Eguchi 1993; Botte et al. 1999; Clark 1997; Riesman 1992). Besides, it has been suggested that the elders' power can be based on their control over the reproduc- tive functions of the community, that is, on their control over the exoga- mous exchange of wives with other communities (e.g. with the dowry practices examined above) (Meillassoux 1991). In Galle Toubaaco, the elders could exercise wide visible and hidden power over decision- making and agenda-setting.

Informants described the elders' authority as natural and unques- tioned. For instance, when asked about the most important person in the community, Amadou Ba Mbaring said: 'There is an elderly person here named Eladji Diao, he is the oldest man in the village' [S1I16ABM]. Penda described the duty of a child as follows: 'A good child is some- one who [. . .] always respects the elders and helps others' [S1I9PS]; and Sidi Ba stated very clearly: 'When changes are made they are made by the elders of the village. We all accept decisions the elders make and don't say anything against them' [S1I3SB]. The elders' power influ- enced the political and social life of the community members. They held, for instance, the power to influence the entire village's electoral vote: 'We hold a meeting to decide who to vote for [at political elections] and whoever the elders decide on, that is the person we will vote for' [S2I12ABM]. They are also recognised as having the right to settle family disagreements: '[The second wife and I] started fighting and our husband came and broke it up, she ran but I didn't and our husband whipped me. After the fight was over the village elders came to help settle the situation' [S1I2FD]. Also, the elders regulated the legitimacy of marriage: 'There are rules here and people do respect these rules. For example, for a marriage to be solidified the elders of the village have to be part of it and agree and bless it' [S1I2FD].

The elders' presence is influential at all layers of decision-making. At the first level, Ndene, the eldest member of the triumvirate, can exercise visible and hidden power, even trumping the authority of the village chief: 'Abdoulaye is the [village] chief but Ndene is the one that makes most of the decisions here' [S2I4PS]; 'He [Ndene] chose him [as village chief] because Abdoulaye didn't know anything so Ndene knew he could manipulate him but he couldn't manipulate the others' [S2IS2OB]; 'Who makes the decisions for the village? Ndene does' [S3I6SD]; 'Ndene is [. . .] the leader of the village' [S2I8FD]. At the second level, the elders' presence is ensured by the fact that they are de facto members of the consultative group of the ruling authorities. They can exercise both visible and invisible power, by contributing to making decisions that would affect the entire community and by summoning village assemblies. At the third level as well, that is, during village meetings, I found a very strong influence of the elders over the decisions taken in the village. In all the assemblies I observed before the HRE programme, the elders contributed with the quasi-totality of the observed interventions.

In sum, the elders cover a major role in orienting the political and social life of the rural community due to their presence and influence at all layers of decision-making. Informants believed this social order to be natural and unproblematic. Fatou, for instance, demonstrated compliance with the status quo by saying: 'I think it [the fact the old people are in charge of decisions] is right, the older people should always be making the decisions, this is the way things have been done here for a long time' [S2I8FD]. Being a male elder in Galle Toubaaco, then, means having access to visible, hidden and invisible power in the family and the society.

Weber (1968) analysed gerontocracies and, more generally, the social status quo dominated by the elders' authority as a good example of social systems dominated by traditional authority. Obedience, in Weber's model, is owed to the elders as persons, rather than to impersonal regulations as in the case of legal authority. In Galle Toubaaco, elders' domination is shaped by the same rules that regulate inheritance and is translated from the structure of the family into the political organisation of the village. Their power is unquestioned and unquestionable: while legal authority (such as Abdoulaye's) can be contested (and members in Galle Toubaaco actually did so by questioning his young age), elders' dominance is based on customs, and cannot be challenged without unveiling the entire issue of power distribution within the community. In other words, the community would need to reframe their entire understanding of community roles to renegotiate the role that age played in decision-making. A similar distribution of power is problematic because social change, as a process in which people abandon quiescence for political participation, requires young members to participate in the political life of their community by exercising visible and hidden power. It would not need an inversion of the traditional structure of the rural community, with the young members taking over the elders' role, that would threaten the elder's role.

While current socio-political patterns in Senegal seem to suggest that roles will inevitably change in the future, with young people gaining individual and political autonomy, this possibility was not included in members' understanding of future development before the HRE programme. Not only did community members not contemplate different concrete alternatives, they also did not understand alternatives as necessary; that is, they did not understand age discrimination as perpetuating political inequality. Community members knew exceptions, as in the case of Djombo (a politically active and clever young member of the community) or Dembaye (who had some political influence), but did not understand other young and female members as capable of being politically active or influential. They did not see young members as able to contribute to decision-making more than the elders, with their knowledge, could do.

OTHER HUMAN RIGHTS-INCONSISTENT SOCIAL PRACTICES

The analysis of the human rights challenges faced by the country of Senegal frames the identification of those practices: child and forced marriages and hazardous child labour. Female genital cutting completed the framework of Senegal's current human rights challenges as analysed in Chapter 3. Data gathered during fieldwork, however, did not allow an analysis of the practice; however, indirect reports (female members who spoke privately with Korka) suggest that the community members had abandoned it a decade before my fieldwork. Due to the sensitiveness of the issue, no data could be gathered to allow an understanding of the reasons behind this abandonment. However, this seems to be consistent with what the nurse of the local health post said, referring to the whole area:

> I have been here four years but haven't seen any ['circumcised' women or girls]; I have talked to some women that said they were circumcised.
> *How old were they?*
> Some were in their 20s some in their 30s.
> *At what age are women usually circumcised [cut]?*
> Around 8 years old. [S3IS1HP]

If the youngest 'circumcised' woman that the nurse met was 20 and FGC happens at the age of eight, that might mean that the practice started declining from 2002. On the basis of the literature on the abandonment of FGC, it can be speculated that the ongoing 'modernisation' process in the country and the end of the social function of the practice brought about its abandonment in Galle Toubaaco (Mackie 2000). CFM and child labour, instead, were social practices in place at the time of fieldwork and are discussed here as a benchmark to understand a potential shift after the programme.

Child and Forced Marriages

The practice of CFM represents a form of gender subjugation and is the result of a patriarchal structure of power that bargains women's reproductive functions with the neighbouring communities (Meillassoux 1973). This subjugation is not necessarily (or consciously) implemented against girls' interest. A series of studies conducted in sub-Saharan Africa analysed parents' motivations behind the practice of CFM (Stockman and Barnes 1997; UNICEF 2001). The studies demonstrated that parents implement the practice in their daughters' interest, genuinely thinking that young girls would be better under the protection of a male guardian or that outside marriage they might risk becoming pregnant from pre-marital sex.

In Galle Toubaaco, the practice of child marriage for girls was extremely common. Until recent years, marriage also used to be forced (generally for girls and, in rare cases, also for boys):

> I have one daughter, she is 13 years old. She has been married for a month now [. . .]. [S1I10AIB]

> The girl I married was promised to me when she was 8 years old. I was 18 and she was 15 when we got married. [S1I3SB]

> I was 23 years old and my wife was 12 [when we got married]; my parents chose [my wife for me]. [S1I16ABM]

> I first saw my husband the day my dad told me I was going to marry him. [S1I5AS]

> I was a little girl, only 16 when I arrived here [after getting married] [. . .] back in those days Fulɓe would just give away their daughters and it didn't matter if she liked the husband or not. You like it or not you will stay because you have to respect your parents and do what they say. [. . .] My husband was well off and was a relative and that is why they forced me to marry him. [S1I1DS]

> My wife is a relative and it's our parents that united us, my dad went and asked my wife's parents for me. My wife was 14 years old but I can't remember how old I was, 20-something. I didn't choose my wife but I was lucky that my parents chose somebody I actually liked. [S1I4MD]

> I did it [forcing someone to marry someone else] but I will never do that again. I forced my daughter to marry someone and it hasn't worked out very well. [S2I2DS]

Informants reported that the community had dropped the practice of controlling girls' decisions; however, they were very inconsistent and unsure about when this had happened. Rather than forcing girls to marry their husbands, community members reported that young girls would now be only 'asked' to do so:

> We no longer force girls into marriages they don't want. This stopped a couple of years ago, after we started listening to the

radio and hearing it's not good to force your daughter to marry; you should ask them first if they actually like the man. [S1I1DS]

[Informant is talking of a couple who had got married eight years before] When she was young it was possible for her to say she didn't like the guy she was going to marry. Things have changed and girls are now able to say no to someone if they don't like them. It was not accepted to say no before but now you can. [S1I5AS]

Our village is evolving and changing, we used to pound our corn for flour all the time but now there is a machine at Mbose or Touba Mbella that we can go and use. Now men and women decide who they would like to marry and before it was the parents that chose for them. [. . .] It's OK for parents to choose for their children but it's OK for the kids to choose too. [S1I1DS]

I was introduced to him on a Wednesday and I was asked if I liked him. After seeing him and talking to him a little that day I decided I liked him. He went and slept at a nearby village and we ended up getting married that coming Friday. [S1I9PS]

Five factors emerged during data analysis suggesting that change in the practice of forced marriage was not yet effective. First, the words that informants used to say that girls were now allowed to refuse to marry someone (they were 'asked' to do so) are the same as used by older female informants to describe their own marriages decades ago. However, those same women then gave an understanding of their marriage as forced; 'old' Fatou, aged 60, for instance, said: 'My husband came to my village and *asked* me if I liked him and I said yes I liked him. I was 13 years old when I married my husband' [S1I2FD]; in a following interview, however, she said: 'I didn't like being *forced* to marry someone' [S2I8FD]. This suggests an unclear conceptual distinction between being forced and being asked (possibly due to the difficulty of translating in Fulfulde the nuance between the two verbs). Thus, one cannot claim with certainty that there has been a real change in the practice over the generations.

Second, the power to say yes or no might also be granted to girls, but that is not enough for them to exercise it. Access to visible power is hindered by hidden and invisible power dynamics (Gaventa 2006). There are at least serious doubts that 12-year-old girls who learnt to respect the authority of the elders as absolute and who had experience of self as a second-class gender would disagree with their parents' opinion, or with what they perceive as such. This might happen, for sure, but only in rare circumstances and within exceptional family dynamics; take, for instance, what Ami said:

> *Can a young woman change her parents' decisions?*
> No, whatever your parents tell you is what you are supposed to do. [S2I11AS]

Third, language analysis of the way in which informants spoke about their girls' right to disagree shows inconsistencies. Ami, talking about her son's wife, said: 'We first mentioned to the girl who she <u>was going to marry</u> at the age of 10 and once she turned 15 she <u>agreed</u> and we brought her to our family home [. . .]' [S1I6AS]. It is difficult to understand how it is possible to communicate to someone who she *will be going to marry* if the choice is still hers to be taken in five years. Being told of *going* to marry someone seems not to leave any room for personal choice; rather, it suggests communicating a decision that has already been taken, and with which the girl will have to comply (to 'agree') at the right time (in this case, five years later).

Fourth, no data exist showing a single case of a girl refusing to marry her chosen husband within the community of Galle Toubaaco. Aisata, for instance, could not understand why a friend's daughter would have said no to a man who wanted to marry her:

> When she was young it was possible for her to say she didn't like the guy she was going to marry but I don't see why she would have done that. [. . .] I have never seen or heard of anyone saying they didn't like the person they are planned to be married to. [S1I10AIB]

Fifth, when this happened (in other communities), informants said it produced isolation, which might be feared by both parents and girls. The old Kardiata said that, in her entire life, she could only recall one episode of a girl refusing to marry a man:

> There was once that I saw someone who refused her marriage and she is 18 years old now and she was 14 at the time. She hasn't found the person she is to marry yet. Nobody has asked for her hand yet since that time. I am not sure why someone still hasn't asked for her hand but I think it might have to do with her refusing her first proposal. [S1I7KS]

Control over marriage choice has the social purpose of controlling reproductive patterns by guaranteeing gyneco-mobility (wives following husbands to their villages) and demonstrating adherence to a patriarchal marriage network of communities that grants the possibility of integrating women from other villages (Meillassoux 1991). Women's choices are controlled because marriage is used as a means of granting reproduction for production purposes. In the complex marriage network, families control their daughters' decisions by virtue of long-term mechanisms of reciprocity in reproduction patterns. Fertility, the reproductive functioning, is maximised by marrying girls immediately after puberty (responding to local challenges of high infant mortality rates, by increasing the number of children that women can have). Dembaye said sadly: 'It hurt to be forced to marry but [. . .] I was too young to understand everything' [S1I1DS]. Like Dembaye, other women in Galle Toubaaco did not like being forced to get married. However, they did not necessarily characterise their situation as unequal, as they had little access to the tools through which they could reimagine social reality unveiling the biases created by invisible power dynamics (Appadurai 2004; Gaventa 2006).

Community members had to renegotiate marriage dynamics between them and with the neighbouring community, and restructure new ways of fulfilling the reproductive needs of their communities. The influence of external factors brought change in the way members of Galle Toubaaco understood CFM. However, that influence produced only a shift in the form (from forcing to asking girls to marry someone) but not in the substance (girls have no real access to the necessary power to contest elders' decisions). The practice is then problematic from a human rights and a human development perspective, and participants might come to take it into consideration during the HRE classes.

From a human rights perspective, CFM infringes upon people's rights to freely choose their spouses (ACRWC Art. XXI; UDHR Art. 16(2); United Nations 1966: Art. 10; CEDAW Art. 16(1a)) and even when they agree, marriage of children is supposed to have no legal effect (CEDAW Art. 16(2)), since children are not yet considered able to give free and fully mature consent. According to human development theory, CFM impacts on girls' capabilities as both a health and an educational issue: it impacts on girls' perinatal health and limits children's opportunities to access formal education. More importantly, child marriage hinders girls' range of capabilities and limits their development as full human beings (Nussbaum 2000; Sen 1999).

Human rights education might give community members the opportunity to reframe their daily practice within a human rights perspective. Whether this brought about change or not (and the implications of it for the reproductive needs of the community) is analysed later in the book.

Child Labour

The Government of Senegal is actively fighting against the worst forms of child labour, yet it still stands as a major human rights challenge in the country. In Galle Toubaaco, children of both genders contribute to family work. The amount and type of labour they carry out in certain cases would take time that could otherwise be employed in playing or for their education:

> As a child [aged six] once I woke up, I would sweep the compound, do dishes, pound millet, cook and fetch water. I have two younger brothers. We would all wake up at the same time, I would do housework and they would go out in the woods to herd our cattle. [S1I11FDY]

> *What are other differences do you see between your childhood and children's childhood today?*

> Apart from having all the toys, the kids pretty much do the same things we used to do. They still go out and herd cattle every day and help out with housework. [S1I12HB]

> Growing up I lived with my uncle and I would herd cattle and work with my aunt around the house, learning how to cook and clean. [S1I1DS]

> [When I was six years old] I would herd our sheep and cattle all day. [S1I14ABY]

Child labour poses problematic challenges; since it occurs because of parents' concern for the household's survival, debate has been spurred over whether it should be prohibited or not (Basu 1998; Basu and Hoang Van 1998; IPEC 2011; Nieuwenhuys 1996). The ILO's International Programme on the Elimination of Child Labour (IPEC) defined child labour in domestic and agricultural work (including herding) as highly hazardous and linked to a very high number of injuries (IPEC

2011). These injuries are related, for instance, to a series of hazards like carrying heavy loads, using sharp objects or isolation that in turn could result in back pain, depression, exhaustion and behavioural disorders. According to the ILO, children are particularly at risk due to vulnerabilities arising from their incomplete physical and mental development.

Nieuwenhuys (1996), on the other hand, argued that children have been ideologically considered as a separate category of human beings excluded from the production of value; the dissociation of children from the performance of valued work has been considered a yardstick of modernity and has its origins in the modern bourgeois society. In her view, child labour would be morally condemned today by Western agencies that attach to it concepts like 'sacrificed childhood'; that view, however, fails to admit child work as a form of self-esteem and functional social interaction (Nieuwenhuys 1996). In Galle Toubaaco, child labour contributes to the formation of children's identity and role within the society. Through their labour, children gain self and social consideration, they slowly gain full membership of the communities they are part of (the family, their peer group, the village).

Nussbaum (2000) studied the various dynamics of child labour and suggested that normative approaches keeping children from helping their families would produce more harm than benefit. However, excessive child labour may be problematic from a human development perspective because it can hinder children's opportunities to develop their full personality (including receiving education that contributes to their human development). Since participation in public life requires knowledge and basic education skills, it is contrary to the essential conditions of participatory freedom on which Sen grounded his approach to development (Sen 1999). A human development-respectful approach to the problem would tackle that part of child labour that hinders children's learning and socialising opportunities. If child labour limits children's access to wider processes of education (and not schooling only), then it limits their capacity to aspire to different alternatives; that is, it hinders their future possibility to question the status quo, to unveil invisible power dynamics that reproduce inequalities and foster unjust social relations (Nussbaum 2011). From a human rights perspective, whilst there are restrictions placed on the dangerous aspects of child labour, child work that does not threaten the child's health and does not keep the child from having time to play and go to school is not legally prohibited (a position that does not take into consideration alternative forms of education). In its worst and most hazardous forms, though, child labour is condemned as a practice that goes against children's right to a fully healthy childhood (United Nations 1989: Arts 24, 28, 32; United Nations 1999: Art. 1).

CONCLUSION

The analysis of power dynamics in Galle Toubaaco offers an understanding of both members' compliance with and resistance to the unequal social status quo. 'Invisible' power dynamics (the way members understood each other's roles) influence members' access to visible and hidden power. Those dynamics are built through different access to resources that shape power in the household and in turn shape women's social and political roles.

A gendered distribution of labour and different marriage patterns in Galle Toubaaco influence members' access to strategic resources. That access dialectically contributes to structuring gender roles and relations. Men control access to land, revenue, knowledge and services, and enjoy a more stable network of relationships. Unequal access to land and revenue shapes the family's economic dependency on the patriarch. Unequal access to knowledge limits the community's capacity to aspire, to conceptualise a different status quo: a woman travelling could pay attention to (and hence take back home) a different set of information than a man (e.g. about women's roles elsewhere in the world). Unequal access to services (e.g. to health structures) contributes to the creation of a wide social gender inequality issue and multiplies men's opportunities of access to an even greater range of resources (e.g. by accessing fast public transportation that could take them to bigger urban centres or other countries). Access to these resources shapes participants' understanding of gender roles and relations (that, dialectically, reinforce the status quo): men are those who take decisions and generate revenue, women are those who guarantee progeny and take care of the family. The way community members socially understand those gender roles and relations creates invisible power dynamics that shape visible and hidden power in the household: the eldest male, the patriarch, controls decision-making and agenda-setting in the family. Women's quiescence with the status quo in the family limits resistance to episodic and isolated events: women understand defiance of male power as exposing them to a greater risk than quiescence with the status quo.

Women enjoy limited power in the family (related to their reproductive capacity, their fertility) and negotiate with their husband within the limits allowed by social norms of gender roles. Rebellion against power (with possible negative consequences, such as divorce) is understood as dangerous and results in episodic actions that, often, generate normative responses (such as domestic violence). Also, resistance is isolated: external gender segregation in the village hinders women's affiliation and their capacity as a group to renegotiate respective social roles with the rest of the community.

Power relations extend beyond the household and are replicated within the social and political arena of the community. Male elders, the patriarchs of the community, control decision-making processes and agenda-setting at different levels: from the subjective interpretation of the rules regulating access to positions of legal authority (election of the village chief) to the control over number and agenda of village assemblies. Female and young male members could not challenge dynamics of visible and hidden power since they could not interpret them as unequal: 'invisible' power dynamics (but with very tangible consequences) structure social norms that hinder their participation in village assemblies and other places of decision-making. Male elders control the political life of the community and regulate their social stability by acting as judges within family discussions. They control the reproductive capacity of the community by regulating the dynamics of CFM that guarantee endogenous gyneco-mobility. The social function of CFMs is that of overcoming conciliatory (rather than predatorily) the internal reproductive limit of the community to guarantee, at the same time, their productive capacity (with men free to leave the household). To fulfil its productive needs, the community also employs child labour. Forms of labour like the one carried out in Galle Toubaaco (from the age of six onwards) have been studied by scholars as potentially threatening young children's human development.

These aspects of the community's social organisation have a negative impact on members' lives in human rights and human development terms. Power distribution in the household and in the society limits the community's empowerment and members' development of capabilities. CFM and child labour are also (albeit differently) potentially harmful for Galle Toubaaco children's well-being and have a negative impact on the community's life in human rights terms. Room for change exists, however; informants made sense of gender roles as traditional (i.e. socially constructed) rather than dictated by religion or biology. Those roles can thus be socially reconstructed: members could build and share a new social understanding of roles and relations. HRE could unveil those social norms and dynamics of power and help participants in questioning them. The next chapter offers an understanding of how Tostan delivered an HRE programme with that aim.

Chapter 5

HUMAN RIGHTS EDUCATION IN ACTION: THE PROGRAMME UNFOLDS

INTRODUCTION

This chapter analyses Tostan's HRE programme in Galle Toubaaco. It provides an overview of the programme by analysing how different factors played a key role in classroom dynamics. I analyse three different features of the programme that were important both in triggering participation and in activating the dynamics of reconsideration of the local reality: the learning context, the content and the pedagogy.

The first section offers an analysis of the context, including the way in which Tostan negotiated access to the village, the role of the facilitator and participants' expectations. Tostan's negotiation of access contributed to there being little resistance to the programme, and avoided misunderstandings or false representations of how the village would benefit from the programme. The selection of the facilitator (who shared the ethnic background of the community but was an outsider) had strategic importance for the success of the programme. And participants' expectations were important because they ensured their consistent participation in the classes.

In the second part of the chapter I look at the pedagogical strategies used in the class and analyse their Freirian nature and their being modelled through an experiential pedagogy. The facilitator engaged participants in discussions about their local reality and asked them to engage in representation of their reality through sketches, poems and songs. I suggest that, starting from their local reality, participants could develop their own understanding of the content exposed and could engage in a critical dialogue concerning their experiences of that reality. The dialogic process was structured as democratic and was facilitated in the local traditional language of the rural community. Both democratic participation and the use of the participants' mother tongue played a key role in fostering contextualisation and adoption of human rights practices.

Next, in the third section, I analyse the curriculum of the Kobi 1, dividing it into three parts. The first part (the introductory sessions) contributed to triggering participation and unity by fostering the nature of the class as a CoP. In the second group of sessions (the sessions on democracy), participants envisioned possible different alternatives to their political and social status quo. The final (and bigger) group of sessions (the human rights sessions) engaged participants in analysing their local reality from a human rights perspective. As the sessions unfolded, human rights became a tool to enable critical analysis of local practices that emerged as key themes from participants' discussions; I explore how they reified the abstract human rights knowledge in their daily lives and explored local understandings of it.

The fourth section of this chapter explores resistances to the programme and offers possible explanations of the reasons behind the lack of demonstrations of such resistance in the data. It is important to make sense of the low level of resistance to understand what in the programme built consensus at community level that then might have facilitated the process by which participants shared their views and perspectives with non-participants.

In the concluding section, arguments are linked together and I suggest that the different components of the programme contributed to a shift in participants' outlooks, which will itself be analysed in the next chapter.

THE LEARNING CONTEXT

Accessing Galle Toubaaco

As stated by the NGO's staff members interviewed in Dakar, in November 2009 Tostan identified Galle Toubaaco as a potential community to participate in the education programme under the requirements of the funding body UNICEF. UNICEF requested that Tostan select for its three-year CEP rural communities where child-harming practices (such as FGC, CFM or poor care of children's hygiene) were likely to be in place. Tostan decided to target Fulɓe communities, since precedent literature and baseline studies suggested that they would satisfy similar criteria. The village's potential for the organised diffusion[7] of the knowledge in other villages also played a key role in the selection process. Galle

Toubaaco satisfied all these criteria and was therefore approached by representatives of the NGO who offered the possibility of participating in the Tostan programme.

Following what they knew to be traditional lines of authority, Tostan negotiated access in Galle Toubaaco with the Imam, the village chief and the local elders. According to both local staff and village authorities, Tostan's representatives explained the content of the programme, that everyone in the community would be invited to participate, and that the community would be responsible for the facilitator's food and accommodation. Tostan also explained that the Kobi 1 part of the programme, which included the HRE classes, would last four months and would then be followed by the other components of Tostan's educational programme (problem solving, health, hygiene, literacy and numeracy, amongst others) in the following three years. Finally, Tostan officers informed authorities that two different classes would be held: one for community members over 21 years of age and one for those under that age. Tostan's age differentiation strategy responded to traditional forms of respect for the elders common to different ethnicities in Senegal (and particularly relevant to Fulɓe communities). These forms of respect regulated norms of interaction among community members and could have hindered young people's participation in the classes because young men are not supposed to contradict an older man.

Tostan requested that community members take care of building the hut that would host the classes, which they did well before the beginning of the programme. The classroom had not been used for any other purpose and would not exist without the Tostan programme. Its presence primed a change in the routine of the village. According to informants, the new class contributed to generating talk about the programme to be and, possibly, it also contributed to the raising of individual and public hopes on what the classes could bring to the community, so that when the HRE classes started, participants had already formulated some expectations of them. Aisata Ba, for instance, commented about the hut that would host the class by saying: '[People have been talking about the classroom because] We have waited for this kind of programme for a long time and now that it's here we hope it will help develop our village in the future' [S1I10AIB]. Informants understood the existence of the class as a first sign of a change in the village. The second sign was community members' participation in the classes. Everyone could see

people leaving their huts to join the classes. To informants, seeing similar differences in the village opened up the possibility for more change
to come:

> *What's going to help the village become as you describe it?*
> Tostan can help; since they got here, there have been lots of
> changes already. Now women, men, girls and boys are going to
> school and that was not happening before. [S1I12HB]

Classes started on Monday, 12 April 2010 and would normally run three
times a week from 4 p.m. to 6 p.m.

The Facilitator: An In/Outsider Role in the Community and the Class

For effective problem-posing education to generate processes of critical
reconsideration of local realities, it is of the utmost importance for the
educator to be a native speaker of the same language as the learners;
that is, to be aware of how learners construct the world around them
and their world of learning (Freire 1970). Freire argued that creating the
world is naming it; the ways people make sense of the world together
and express their understandings of it through their language are inex-
tricably correlated.

For the entire duration of the course, participants would have the
same facilitator: Kebe, a 40-year-old man originally from Fouta Toro, the
Northern Fulfulde-speaking Tukuloor part of the country. Consistent
with Tostan's requirements, Kebe both shared the ethnic background
of the local community members and was born and raised in a fairly
distant community. According to the NGO's headquarters staff, Tostan
required facilitators and participants to be part of the same ethnic group
to ensure that facilitators would have the necessary background to fully
make sense of the community's understandings of the world and the
classes. On the other hand, Tostan employed outsider facilitators so that
they would be able to construct with participants an educational and
authoritative role without having to deal with participants' pre-existing
biases or with the facilitator's past actions or behaviours that would be
inconsistent with the content of the programme. Kebe's external origin
seems consistent to transformative education practices with regard to
two aspects.

First, the facilitator might have conflicts of interest that would lead
his educative action in one direction or another. As seen earlier, the

Freirian educator gives to participants the means to rename their reality, rather than tools to shape their views over his. The facilitator's conflict of interest might shift the focus of the educational action: from fostering participants' cooperation towards what they define as a better community, to aiming for the facilitator's vision of a better community that he has developed in the local community. Of course, this argument could also be raised with regard to outsiders entering the community: this dynamic is also one of approach and is not limited to the ontological characteristics of the educator. However, the facilitator's 'outsiderness' contributed to reducing the risks related to, using Freire's (1970) words, the educator 'filling' the world into participants, controlling and giving direction to the educational process rather than helping participants discover what is inside them and remake sense of the world around them together.

Second, Kebe's extraneousness to the community of destination helped him see himself as a learner, rather than a teacher: new people and relations created a learning challenge: 'Here I am like you – Kebe told me today – everything is new to me and I have to learn everything' [Diary, 28.03.2010]. Kebe seemed to possess, in his approach to the classes, the humility and availability to listen that are key in problem-posing education. His approach as learner, rather than 'teacher', resonated with the role that educators have in liberating processes of education: one of critical educator.

Tostan recruited Kebe in 2007 and employed him elsewhere in the country in the period 2007–10. In 2010, then, he was included in the roster of the facilitators working on Tostan's new UNICEF-founded CEP and participated in the one-week training course on the Kobi 1 held in Kaolack with the other facilitators working in the region. According to Tostan's local training team, the course aimed at making facilitators familiar with the first three months of the programme. Also, the training discussed with facilitators the degree to which they would be allowed to adapt the programme to their own abilities and participants' needs, and the educational approach that facilitators should adopt (participant-centred, flexible, interactive and respectful of the dignity of all participants). At the end of the training, each facilitator was paired with a village. Kebe was assigned to Galle Toubaaco: his intention to collaborate in the present research was then explored; he agreed to participate and negotiated access to the classes that he would run in Galle Toubaaco.

Kebe moved to Galle Toubaaco in March 2010. He earned the respect of the community relatively quickly. He was held in repute alongside the *intellectuels* of the village (as his sitting position during the observed village meetings, on a chair beside the elders, suggested). Community members, independently of their participation or not in the classes, showed high consideration of Kebe's education and his ability to transform that knowledge into a concrete benefit, that is, a job as a teacher with Tostan. This esteem allowed him to access hidden and visible power mechanisms in place in the community: Kebe could suggest topics to be discussed during village meetings and could influence the community's decisions on those or other topics. Being aware of the power he could have in influencing the community's political decisions, he consciously refused to give it when members asked for his opinion on what they should do. After one of the meetings observed, when asked about the reasons for refraining from doing so, he replied by saying: 'It's their village, not mine; they have to take the decisions, not me' [Diary, 10.04.2010]. Yet, during the meetings or other informal moments, he reminded participants of the discussions that they had in class as, for instance, when suggesting the existence of democratic voting as a means to make decisions. In that specific case, participating members explained to non-participants the reasons explored together in class and tried to convince them of the benefit that came from voting. Thereafter, in the other observed meetings, the rural community replaced tacit consent with a show of hands as the standard decision-making procedure.

Kebe made various efforts to respect community members' decisional autonomy. He did not take their place by telling them what they should do or offering rewards for doing as he suggested. Rather, he showed participants ways of analysing alternatives to their reality and primed the results of their discussions in their daily life (when community members asked his advice about the decisions they were taking). In doing so, possibly following the NGO's instructions given during the training, Kebe seemed to consider community members as exclusively responsible for giving direction to their community's development. His role, then, was to be that of an indirect helper. In class, his presence created a new audience for speech. He could elicit participants' discussions, without which the Tostan programme could not work. He could generate the dialogue by being a kind human being towards participants, who were entering into education for the first time.

The observed facilitator–participants and facilitator–community relations were in line with the basic principles of problem-posing human rights education: indirect, non-intrusive and participant-centred.

However, on a few occasions, Kebe's role in the class and in the community diverged from the indirect approach he adopted in other moments:

> Session 12, young people. Today Kebe looks very tired. I don't
> think he prepared for the class as he usually does. It's very hot
> outside; everyone seems to be suffering from the incredible
> heat. As he did in other classes, Kebe asks participants to mix
> amongst different genders, trying to break norms of segregation
> in the class. The first who has to move is AB, who after being
> asked repeatedly to move, eventually stands up, in silence,
> slowly, and looking seriously at the ground. He changes place
> unhurriedly, shaking his head, annoyed. His sunglasses and hat
> on, he finally sits amongst the girls. [. . .] The class starts; there
> is not much playing today. Kebe is doing much of the talking
> and asking participants from time to time their opinion. Their
> answers are limited to choral 'yes'. [. . .] It's the final summary:
> Kebe asks participants to summarise. The class ends. [Diary,
> 16.04.2010]

In the class above, Kebe's approach was more direct and non-participative than usual. Yet he used the drawings and tried to involve participants in the discussion and, possibly, participants' reticence motivated him to do most of the talking.

In Freirian terms, the tendency of the class to assign to the educator the role of talker must be deconstructed by the educator. The oppressed look to authority to be told what they need to do or say (similarly to what Belenky et al. 1986 argued regarding the silent women). The educator can be seduced by that power since he does not have to struggle to obtain it: the oppressed spontaneously offer it to him. In doing all the talking, Kebe deviated from the very core of problem-posing education: the importance of a critical dialogue. In a fruitful critical dialogue, educators and students create the truth together. When he refuses the seduction of the power that the class offers to him, the educator does an act of real love. When he accepts it, it is an act of domination; while love generates freedom, domination generates oppression (Freire 1970). However, the training received and Tostan's facilitator's manual provided Kebe with a constant benchmark against which he could evaluate his educational practices. Tostan's requirements and periodic evaluations ensured that Kebe's pedagogical strategies were sufficiently consistent with the Freirian model for participants to develop critical analysis of their reality, but they were not always in line with the principle expressed by Tostan's general educational approach.

On another occasion, Kebe had to decide either to hold a class with the majority of the participants, or to respect a woman's decision to participate in a baptism on a normal class day:

> Last week, after having obtained Kebe's permission, Fatou Diallo publicly invited in class all participants (and more generally all members) to the baptism of her nephew, to be held next Wednesday. A part of the village, however, didn't want to participate in the celebration. Fatou told me in an interview that they were in conflict with one of her close relatives (Ndene, her cousin). Yesterday (Wednesday), many participants went to the class as usual. Kebe was resting at home. He knew that a baptism was going on that day and that therefore nobody would be in class. He was called by participants to hold the class anyway. Arriving in class he saw a large number of people willing to attend class as normal. He decided that, since the majority of the class was present, it would be fair to hold the class. [Diary, 18.05.2010]

It is difficult to make sense of Kebe's decision to hold the class anyway that day. His decision might then be motivated by the desire to positively reinforce a democratic attitude. In this example, as in some others, what could be perceived as deviant by an outsider could possibly have coherence from a local understanding of it. Fatou showed sadness for community members' decision to go to class:

> we had already learned about human rights and about discrimination before the baptism but the women continued to discriminate anyway and decided not to go to the baptism. Before the baptism the teacher said there would be no class because of the event, so he will give everyone a chance to attend the baptism. All of the women decided to show up at class anyway instead of going to the baptism so the teacher taught the class. I went to the teacher and told him they violated the human rights rules but the teacher said the majority of the students showed up to class. I told the teacher this is discrimination and you should not have taught the class. [S2I8FD]

Fatou's report of the events highlights her capacity to reprehend Kebe towards the end of the HRE classes. That suggests that Kebe's role was

understood as authoritative but not unquestionable. Fatou's willingness
to stand up and defend her human rights against the facilitator dem-
onstrates that she was convinced of the rightfulness of human rights
by the moral authority of the content, rather than by the charisma of
the facilitator himself. While Kebe's behaviour could be understood as
deviant from Freire's compassionate model of educator, it offered an
opportunity to Fatou to demonstrate (*in primis* to herself) her capacity
to argue and defend her dignity using the moral values primed in the
class: 'People have changed, I have changed. I know my rights now and
can defend them as I did with the teacher [. . .] on the occasion of the
baptism' [S3I11FD].

It is difficult to fully assess the impact of similar episodic deviations from the Freirian ideal of a kind and compassionate educator.
It is impossible to offer an honest understanding of those deviations
without acknowledging that they might have resulted in participants
standing up for their own rights. However, not many other examples
like the two offered above were witnessed during fieldwork and most of
the observational data show a kind and human facilitator caring about
participants' human rights and centrality in the way he planned and
implemented the HRE classes.

The Participants: Gender Participation and 'Self-deprecation'

A total of 30 adult participants registered for the classes, 21 women
and 9 men. A class for young people was also organised, with 67 young
participants, 37 girls and 30 boys. It helps to make sense of the number of female participants (surprisingly high considering the gender
relations described in Chapter 4) by the fact that many adult female
participants were enrolled on the programme by their husbands (often
without being aware of their husbands' decisions) or, alternatively, that
adult female participants enrolled with their husbands' permission.
Aisata, for instance, was happy to participate, but she did not even
know that the programme was coming to the village. In her interview
she explained:

Are you taking the classes?
Yes, I am taking the Tostan classes, when they were signing up
people to take the class, my husband signed me up, I wasn't even
here that day. When I came back my husband told me he signed
me up to take the classes. [S1I10AIB]

In Galle Toubaaco, non-participating husbands generally encouraged and supported their wives' participation. As explored in Chapter 4, wives and husbands bargain power and roles in the household within a set of pre-existing possibilities that social norms contribute to shaping by activating invisible power dynamics. The patriarchal structure of the family might foster family members' dependency on the eldest male who, in turn, could subjugate family members to his will. In Galle Toubaaco, husbands were aware of the benefits that the programme would bring to their family. Samba, who could not participate in the classes because of his work, said: 'I am not in class but I am behind it 100 per cent, my wife and my kid are taking the class and I encourage my wife and kid to go to class every day and work hard in class' [S2I15SD]. Another example was given by Mas, who said:

> *You told me you are happy your family is participating in the classes, since you can't. Why are you happy?*
> If they work hard one day everyone can learn how to read and write. An education can help teach a person how to better take care of his cattle and can give him new ideas on different ways to herd. [S1I4MD]

Their compliance with their wives' participation is linked to the benefits that they perceived as coming from the programme for the entire household. Yet before the programme, Tostan representatives and the facilitator discussed the content with the community. Community members (like Mas above) were then aware that, probably sometime in the future, participants would have a chance to learn literacy and numeracy. They did not want their family members to miss that opportunity: the entire family would benefit from having an educated member since he or she would be able to do maths, administer money, read documents and write letters, as well as teach others what he or she learnt. Amadou Ba Mbaring, for instance, said:

> I am happy [my wife is taking the classes] and if I wasn't happy about it she would not be taking the class.
> *Why are you happy about that?*
> I am not taking the class, so she needed to take it. [S1I16ABM]

The case of Amadou Ba Mbaring offers a good example for analysing a husband's motivation for his wife's participation. He was a young husband; he and his wife had no children yet. He could not take the classes, because he worked as a middleman in the weekly markets and hence was seldom present in the village. Therefore, his wife was the only person that could go to class: she *needed* to take the classes since Amadou could not. Amadou said she needed to because he recognised that he (and possibly their future family) would benefit from her knowledge. Only one man was reported as participating in the programme but keeping his wife from participating, deeming his own participation sufficient.

The 'young' Fatou Diallo, who wanted to participate in the classes, could not:

> *Are you taking the Tostan class?*
> No I am not. My husband and his brother are taking the class. My husband didn't sign me up. He thought I was too busy and wouldn't have time to do that. [S2IF5DY]

In the remaining cases, the entire family of participating informants supported them. According to informants, other members, especially children, helped their mothers by assisting them in their tasks. Hawa talked of the entire community, when she said:

> The women are cooking a lot earlier than they used to, the young people are fetching water for the family earlier and taking baths before noon so they can get ready to go to school. [S2I6HB]

The husbands supported their wives by giving their consent to their participation and by tolerating a change in family behaviours: for instance, eating earlier or later than usual and allowing women to leave the house. This form of support is what was available for the husband in accordance with the norms regulating family and gender roles (nobody could at this stage seriously expect husbands in Galle Toubaaco to cook for their families while women went to class).

Tostan encouraged both women's and men's participation. Aware of gender dynamics likely to be in place in the community, though, the facilitator was prepared to meet initial resistance to women's participation. Kebe approached male members who showed resistance to try to understand their concerns and reassure them about the nature of the programme:

Are you taking the Tostan classes?
My wife and two of my kids are taking this Tostan class. I am
so happy they are taking this class and if I wasn't encouraged
by this Tostan programme they would not be taking the class.
I myself would be in class every day but I have too much to do.
I see uplifting and realisation from an education. [S1I4MD]

Tostan's approach to women's participation was consistent with indirect
approaches to development analysed earlier. In Galle Toubaaco, Tostan
did not challenge local authority. It could have done so, for instance
by trying to convince women to resist men's authority and demand
their right to participate in the classes. Instead, Kebe approached the
local community from their perspective, offering them an opportunity to lead their own human development, treating them as 'ends in
themselves', rather than using them to reify his (or Tostan's) view of a
'more just' community. In Ellerman's (2006) terms, Kebe started from
where the doers (community members) were and saw the world with
the doers' eyes; that is, he did not impose change on the doers, rather
he approached community members by respecting their local reality,
their norms and practices and from there he built the premises for the
programme to happen.

Women's participation represented a first challenge to the way they
were perceived in families. Certain women were the only participating members of the family: they were doing something independent
and outside the household, and on which the family set part of their
hopes for a better life. This role for the women was a novelty in the
daily life of community members, compared with the role described
in the previous chapter. Husbands might well have perceived wives'
participation as part of their reproductive functions (the women gain
experience that benefit the entire family) but the process of reconsideration of gender roles was nonetheless triggered by women's participation. In cognitive terms, new clues in people's experience were
activated, pre-existent schemata were being challenged and others
would later be produced by men's observation of women's participation during the classes.

Male members participated less consistently and in smaller number.
However, their participation was of paramount importance: men could
observe women doing things they never saw them doing before (talking, taking decisions, laughing) and, in so doing, their previous biases

about what women could do started to be challenged. Men's presence gave women a reason to conceptualise their condition, to explain their challenges to someone alien to the way they made sense of their life in the community. Men's presence offered an opportunity for the women to become aware of those challenges and for the men to become aware of the women as full human beings. In Freirian terms, as described earlier, the presence of men represented for women the challenge of the *non-I*, requiring the conceptualisation of the *I* and the problematisation of the themes that would emerge as related to it.

Both male and female participants expressed an unspecified faith in education, metaphorically referring to the programme as something that would wake them up, help them find the right path, find light in the dark: 'we need education because we the Fulɓe are lost people' [S1I2FD]; 'education can wake us up, we are like sleeping and not aware of the world around us' [S1I15SD]; 'I feel like I need to get an education because if you are not educated you are a person that is lost' [S2I3OB].

The three factors that played key roles in the learning context intertwined in the social change process that HRE facilitated. The indirect approach with which Tostan negotiated access to the authorities both made them the protagonist of the community's empowerment and showed Tostan's interest in working together with the authorities and not against them. The strategic choice of the facilitator also drove the programme in the same direction. The fact that Kebe could anticipate community members' shared cultural expectations, due to their common ethno-linguistic identity, allowed him to find ways to engage participants in the programme, respecting local roles of gender and relations of power in the household and the community. Besides, he was originally from another, more distant community. His being extraneous to past dynamics and events allowed him to build up his authoritativeness as educator, although he did not translate this into banking authority (both in the class and in the village). Finally, participants' interest primed their motivation to participate in the class. Whatever their husbands' interest might be, women's participation was a concrete symbol of changing gender roles that all community members could witness from the first class. Their participation in the class was even more meaningful due to men's presence. Men's presence in the class required women's effort to problematise their situation, having to explain it to the different, to the non-I, throughout the human rights curriculum.

THE EXPERIENTIAL LEARNING

Throughout the interviews, informants talked about what they found interesting in the classes, what they learnt and what surprised them. Their answers were analysed together with observational data from the classes, and helped identify instructional strategies and understand what stood out about the course content. In the second and third sets of interviews (respectively during and at the end of the HRE programme), informants reported they had benefited in particular from the experiential aspects of their learning. Observational data confirmed that experiential learning strategies continuously triggered participation. In particular, three pedagogical factors had a key role in eliciting active critical participation: interactive and participative pedagogy (the use of pictures and role-playing exercises, including theatre, designed to simulate familiar situations; facilitator's examples making reference to local familiar practices and events; small group activities); learning through discussion (discussions with other participants and communal sharing of anecdotes on village life); and the use of Fulɓe traditional values and language.

Applying Interactive and Participative Strategies

Each class started with the facilitator showing a picture introducing the human rights that would be discussed that day, encouraging participants to comment on the picture. An example of this educational tool is offered in Figure 6.1, where people of different skin colour, religion and gender share the same space. The panel was used during the class on the right to non-discrimination.

Informants' reference to the tool suggests that its use was effective in drawing participants' attention and eliciting their participation:

> The teacher used cards with pictures to teach us and that really helped me because it's great to talk about it but if you can see it too it's good. [S2I8FD]

> The photo with people of different colours is very interesting. [S2I2DS]

> [The class] has changed people by teaching and showing people (drawings) how to keep clean, work together, take care of one's health and respect one another. I believe the images caught people's attention and made them believe if they act in a certain way they will benefit and it has been working. [S3I2PS]

Figure 6.1 Drawing used to introduce session on human right to non-discrimination (reproduced with permission of Tostan)

The facilitator would use the pictures to spark the discussion with participants about what they saw in them.

On other occasions, as part of interactive strategies, participants engaged in short sketches to depict social or familiar problems and issues that required solutions. This educational technique goes under the name of theatre of the oppressed, and was developed by Augusto Boal as a strategy to translate Freirian theories into action. Boal (1979, 1995) created a tool through which people could question the social status quo, overcoming the divide between actors and audience: participants simultaneously act and discuss what happens in the scene. Theatre can liberate participants from social roles and social responsibilities. A woman who would not normally stand up publicly against her husband can do it in the scene, naming and shaming his misbehaviours while raising issues and concerns that the entire class will be able to discuss afterwards:

Sixth sketch today. The skit starts with two women fighting. One of the two women takes a stick and starts beating the other. Another woman walks in and tries to settle the issue. OB (a man) – with the role of the husband – walks onto the scene and orders the first woman to stop. She refuses. The man threatens her physically. The first woman seems to get genuinely scared – she says something smiling. The public laughs. The third woman succeeds in getting people talking and bringing peace in the group. The first woman drops the stick. Applause. [Diary, 29.04.2010]

Participants were invited to express their opinion after the sketches finished; the facilitator encouraged them to relate the content of the sketch to their own experience. Participating informants referred to the experience overwhelmingly in the interviews. Non-participating informants also reported indirect mentioning of the technique as one of the motivators of participation. 'Young' Fatou Diallo, for instance, said:

> *Did Penda tell you anything when you asked her [about the class]?*
> She did tell me it was good and teaches them a lot of life skills and told me they would do theatre in class. [S3I8FDY]

As another instructional strategy, the facilitator encouraged participants to contribute to the discussion with concrete examples from their own life. According to informants, listening to concrete cases helped them to understand and memorise the new knowledge they came across. In one class, for instance, Penda explained with sadness how she had lost a child:

> [In the class] we learned to be decisive [. . .] After taking these Tostan classes I know I was not decisive during my first preg-nancy. I told in class what happened: I didn't go to the doctor once, I had the baby and she lived for nine months and at the tenth month she got sick, I took her to the hospital but it was too late. The doctor told me there was water in the umbilical cord and if it got to her head she would die. Sure enough three days later she died. Now I know the importance of getting regular check-ups while pregnant and once your kids are born make sure they get all the necessary vaccines. [S3I2PS]

From a concrete experience (having lost a child), Penda drew a dif-ferent understanding of healthcare. Experiential learning built new knowledge from what participants already knew: their own experience and life. It helped connect the concrete and familiar to a more abstract knowledge, as in the case of the informant above. Consider what Ami said, for instance:

Can you explain discrimination as you understood it in the class?
Discrimination is like having two wives and treating one better than the other or having two kids and putting one into school and keeping the other at home to work. [S2I11AS]

Ami derived abstract knowledge on equality from a concrete experience that she came across in her life (discrimination in the family).

Another informant, Omar, said: 'After [. . .] seeing examples of discrimination in our village [. . .] I know it's not good to discriminate' [S2I3OB]. Abstract knowledge was activated from concrete examples from participants' daily life, engaging them in concrete discussions to which they could easily contribute. There is a genuine increment of knowledge in participants' experience in the classes. That knowledge was generated from the familiar, started in the vernacular, by 'wrestling with the conditions of the problem at first hand' (Dewey [1916] 1966: 92):

What did you think after first learning about this [human right to non-discrimination]?
The first thing that came to my mind was that this is something for me and I believe in it. [S3I3AIB]

The 'material' of the new knowledge preceded the classes. The problems were not new. The experience of those problems instead was novel: the operation that led to participants' coscientisation about their reality is where the new knowledge was produced. Experiential learning is intrinsically tightened in problem-posing pedagogy: only seen in local terms, the reality becomes problematic and participants can challenge the status quo (Freire 1973). In experiential learning, the educator rediscovers the material. Kebe knew what he would teach before the classes but exposing the content to participants' vernacularisation he relearnt it. The epistemological process was dialectical: participants and facilitators engaged together in a path of critical renaming of the world. They rediscovered the material together, rather than it passing from the educator to the students (Freire 1973). In other words, Kebe did not own the object he studied with the students. They illuminated it together through the experience of the participants: problem-posing education starts with reality to overcome it (Shor and Freire 1987).

For this process to be effective, Freire recommended reducing discussion groups to small groups. In Galle Toubaaco, Kebe split participants into groups on different occasions. He asked participants to mix, creating mixed-gender groups. In small groups, participants gained confidence and exercised their public speaking skills. Observational data show that some initially led small group discussions, while over time more people started contributing to the group discussions. In turn, participants gained confidence in their speaking skills that diffused to the class first, and the entire community after.

Democratic Participation

Both Dewey and Freire considered democratic participation in the class as a fundamental characteristic of effective transformative education (Dewey [1916] 1966; Freire 1970). To Freire, by thinking and acting democratically, students become aware of others as subjects of the world and as equally deserving of dignity and respect. Democratic participation allows students to challenge dynamics of power that would otherwise hinder the process of students' coscientisation by limiting the reconceptualisation of their world (Freire 1998). To Dewey ([1916] 1966), democracy is a fundamental aspect of liberative education. The class, as ideal metaphor for the society, should make provisions for participation of all students on equal terms. Democracy in education allows the emergence of students' internal aims, and structures processes in which the students can have genuine problem-developing (and problem-solving) experiences.

Kebe structured a norm of democratic participation in the class, one where everyone was encouraged to contribute and everyone's contribution was valued and never diminished. Participants learnt about democracy not only through the content of the sessions, but also by experimenting with it in class:

[The class] taught us democracy, about not discriminating against one another and to respect each other. Kebe was a major reason why things have changed; he involved everyone in the classes emotionally, educationally and religiously. He is such a hard worker. [S3I7OB]

Asked about the most interesting thing he had learnt in the class, Omar answered 'democracy', and connected it with the facilitator's efforts to elicit participants' dialogue and collaboration. Participating informants described the class as a place where they could speak to people with whom they would not have previously had proper conversations and where they could learn and practise better ways of talking to each other:

> What we are learning now will change things a lot.
> *Why would the class change things?*
> The classes have brought people together and taught them how to talk and listen to each other and help one another. [S2I3OB]

Informants stressed two reasons for being enthusiastic about talking with others in class: first, some informants (such as Penda and Ami below) said they were happy to get to know each other better and to learn from each other: 'There are some people whom I did get to know a little better. With class we have a lot more time to talk to one another and get to know each other' [S2I4PS]; 'There are a lot of people I got to know in class, Ndene is one of these people I didn't know him much before but now we talk and joke around' [S2I10AIB]. Second, they were surprised by the fact that everyone was learning to both speak in public – especially women – and respect other people talking. Djombo, Omar and Ami, in particular, said:

> people here are used to having a conversation with three people talking at the same time but in class when that started to happen the teacher would tell us we had to speak one person at a time. [S2I7DS]

> I find it [the class] very interesting because I am learning many things I didn't know before. Now people here are much closer to one another, they talk to each other all the time, help each other and exchange ideas. [S2I3OB]

> [. . .] before if it wasn't for a marriage, baptism or a funeral people would not get together but now people do a lot of things together and help each other. Now women talk about what they learned in class and about their finances and how they can help develop the village. [S3I3AIB]

Also, other informants said they were positively surprised by being together in the class and sharing ideas with each other. The 'young' Amadou said: '[classes are good because] People have less time alone, they spend more time together in the classroom' [S3I10ABY]; and the 'old' Amadou confirmed: '[thanks to the classes] People now spend less time on their own and talk together in class, everyone can talk' [S2I9AB]. Observational data show a gap in gender participation in the first classes with men talking much more than women: 'Session 2 today. [. . .] It's almost the end. An old woman, encouraged by the facilitator, stands up and talks. I realise this is happening for the first time since the beginning of the classes' [Diary, 15.03.2010].

As also acknowledged by informants, women started contributing more and more to the discussion over time, while at the beginning most of them refrained from talking:

Do you think the women talk the same, more or less in class now?

The women are participating a lot more in class now. [. . .] They are gaining confidence from the class.

Why did they not talk before?

They were too shy to speak. [S2I2DS]

I am speaking a lot more because I am learning a lot and I have more confidence in myself. [S2I11AS]

The women are talking a lot more [now compared with the first classes].

Why are they talking more now?

They are starting to learn from the class and develop. [S2I4PS]

Informants made sense of women's lack of participation as shame or lack of habit. Ami, for instance, talking of lack of participation of women in the village meetings and the first class, said: 'If you are not educated it's hard to speak especially when your children are around' [S1I6AS]. Sidi Ba also expressed the opinion (in line with that of other men) that: 'women are too shy and don't speak up and sometimes they are afraid to speak because they are women' [S2I1SB].

In the quote above, Ami established a direct link between being educated and having the capability to talk in public. To her, uneducated people would not participate in a discussion. However, the male elders, who were not necessarily more educated than the women, did most of the talking in the community. Ami's was an attempt to rationally justify women's silence in public meetings; she could not conceptualise women's absence from the talking as conditioned by hegemonic invisible power relations. On the other hand, Ami's quote reveals her hope that an education would help her learn public speaking skills that she would then apply without shame. Interestingly, she referred to the shame she would face by speaking in front of her kids who represented her family and household. It is in the household, in fact, that her subjugation to her social position started, shaped by invisible power dynamics that reproduced themselves generation after generation.

Belenky et al. (1986) drafted a theory of silent women that might help make sense of women's lack of participation during meetings. Women who are socially, economically and educationally deprived develop language but do not explore the power that their words can have. Women experiencing patriarchal authority as all-powerful obey without asking for explanations, for rationalisation. They learn not to trust their ability to understand the 'why of things' and rely on the presence of an authority to guide their actions. Women learn, in other words, to maintain a woman's place. As to how they learn their role, I suggested an explanation in the previous chapter, by analysing invisible power dynamics, social norms and access to resources. Ami, and the other women who linked their not being educated to their lack of public speaking, might have self-deprecated themselves because they internalised the opinion shaped by the social status quo. Freire analysed direct forms of 'power-over' shaping peasants' perception of self on the active depreciative talking of the bosses. What happened in Galle Toubaaco is different; yet, Freire's analysis is useful. In Galle Toubaaco, the invisible power dynamics analysed in the previous chapter created a norm of female 'silence' (in Belenky's term) and subjugation for women. Women, lacking capacity to aspire to a different reality, understood themselves as facing a self-reproducing scenario and could not see themselves as active agents of social change. Kardiata's sentence quoted earlier re-emerges with new perspective: 'We will ask the men to work hard and allow everyone to have a voice' [S1I7KS].

Women in Galle Toubaaco did not demonstrate an understanding of themselves as talkers. They listened to the voice of others in the class. Amongst those 'others' there were Kebe, the men and the women that they modelled (particularly the elders). They started with a little talking at first and saw that others valued their opinion. Then they spoke more and more. In class, they experienced a different self, one as a talker. In the family, then, they also experienced a new talking role, one of a teacher that shared what they had learnt in the classes with non-participating members. As the classes went on, women got used to talking in front of a public audience. Men were surprised at the new capabilities that women demonstrated they were developing; Amadou, for instance, said: 'They [the women] are talking a lot more now, before they would sit around and not say anything but now they talk all the time' [S2I9AB]. However, as Omar remarked, half-way through the programme women's talking was still limited to the classes: '[Although the women have learnt to talk in the classes] The women talk a lot more in class than they do in meetings. In most meetings men are the ones that speak' [S2I3OB].

The democratic environment of the class created by Kebe helped women to produce a new understanding of themselves as talkers. This new understanding was also acknowledged by men. New aspirations entered the field of women's possibilities. The traditional role of women as listeners was challenged by the development of new capabilities and widened members' capacity to aspire, to imagine alternative courses of action. This capability was then translated into village meetings, generating surprise amongst community members and further contributing to challenging traditional gender roles. The results of this process are explored in the next chapter.

Using Participants' Mother Tongue

Language plays a critical role in problem-posing education, since it can be used to make social inequality invisible or to unveil it (Freire 1970; Freire and Macedo 1995). Through the use of Fulfulde, Kebe activated local values and triggered common understandings of the world. Every class started with a Pulaar proverb to frame the content of the class over a traditional positive value. One of the first classes on the importance of working together, for example, started with a Fulɓe proverb stressing the importance of cooperation: *Conflict does not exist; only a lack of dialogue exists.* At this stage, the classes did not include learning to read and write. Literacy comes later in the programme. Participants were aware of the curriculum progression and set their expectations on it. Since the beginning of the programme, however, they could learn Fulɓe words that they had lost in their contact with the Wolof ethnicity. As demonstrated by informants, the fact that classes were given in their own language was a strong motivator of participation:

> There are lots of young people and older people in the class and they are all learning new things. [. . .] they are getting an education they didn't have before; they are learning words they didn't know before. [. . .] For example, they didn't know the Pulaar word for onions. [S2I1SB]

> [It's good to learn in Pulaar] because it [Pulaar] is a sacred language, it's a language sacred to human beings. [S2I13MS]

> We have been learning a lot of words in our language that we didn't know before. Words like *niamakou*, hot pepper. The class will change people, for example there can be a change in use of the words where we stop using Wolof words in our language. We are learning many Pulaar words in class that we didn't know before and we'd rather speak pure Pulaar than use Wolof words when speaking Pulaar. [S2I14ABY]

Academics and practitioners in the field have acknowledged the importance of using mother tongues in education to enhance the quality of the education delivered and to protect minorities from losing their linguistic identity (Benson 2004; Phillipson 1996; Skutnabb-Kangas 2000; Van Dyken 1990). Other scholars, though, have argued that linguistic human rights based on mother tongue education have relied too much on notions of identities, excluding the minorities they are intended to protect from the knowledge needed to interact with the globalising world around them (see, for instance, Stroud 2003). In Galle Toubaaco, the use of Fulfulde in the classes was strategic for three reasons. First, the language identity of the participants was strongly connected to their ethnic identity. Participants acknowledged the importance of rediscovering or getting closer to that linguistic identity by learning their language. Delivering HRE in Fulfulde enhanced participation by triggering participants' desire to reintegrate their ethnic identity.

Second, participants in class critically analysed local practices regulating their social behaviours. To do so, they needed to use the words linked to those behaviours to reframe their own meanings of them. Freire (1970) stressed the importance of the relation between words and actions. Words construct the world, not vice versa. To deconstruct their social status quo, participants needed to summon shared values, practices and words that name those practices and values. In the HRE programme, participants looked at their daily life and made sense of it together, in their own language and through commonly shared social assumptions and schemata.

Third, receiving education in one's mother tongue is a basic human right of every human being (contained, for instance, in the ICESCR – Article 27 – and the CRC – Article 30: United Nations 1966, 1989). As seen earlier, HRE is by definition delivered with respect for human rights, and it could have been detrimental, and it certainly would have been incoherent, to ignore the right that people have to develop their personality and analyse the world in their mother tongue.

THE CURRICULUM

The Preliminary Session: Creating a Community of Practice

Situated learning theory identified three characteristics that communities of practice share: mutual engagement, joint enterprise and shared repertoire (Wenger 1998). In the first sessions of the programme, Kebe asked participants to reflect on their identity and set their own goals for the programme. In the first session, he invited participants to travel to the village of knowledge:

> First session today. My interpreter explains to me that Kebe told the story of four friends travelling to the village of knowledge: some of them are tired, some others complain, some others are tired but focused on their goals and they feel proud of the sacrifices they are making because they are reaching the village of knowledge. After the story, Kebe asked participants to answer some questions in groups, discussing their opinions on the different characters travelling, and if they would consider it a successful journey or not if only one person in the group reached the village of knowledge. [Diary, 02.04.2010]

The content of the story elicited the idea that rewards in the future justify smaller sacrifices in the present. The following active discussion acted as a trigger for the participants to discuss concretely the supporting reasons for the idea that sacrifices can be made envisioning a bigger success.

Omar then suggested that, as it was for the travellers to the village of knowledge, so it was for their village: they were travelling to the village of knowledge and the classes with their sacrifices represented an investment in the future since education is always useful. Then, Kebe asked participants to discuss some local proverbs such as, for instance, *If ten dig a hole and ten fill it, there is a lot of hole but no dust; Conflict does not exist, only a lack of dialogue exists;* or *People are people's own medicine.* Participants agreed about the importance of collaboration as a part of their traditional values and their ethnic identity, and related this to the story discussed earlier.

Mutual engagement, 'the source of coherence of a community' (Wenger 1998: 73), ties participants into the practices of their community. The first session, with participants reflecting on their need to participate for the greater success that will follow, enabled participants' engagement with each other: the journey to the village of knowledge is useless if only one person reaches it; everyone must arrive at the end of the journey for the greater benefit of the group. In the following session, Kebe primed the importance of participation through a game:

> Second session today. The facilitator gave a ball to participants and asked them to pass it to each other. He then asked participants to think of the game as a metaphor of a discussion: everyone must play and the ball must not go from participants to facilitator only. [Diary, 04.04.2010]

In the class, everyone started being 'included in what matters' (Wenger 1998: 74), that is, in the class participation. Kebe adopted a dialectical approach, encouraging participants to talk and recalling, from time to time, local proverbs triggering the values of collaboration, participation and engagement. Wenger called similar processes the coherence that transforms mutual engagement into a CoP. In the same session, Kebe asked participants to choose an animal that represented them, finding positive and negative traits of those animals and asking participants for strategies for promoting better interaction and dialogue in the class (since the lion can be patient, or the turtle can be shy, for instance). In this second session, then, participants began to explore their heterogeneity, what Wenger (1998) called their diversity and partiality that gives unique significance to each participant's life.

The second characteristic of a CoP, joint enterprise, is a relationship of mutual accountability among participants towards a common goal (Wenger 1998). In the third session, Kebe asked participants to draw their village of the future. He put a big piece of paper in the middle of the classroom and distributed some markers. Then, he invited participants to envision the future of their community on the paper. Many participants drew a health post, others drew a millet-peeling machine, others drew a school, and so on. Kebe then asked participants to discuss in small groups the changes their community would need in order to achieve their envisioned ideal village. Situated learning theory called the creation of a stated goal the beginning of a negotiated enterprise. With it, participants also share relations of mutual accountability that is both accountability for participation and moral accountability. According to informants, when some participants did not come into class, other participants required them to explain their reasons for not coming: they shared the accountability for their presence in the class. Besides, participants constructed reciprocal moral accountability to respect (in their daily life) the behaviours understood as morally correct in the classes. What was agreed in class, since it was for a better future, became everyone's responsibility to implement and protect. In the words of a female informant interviewed towards the end of the Kobi 1:

> *What did you like the most in class so far?*
> The most enjoyable thing so far has been learning about the right against discrimination and violence. Learning about it in class can help diminish the cases of discrimination in class. [. . .] With the class, people will know what is good and what is bad, everyone sees them now if they discriminate. And for those who don't know, people who attended class will tell them. [S2I9MB]

Session 4 was not observed, but it was likely to have contributed with the others to building up mutual engagement, since it dealt with the importance that every human being has in a human community. The facilitator reported he was very satisfied with that session. According to him, participants were impressed when reflecting on their roles in the world and the impact they could have on their community. The act of reflecting on the changes that famous people had made in the world (as participants were invited to do during session 4) gave credit to the idea that everyone mattered if they wanted to make the village better:

if a human being could change the world alone, they could definitely change their village together.

The third characteristic of a CoP is the shared repertoire of resources. Kebe made continuous reference to Fulɓe proverbs or stories. Participants responded to the priming of the Fulɓe *common sense* by locating customary Fulɓe views of the world (that they recognised as being part of their ethnic tradition) in their daily personal experiences. Participants, encouraged by Kebe, shared their history and their stories; in Wenger's terms, they shared resources of mutual engagement. Anecdotes, untold stories, and participants' similar and diverging views of community life represented the resources through which the CoP'class' recognised their common identity. Then, after the programme, the new views of the world unleashed by the programme represented a new set of resources available to participants. Participants used these resources to reconfirm their common membership outside the classroom: in the village. In the formal and informal meetings, participants shared human rights knowledge, anecdotes and stories that raised their awareness of being members of the CoP-class.

Their role in the class and the set of resources acquired slowly equipped them with new terms of interaction with non-participants. They could teach them and, in doing so, they would discover themselves as teachers, they would reach a different awareness of self as talkers:

Is what you learned today useful at all?

Yes it can benefit me because now I can teach my family and friends and all that is beneficial. [S3I11FD]

Now women are gaining more confidence and are starting to talk more, they participate in the classroom and when they come home they tell us what they learned. It's nice because I am not participating in the class but I am learning from them. Sometimes after class they all get together and talk about what they learned and how they exchange ideas. [S2I1SB]

Legitimate participation theory of learning in CoPs argued that members in the community could be either full or peripheral. Full members are those who grant legitimation to the newcomers that, demonstrating their capacity to act and speak as the old members do, slowly access more central positions and gain full recognition as legitimate talking members of the community (Lave and Wenger 1991).

The class was a new environment, it offered an alternative setting hosting people's relationships, and as such offered people an opportunity to engage in new forms of membership. Observational data show that the number of people actively participating increased over time. While at the beginning a few men (particularly the elders) did most of the talking, session by session the women gained confidence: data show, in the first session, that 90 per cent of spontaneous talking (i.e. non-primed, e.g. women being asked to report on their group's work) came from men. In the last sessions observed (three months later), that balance had reached an impressive 60/40 in favour of the women (who, though, as seen above, significantly exceeded men in number).

In Galle Toubaaco, the only potential old member of the community was Kebe, since the content of the classes was unknown to all other members. In response to this situation, participants tried to obtain legitimisation from Kebe, checking his agreement with what they would do or say. Kebe, though, refrained most of the time from doing so. In Freirian terms, participants tried to bargain their legitimation with the facilitator motivated by self-deprecation that fostered the idea that knowledge could only be received, not generated. Kebe, however, remained firm in the pedagogical position enforced since the first session: everyone's participation was important and every contribution was unique. Rather than looking for the right or wrong answer, the class would be a place where people could share their views without fear of being evaluated or judged. Kebe gave participants the tools to legitimate their membership by themselves or, to put it in another way, he legitimated everyone's participation equally.

Such a process was a new one for people in the class. They were used to the hierarchical relations analysed in the previous chapter. Hence, they responded by adapting their actions to the way their current cognitive schemata suggested: bringing the relationships learnt outside into the class. In their understanding of gender roles, men would be the talkers and the decision-makers, women would be the listeners and the decision-followers. As the class went on, however, women discovered a different self to what they were used to: they could talk in front of others in small groups, they could represent their group and report to others and they could obtain other people's agreement in the class with what they said. Aisata, after the classes, could recall something a woman had said – and the consensus she obtained – without hesitation:

Do you remember something a woman said in the class?
A woman said that taking care of our children is important.
Everyone in the class agreed with what the woman said.
[S3I10ABY]

The men witnessed women gaining public speaking skills and implicitly acknowledged their capacity by speaking to them (agreeing or disagreeing with them). In situated learning theory terms, participants inverted the process of legitimation of their membership and built their own legitimation through what Gaventa (1980) defined as a series of growing successes that allow people to unveil and contest invisible power dynamics. Rather than having to ask for legitimation of their membership, participants in the class built their own legitimation. Village relationships, with some members holding talking power and others being relegated to silent roles, were reconceived in the class into a new understanding of them:

> Session 8. Today for the first time I counted more female participants than male participants intervening in the class. Also, today for the first time a female participant disagreed with what a male participant said and all other participants, both men and women, backed up what this woman said. She looked very happy, as if she was feeling important. [Diary, 21.04.2010]

In Freirian terms, the dialogue that occurred in the class liberated participants (or at least many of them) from the oppression that limited their understanding of the self as capable of meaningful contributions. The CoP had been positively built on rules of democratic participation since the first sessions. The dynamics that enhanced everyone's participation were reactivated in each of the following session. In these sessions, participants, aware of the importance of their mutual engagement and their goals, critically analysed local practices and behaviours from a human rights perspective.

The Sessions on Democracy and Human Rights: Analysing Local Practices

The four preliminary sessions analysed above engaged participants in discussing collaboration in the class and set the groundwork for a vibrant, democratic CoP. The following six sessions dealt with the justification for the existence of government and the law. In session 5, Kebe asked participants to imagine they were in the 'Island of Tomorrow', and invited them to discuss a possible organisation for their society.

Rather than summarising participants' reactions to each and every one of the six sessions on democracy, it seems more useful to remark that, generally speaking, during these classes participants were engaged in discussing everyone's role in the village. For instance, they discussed the importance of living in peace as a group and the reasons for having government and laws. What stood out during observation was the 'Democracy Game' played in session 9. Kebe split participants into pairs (they were still in the Island of Tomorrow) and asked them to evaluate a concrete situation each:

> Kebe had a series of situations (he will tell me later he took those from the manual) including, for instance: the government of the Island of Tomorrow declared that elections cost too much and is shutting them down; the government starts a programme to be sure that girls go to school; the government favours one national language to the detriment of others. Kebe tells me he had many situations, but he chose the most relevant to Galle Toubaaco. [Diary, 25.04.2010]

As seen in detail in Chapter 2, Freire (1970) called topics of great concern or importance to the learners 'generative themes'. Human beings are able to reflect on their existence and the historical characteristics of that existence. In doing so, they can experience their field of social possibilities, what Freire calls 'limit-situations', as obstacles to their liberation. When those barriers are perceived as insurmountable, human beings lose hope of changing the status quo. For participants in HRE, then, exploring social norms and invisible power dynamics is not enough: students must look at them with the positive feeling of being able to change them. The educator – Kebe in Galle Toubaaco – should help learners understand those limit-situations by investigating with them their thematic universe. As he would do many times during the course, in session 9 Kebe chose to challenge participants with particular problems, investigating possible generative themes that had emerged in the previous classes. Participants responded to Kebe's challenges in their own way, by exploring their local reality and translating the abstract knowledge on democracy into a problematic understanding of their local reality: 'Kebe told me he was surprised because participants spoke about the fact that they didn't elect their village chief. By the way he speaks about it, it seems that participants were quite critical of the issue' [Diary, 25.04.2010].

At this stage of the process, participants started experiencing limit-situations as problems encountered during their life. However, solutions were still not in the field of possibilities. On the one hand, then, participants already problematised their need to cooperate in order to reify their ideal better village. During another of the following sessions (session 10) participants started to talk about the coordination they needed to reach the future that they envisioned. However, similar forms of coordination lacked references to dignity, equality, rights or responsibilities. Participants had critically reflected on everyone's role in their journey towards a better village; however, discussions on how people needed to be treated for them to be able to positively collaborate for that journey did not emerge yet. They could envision their goal and understood their need to cooperate, but the problematisation of their working together – that is, how participants could reify that cooperation – still had to undergo critical analysis.

Sessions 11–24 explored certain human rights:[8] the right to life; to be free of all forms of violence; to be protected against all forms of discrimination; to peace and security; to health; to education; to water, food, housing and clothing; to a clean environment; to work; to a family and a nationality; to marriage; to free expression, opinion and information; to free association; and to vote and to be elected. These sessions elicited participants' discussion about their view of human rights, their local interpretation and understanding, their vernacularisation. Amongst the sessions observed, three in particular stood out for their significance and because they unleashed powerful dynamics in the class. These were sessions 13, 14 and 17: the right to be protected against any form of violence (13), to any form of discrimination (14) and to health (17). The classes reached a high emotional level, with participants cheering, singing, clapping and some even crying. Session 13 began with Kebe asking a participant to summarise what had happened in the last sessions. Then, Kebe asked participants to comment on a drawing representing a group of men and women peacefully talking together.

> Session 13 'Jojjande reenedi e kalambadi musik' [human right to be free from all forms of violence] has started and the women are much more reactive in interpreting the drawing. [. . .] [*After the initial discussion*] My interpreter and I are trying to take note

Figure 6.2 Drawing used to introduce session on human right to be free from violence (reproduced with permission of Tostan)

as much as possible of things that people are saying, but the conversation is escalating, people seem to pass from enthusiasm to anger, then to happiness. Their contributions follow incredibly fast one after the other. A man takes the floor, I think he is trying to argue something but, it's the first time I see this, a woman interrupts him (again: it's the first time this happens) and says something that sounded like 'Musiki ɲe ɲa fai ɗe66o [bad things are being done against the women].' All other women start talking together right after; it's the first time that the class is participating so actively and disorderly at the same time. Kebe intervenes, looks at the men in the class and says something. Men and women laugh together. Tension seems gone. Ndene takes the floor: 'Kebe hali gonga [Kebe has spoken the truth].' Ndene is defending women's rights. [. . .] My interpreter helped me make sense of what happened in class today: a woman started talking about violence against women, which raised a great consensus amongst other women. Kebe asked the men what they thought and a man said something like – I have never thought about this; I have never realised the way they felt. [Diary, 29.04.2010]

Participants were asked to reflect on forms of violence in the world. After the initial conversation, they moved the analysis to their local reality. A woman spoke about gender-based violence and the other women joined her. More silent participants had experienced public speaking skills in the earlier sessions and, by this session, had acquired enough self-confidence to exercise that capability as a group. In Freirian terms, a generative theme emerged from a critical discussion about gender violence and women reacted with strong emotion to that emergence. The theme emerged as an obstacle to the realisation of women as full human beings, probably for the first time publicly in the life of male and female community members. For the first time, community members were requested to think about this issue together, to express their opinions in front of other members. The theme represented one of the limit-situations described above that trigger people's coscientisation: the critical awareness of a social problematic that in turn generates a different (and higher) awareness of self and the world (Freire 1970).

Informants overwhelmingly referred to this class in their interviews:

Is there violence towards women here?
It did happen before, if a woman did something that her husband didn't like he would beat her and the parents also beat their kids all the time but that doesn't happen any more.
When has this changed?
The class brought this change, they learned that it's not good to discriminate and violence is not good, it's better to talk to one another instead of fight. I think everyone here tries to be a good person and after learning about this stuff in class they realise how bad violence is and how much it can affect a relationship. [S2I10AIB]

Session 14 – on the right to be protected against all forms of discrimination – was just as present in informants' narratives. Although it was less charged with emotional participation in the class, all informants referred to the session as one of the most important:

Session 14 today, non-discrimination. [. . .] Kebe shows a drawing of various people: young, old, male, female, Muslim, Christian, disabled, European, African, Asian. Kebe asks participants what they could see and what the figures had in common. The class answer they were all humans. Kebe asks participants if they thought these human beings are all necessary in creating a better society and what happens if some people are excluded. Participants discuss the issue and they agree that their exclusion could be deleterious to the community. The excluded could hinder the progress of the community. A man says: they are part of that community so they need to contribute. A woman also says: they could remain behind and with their behaviour they could hinder the progress of the community. Another woman adds: a community working together works better: *if ten dig a hole and ten fill the hole there is no hole but a lot of dust.* Kebe asked what do these human beings have in common. Participants discuss in pairs and then in groups of four. They respond by eliciting body characteristics first and then they move to intellectual characteristics: they love, they care about their families, they are rational, etc. The class conclude that since those beings all feel the same and live, they all deserve the same respect. They need to be treated in the same way. [. . .] Kebe asks if human beings in the world are treated all the same. Many participants say no and start talking about their community. [*A series of sketches followed.*] [Diary, 31.04.2010]

The class started with offering examples of indignities suffered by self or by others. The strong Islamic norm commanding equal treatment of co-wives and their children was easily available to participants. At first, then, participants could problematise the abstract norm into a local (in this case religious) one. The human rights-inconsistent behaviours were initially conceptualised as contrary to the religious norm: in fact, the different treatment of two co-wives can be understood both as a violation of the Qur'anic norm recommending their equal treatment and as inconsistent with the abstract international human rights norm of non-discrimination. By analysing their daily family and community life and its being inconsistent with the religious norm, participants moved to analysing it along with its inconsistencies with the wider norm of non-discrimination.

Dewey argued that, in posing a problem, the educator must offer a perplexing situation that can resonate with 'situations which have already been dealt with' ([1916] 1966: 81); the challenge of problem-posing education can thus create new problems 'large enough to challenge thought, and small enough so that, in addition to the confusion naturally attending the novel elements, there shall be luminous familiar spots from which helpful suggestions may spring' ([1916] 1966: 81). The human rights norm was bound to the familiar – to the luminous spots of knowledge – in the session. Participants could explore it from their point of view, and widened the discussion by pooling experiences of discrimination based on gender, ethnicity, social status, and so on. In other words, indirectly, the human rights norm was vernacularised by participants because it was presented to them from 'where they were', understanding it through their eyes (Ellerman 2006; Merry 2006). Informants made wide reference to the session during the interviews:

> *What is the most important thing you have learned so far?*
> I learned about human rights and how discrimination is a bad thing. [S2I10AIB]
> *What is the most interesting thing you learned in class?*
> I learned a lot of things but I forgot many but the [. . .] [*session on discrimination was*] very interesting. [S2I2DS]
> *What have you heard in class that you agree with?*
> That people should always be treated as equal no matter age or gender.
> *Why do you think that is right?*
> Because treating people equally will only help a community. After learning about it in class and seeing examples of discrimination and how it can have an effect on people I now know it's not good to discriminate. [S2I3OB]

The class on non-discrimination elicited talking about equality that resulted in participants critically reflecting on human dignity. Freirian scholar Mergner (2004) suggested that problem-posing education can be revolutionary because it has the potential for inviting people to recognise common dignity. In Galle Toubaaco, the recognition of common dignity led in the class to talking about the equality of human beings and the advantages for the entire community of respecting that equality. In class, then, participants experienced together the discovery of equality. Aminata, for instance, said: 'It's not right to discriminate and anyone who discriminates should be told to stop. I didn't know about discrimination before the classes' [S3I10ABY]. While for most participants discrimination was a new discovery, few had said they had an idea of it before the classes. Omar, who on other occasions demonstrated an outstanding level of knowledge of political and social issues, said: 'Personally I knew what discrimination was but there are many people here who didn't differentiate what was and what wasn't' [S3I7OB].

According to informants, before the programme community members did not ever publicly embody the equality of all human beings in concrete actions or speech. Nor did they ever publicly recognise the political and social implications of that equality. In the way participants talked about equality and discrimination, any reference to the public acknowledgement of equal dignity amongst community members was absent. The class created a space where that equal dignity could become the object of critical analysis and be publicly acknowledged. Once the entire class agreed on human beings' equality, there was no way back, there were no excuses for inconsistent behaviour:

> [The practice of discrimination] is going to change over time, as we learn about it, people will talk about it more and if a husband doesn't stop discriminating between his wives he could come to class with his wives one day and the whole class would hassle him about it. [S2I2DS]

Participants' concept of equality grew within their understanding of it; that is, over local values such as, for instance, working together to improve the quality of life for the entire community.

Another two values primed by the human rights knowledge were participants' love for their children and expectations of mutual reciprocal positive behaviour:

> I have kids and grandkids and [. . .] I don't want them to be discriminated against. [S3I12AS]
> *You just said that if people know what discrimination is they will stop doing it. Why?*
> Because nobody likes to be discriminated against so they won't want to discriminate against others. [S2I9MB]

In the session above, participants developed the capability of community cooperation based on equality and recognition of reciprocal respect and dignity. The preliminary sessions primed the importance of cooperation. In this group of sessions, then, rights offered participants new strategies of cooperation based on dignity and equality.

Session 17, the right to health, offered a good opportunity to practise a dignified form of cooperation:

> Session 17 started. As usual, men sit on chairs. Omar stands up to leave the place to my interpreter. [. . .] A song is made on 'Jojjande Ciellal [the right to health]'. [. . .] The discussion is now on family planning. Men declared to be against family planning, women

explained their positions and their needs. A sketch is put on scene, where a woman keeps having babies and cannot take care of them. Omar shares his opinion: women are right, they cannot have a child every year. Euphoric applause from the women. Some men are still against. [. . .] Men and women are now debating freely, there is an outstanding difference compared with the beginning of the classes. Dembaye in particular is leading the discussion. She even talks over the other men. [. . .] The class is almost over, the women look very happy. Kebe is concluding the class asking the Imam if the Qur'an prohibits family planning. He says that there is no mention of this in the Qur'an, that family planning is not prohibited. [Diary, 01.05.2010]

The abstract knowledge on the right to health generated discussion about themes that mattered from participants' perspectives. By this session, women were assured of the respect earned in the last sessions and confident of both their right to speak and their capability of doing so. In this session, they had the opportunity to talk to men about family planning, expressing their concerns and explaining the reasons behind their need for the practice. The dialogical Freirian pedagogy of the programme allowed women and men to understand each other's positions, unlike passive or banking education strategies.

An example is offered by the case of family planning: in a class towards the end of the programme, participants were introduced to international human rights instruments protecting the right to health. Participants soon started focusing on women's right to health. The facilitator then introduced the topic of contraceptive practices that can help to avoid unwanted or dangerous pregnancies, asking participants to create a skit to show the community's approach to those practices:

A skit today: a wife is lamenting that her husband doesn't allow her to do family planning. The husband (angry) enters the scene and says that he married her to have children. But the wife insists: pregnancies are keeping her from taking care of the house, of her and the children's health [she makes reference to diarrhoea]. They keep fighting until another woman enters the scene. She explains to him what family planning is really about. The husband says that she is wrong: his wife only wants to practise family planning to have sex with other men [and pretends to beat her]. The wife concludes by saying that 'men never listen; they must always be right'. [Diary, 08.06.2010]

Following the skit, the facilitator asked participants for a critical reflection of what they had just seen. They engaged in a discussion about the reasons for practising or not practising family planning. In the discussion, they could understand each other's opinion and difficulties related to family planning. Women could explain their reasons and link them to events in the past, including the death of a female friend. This description moved to tears an old male participant [Diary, 08.06.2010]. Men could be reassured that women's intention was not to seek extra-conjugal sexual relationships, and understood the health implications of unwanted pregnancies.

Until the HRE class enabled participants to understand family planning together – that is, to name it as a problem (Freire 1970) – community members had never come to an agreement on the practice. The issue of family planning had been raised before, following a radio programme:

Did you talk about family planning before the class?
We heard about it on the radio before and when we told our husbands about it they didn't understand what it was so they didn't agree. The men thought it would stop a woman from having kids. [S2I10AIB]

However, the radio programme could not structure a space where participants' discussions were mediated by a facilitator guaranteeing their democratic participation in the dialogue. The radio programme aimed at tackling one issue, but could not help participants engage with the structural dynamic that generated it. Rather than motivating human development, the radio programme only aimed at eradicating one particular practice.

In their interaction, participants became aware of both pregnant women's burdens and men's concerns. The human rights content allowed mutual concerns to emerge and be addressed. Participants of different genders could reciprocally reassure each other. According to informants, participants were then able to address those concerns in the family, possibly widening the field of topics that could be discussed at home and taking back from the classes possible concerns of other family members:

Have you heard of family planning?
Yes I have heard about it.

Does it help a woman?
My wife explained it to me well now [*after the class*]. It's good for the woman's health, the children's health and it also helps the husband because if his wife and children are healthy he won't have to worry about hospital bills. I thought women wanted to have relationships [sexual intercourse] with other men [*laughs*]. [S2I13MS]

In class, participants learnt public speaking skills. The class helped them understand possible concerns that other family members could have about certain issues (e.g. about family planning), providing them with the tools to approach those issues in the family. Observational data report non-participating family members talking with participating members over topics that, according to informants, had been excluded from family discussions before. Slowly, norms of silence started being challenged. Women started perceiving themselves as talkers in the family, and not just in class. The women studied by Belenky et al. (1986) were surprised to be able to have a conversation and make themselves understood by other people. One would imagine the women of Galle Toubaaco also being surprised at themselves when realising that they possessed the arguments to explain their position to the men and, where necessary, to reassure them.

In sum, the human rights curriculum played a key role in the process of reconsideration of local practices. Human rights were hooked to the local experience of daily challenges, to 'luminous' points (in Dewey's words) that helped participants approach new problematic challenges. Liberating themes emerged from the dialogic process of collective participation in the classes. The curriculum itself would not be sufficient, however; the facilitator played a key role in the way the curriculum was critically delivered through a series of experiential learning strategies.

RESISTANCE TO AND LIMITATIONS OF THE TOSTAN CLASSES IN GALLE TOUBAACO

I have identified three limitations in the pedagogy applied in Galle Toubaaco. Before discussing them, however, it is interesting to note that no resistance to the programme was found in the village and the reasons for this to be the case. No community member was observed showing disagreement or being uncomfortable with the Tostan classes. Some resistance can possibly be speculated, but it is difficult to imagine how significant levels of wariness or confusion over the programme could have remained hidden during both interviews and observations. There are three possible factors that could have intertwined in reducing resistance to very low levels.

First, community members expected to benefit from the programme and demonstrated high regard for education. The Tostan programme was free and voluntary. They could withdraw (or ask family members to withdraw) without having to offer any explanation. However, members knew that their village would benefit from the programme: for instance, people would learn how to work together, how to read and write, and they would learn health practices that would benefit the lives of their families. They possibly saw the human rights education part of the programme as something they needed to go through to access more concrete and useful topics, and learning about these would benefit the entire family and community.

Second, people coming back from class were able to teach other family members Fulfulde words that they did not know before. They possibly spoke about Fulɓe proverbs and stories. It is possible that, for this reason, non-participating family members perceived the programme as consistent with their local tradition and values, rather than as threatening their ethnic identity or status quo. The programme, in its indirect approach, not only respected participants' autonomy, it also posed the conditions for resistance as being meaningless: the programme was not perceived as changing people's minds since people were changing each other's minds.

Third, as seen above, the Tostan programme approached the village authorities first. Tostan representatives offered to village authorities the opportunity to invite Tostan: authorities not only gave permission, they requested the classes and were proud of doing so to help their community. Male elders, for instance, said they were very gratified because, at the end of the Kobi 1, outsiders from other villages visited Galle Toubaaco and were jealous of the change they saw: clean roads, showers and latrines, for example. In sum, the programme did not challenge local forms of authority and, possibly, community members showed them their gratitude for the benefits coming from the programme.

Even though very little resistance was observed, the programme in Galle Toubaaco showed some limitations. First, the number of women in class (about 20) greatly outnumbered that of men (five or six). Male informants said they were unable to go to class because of their work commitments outside the village; however, men in the village were often observed doing nothing at class times and still did not participate. I identified two possible reasons explaining their lack of participation. The first one is structural: men did not want to commit to a long programme that sooner or later would clash with job commitments. The second is social: the role of a man in Galle Toubaaco is to seek a source of revenue outside the village. Men might have been afraid that if they participated in the class, other community members would think they did not care about generating revenue for their family or were not capable of doing so. Also, the programme requires formal enrolment, so that occasional participation is subject to an official act of joining the classes. Men might have refrained from enrolling officially for one of the two reasons above, or for other reasons that fall beyond the scope of my work and which are left for future research.

A second limitation was the length of the sessions. In some cases, sessions lasted up to two and a half hours. I have no hard evidence to assess how participants coped with the heat and the length all together, but I often saw, towards the end of the class, tired participants, some of whom were falling asleep. Due to a possible decline in participants' concentration over time, the length of the classes might reduce the potential of the programme. For instance, participants' tiredness might exacerbate conflict and lack of understanding at later stages of the programme, when they are more accustomed to talking together. It would be important, then, to address similar issues by ensuring a participative and engaging methodology and by fostering participants' democratic and constructive dialogue throughout the entire programme.

Third, I observed a relative lack of in-class supervision for the facilitator. The facilitator represents a key feature of the programme: he or she can transform problem-posing generative dialogue into authoritative cultural imperialism. A Tostan supervisor coordinated facilitators operating in the same area. Although Kebe joined other facilitators in training events and supervision meetings, no supervisor ever oversaw his classes in Galle Toubaaco for the duration of my fieldwork. There might have been reasons for this, of course. For example, the supervisor might have preferred not to intervene in class dynamics in the first months of the Tostan programme (possibly worried about undermining the facilitator's role); Tostan might not have had the necessary economic resources; or the supervisor might have had other monitoring mechanisms (e.g. self-assessment sessions or reports from the village chief).

However, the facilitator seems to play such a key role in the pedagogy that the occasional monitoring presence of the supervisor would probably help maximise the pedagogical potential of the programme.

CONCLUSION

This chapter has offered an understanding of the Tostan programme in Galle Toubaaco. Its different components played a role in motivating participation and the changes that will be analysed in the next chapter. The overarching theme in the way the programme was delivered is Tostan's indirect approach. Tostan negotiated access to the community by engaging local authorities in a discussion about the content and the modalities of participation of the programme, securing their preliminary agreement with the classes. Relations with the authorities were always constructive, even after the beginning of the classes.

In Tostan's indirect approach, the role of the facilitator played a key role. The selection of a facilitator from outside the community contributed to fostering a humble attitude in the way the facilitator approached the community. At the same time, the facilitator was selected from people of the same ethnic group, to guarantee that he could make sense of participants' local concerns and understanding of the world and could work with them in the generation of the themes that mattered to them. His relationship with the community was indirect in that he refrained from leading the community in one direction or the other. Rather, he showed possible alternatives and ways to adapt those alternatives to the local reality. His relationship with the participants benefited from his determination to try, as far as possible, to resist that 'power of domination' that 'oppressed' participants tend to offer to educators. Although his struggle was not always successful, he managed to succeed often enough for participants to move from self-deprecation to recognition of reciprocal (and self-)dignity.

In this process, the curriculum played a key role by offering participants an opportunity to visualise their collaborative potential and by inviting them to challenge their understanding of the social status quo through a vernacularisation of international human rights norms.

Finally, the use of participants' native language also proved to be of the utmost importance in linking views of the world and the dialogue that allowed a new understanding of them.

Through the process described above, participants experienced new skills: they learnt how to cooperate and how to contribute to public speaking. Through the four months of the programme, they challenged the way in which they (and others) understood their selves (and themselves) and contributed to initiating a change in the way other community members conceptualised their potential as human beings. The results of this process were observable in the way community members understood gender roles and relations after the programme. Data also suggest a shift in the participation in hidden and visible power dynamics and report the reconceptualisation of local human rights-inconsistent practices into new behaviours. The next chapter analyses this shift in detail.

Chapter 6

THE 'NOW-WOMEN' AND OTHER CHANGES:
A WIDER HORIZON OF POSSIBILITIES?

INTRODUCTION

This chapter explores the outcome of the HRE programme in Galle Toubaaco. Here, I look at what changes happened as a result of the programme: how did community members make sense of gender roles and relations, decision-making and other human rights-inconsistent social practices after the HRE sessions? Participants challenged invisible power relations that relegated women to stereotyped roles and limited their access to visible and hidden power dynamics. In class, new possible roles were experienced that influenced women's behaviour outside of the class. Community members saw a difference in how the women behaved and spoke in the community, and acknowledged that difference. Traditional invisible power relations were challenged by new roles for women. The result of this process impacted on women's capacity to reify those different roles in the decision-making arena by exercising visible and hidden power.

The first section analyses the visible changes in the village and how they acted as motivator for community members' capacity to acknowledge a change process in the village. After the programme, community members of Galle Toubaaco described their community as different. What is more, their community could be perceived as different: observable changes included structural changes that could be easily observed by visiting outsiders (e.g. the presence of more latrines or the increased cleanliness) and changes in the everyday language used by community members, observable in community members' everyday interactions. I argue that the concrete changes that affected community members after the programme contributed to raising awareness of a social change process.

174

The second section argues that after the Tostan classes, women understood themselves differently and reported on a series of new actions they could carry out and new possibilities they had. I suggest that the relation between their identity and the interaction with the factual world around them contributed to their shifting understanding of themselves. I analyse how they made sense of that self and how a category emerged in all informants' interviews when talking of women: that of the 'now-women'. I analyse informants' choice of words in their description of women and suggest that a shift in their understanding of women was instantiated into the now-women terminology they adopted.

The third section explores the concrete implications of new roles available to women in the decision-making practices of the community. In this section, I argue that after the programme women could challenge traditional norms of silence and discover themselves as talkers and decision-makers. Evidence also suggests an increased participation of young community members in decision-making processes, although differently according to gender.

The last section analyses two examples of how participants concretised the human rights knowledge in negotiating different understandings of child-harming practices (child marriages and child labour). The section acknowledges the complexity and deep roots of the practices and suggests an interpretation of how the emerging human rights sensibility could contribute to a modification or abandonment of the practices in the future.

GALLE TOUBAACO

Observational data suggest two remarkable differences in Galle Toubaaco at the end of the programme. First, as immediately noticeable by outsiders, the village had changed: the area was cleaner, latrines and showers had been built and mosquito nets were hung in the houses. Second, less visible to outsiders visiting the village but noticeable by insiders, people's content and quantity of verbal interactions had changed. What is relevant about these differences is their degree of visibility and their indirect role in widening human development opportunities to community members. The visibility of these changes is key because it generated wider public awareness of the change process.

The first visible change, cleanliness, stood out both to community members and to outsiders. Towards the end of the programme:

Mme Ndiaye [the interpreter] reached me [coming to Galle Toubaaco] to conduct the last set of interviews. She arrived with the driver Diouf at 6 p.m. [After greetings and salutations] we went for a walk escaping the smoke produced by the women's cooking. Mme Ndiaye keeps looking around so I ask her if she is surprised by something. She says, 'Ben is it you that cleaned the entire village?' and laughs. I laugh and realise that it's actually true that the village is much cleaner; I don't know why I didn't notice this before. [Diary, 25.05.2010]

Korka, who had not been in the village for a while, immediately noticed a difference. Informants also reported this, updating me about what had happened during my absence. The 'young' Amadou, for instance, said:

What are the most interesting things that have happened in the village the last weeks I was not here?
We had a huge party not too long ago where the whole village got together and cleaned up the school, the mosque and our neighbourhood streets. We wanted our village to be clean and we said we need to do this together or nobody will do it.
Who had the idea of doing this?
The people who are taking the Tostan classes.
Has this ever happened before, cleaning public spaces together?
No this is the first time this has happened. [S3I10ABY]

Samba Diallo also said:

I see some positive change already, now I see the women getting together to talk so there is more of a unity amongst the women and everything in our neighbourhoods gets cleaned and this only started after the classes began. [S2I15SD]

Moudi, who did not participate in the classes, gave his opinion on the effect of the classes on the village by saying: '[the village benefited from the classes] because now our streets are clean, there is unity amongst everyone, people talk to each other, help each other and share laughs with one another' [S2I13MS].

Members' informal accounts, analysed in parallel with data coming from class observation, allowed understanding of the dynamics of this change. They helped explain why community members did not get together earlier to clean the village. They also explained why the village 'became' dirty in members' eyes only at a certain point and why nobody ever problematised the issue, transforming concerns into actions. First, participants had discussed in class the right to health and a healthy environment. They had analysed the benefits of a clean environment and problematised the reality of their village through critical dialogue. The dirtiness of the public spaces emerged as a theme that mattered to participants: experiential problem-posing learning helped them translate the abstract knowledge into its concrete local understanding that mattered for their lives. The village actually 'became' problematically dirty when someone said something like, 'Actually, this village is very dirty, this is unhealthy,' and everyone in the class agreed; Freire (1970) called this the process through which students problematise their local reality and understand the limit-situations in it.

To challenge the limit-situation, the class primed the importance of their reciprocal collaboration in 'travelling' (like the protagonists of the story presented in the first session) towards the better village they had visualised at the beginning of the programme. Members' potential as agents of change had already been explored in a previous session so they committed to cleaning public spaces together. Then, according to informants, they summoned a village meeting and explained to other members their concern and the solution they had identified. They discussed the practicalities together and agreed to meet to clean the village. Then, community members agreed to organise public cleaning days, where everyone available (whether man or woman) would collaborate in the cleaning. The public visibility of everyone cleaning is important for two reasons.

First, the event set a norm of expected and acceptable public behaviour. As seen earlier, social norms are beliefs about the beliefs of others (Bicchieri 2006). The decision taken in the meeting was not enforced by a law; it was enforced by expectations. On the one hand, all community members expected everyone else to contribute. On the other, however, everyone leaving the meeting thought that – after the meeting – everyone else would expect him or her to be at the public cleaning contributing to it. Elster (2007) argued that collective action is 'hindered by an 'unravelling problem'. The problem is that people are willing to contribute to communal good only if everyone else does so, but, on the other hand, collective action is effective only if everyone contributes. Seeing everyone actually contributing to the cleaning reinforced the norm, translating it into a living practice. More importantly, the fact that everyone could see everyone else contributing to the cleaning created a set of expectations.

Second, the public experience of a collective change signified the importance of that change for the entire community. Not only were community members seeing a change in their community, they were also seeing others seeing the same change. The event was, in sum, public and as such generated talking about the change in the community. Mas, who did not participate in the classes, for instance, said:

> I hear them [participants] talk about things they learnt in class and how things can change, they didn't talk about this kind of stuff before, all this started after the Tostan classes came here. In particular, sanitation; people's homes have become much cleaner and now people get together and sweep the streets. [S3I4MD]

This process, in turn, reinforced the norm of cooperation that was first established in the class and possibly widened up the debate about the change in process in the village and its potential. This process was similar to when, before the beginning of the programme, the existence of the new hut for the classes (and the fact that participants could see each other looking at the class or could imagine them doing so) generated talking about the programme and fostered the emergence of hopes and expectations:

> Things have changed a lot; [. . .] you can see that the village is much cleaner now. [S3I1DS]

> Human rights are good because it's about being clean. [S2I1DS]

> I personally think [human rights] is good; [. . .] We learnt about [. . .] cleaning our streets. [S3I2PS]

Among the men available in the village, only some were cleaning with the women. However, nobody could expect all men to be cleaning the streets together at this stage: cleaning pertained to women, as cooking did. In the cognitive terms of Strauss and Quinn (1997), the new experience of some men helping in the cleaning up loosened members' schema that upheld the existent norm of cleaning as a women's task and started creating the possibility for change. Many more similar experiences would then be required for both men and women to conceptualise and accept cleaning as a 'normal' practice for both genders.

Interestingly, publicly restoring order (as these people did when they were cleaning up the village) has also been demonstrated to result in greater prosocial behaviour of the people who see order being restored. Keizer and colleagues (2013) tested the hypothesis with a series of experiments: the strongest driver of people's prosocial behaviour was witnessing order being restored by research confederates (e.g. picking up flyers or oranges from the street). That village members in Galle Toubaaco publicly cleaned up the village, then, was also important because it was strengthening norms of prosocial collaboration among all people in the village, including those who did not participate in the cleaning. A norm of cooperation was being established, and would became more and more solid because community members could see the benefits coming from that cooperation. Participating informants were the first to link cooperation and concrete benefits. After the experience of those benefits (e.g. a cleaner, healthier village), non-participating informants would understand cooperation and respect as necessary preconditions for the development of their community. Samba Diallo, for instance, discussed the issue by saying:

> There needs to be solidarity among the people, development starts with everyone working together for a common goal, respecting one another and helping one another. After seeing what working together made possible in the village we know this is true. For our village to become somewhat modern we need a health post, a school, flour machine and especially a store. The closest store is ten kilometres away. It would be nice to have a store here where we can buy rice, sugar or oil, having just a store here would be a big step forward towards development. [S3I6SD]

The second observed change in the village was that community members would summon the term human rights often in their verbal interactions. Human rights did not simply become a topic of conversation; the phrase *human rights to* ... was repeated as a mantra by people laughing, playing, singing and dancing:

Tonight I was having dinner with the family of the village chief. AB looks at me, smiles and says, 'Jojjande reenedi e kalambadi music [human right to be protected against any form of violence].' I smiled and repeated it. Then he looked at the food, smiled again and said: 'Jojjande Lacciri e Maro [human rights to cous cous and rice].' I smiled. Then I summoned another fictitious human right [human right to the night] and then his wife and his son began. And so everyone again and again. We did this for at least half an hour! This event set my interest for seeing how much talking people do on human rights. I noticed that, now, participating members summon human rights in the most disparate moments: when cooking, cleaning, drinking tea; often when this happens they seem happy and sometimes celebrate with a laugh, a little dance or a song. [Diary, 20.05.2010]

It does not matter whether participants were actually using the term human rights to debate about their local reality. What matters is much less complex: the term human rights replenished the day of every community member, participating or not, and in turn both elicited the talking about what human rights were and symbolised change to non-participants.

Sidi Ba and Mas, both non-participating informants, commented on human rights:

Have you heard of human rights?
I did hear them talk about it but I don't know what that is. They started talking about it after taking some of the Tostan classes. [S2I1SB]
Have you heard of human rights?
Yes, this year I started hearing it from the people who are taking the Tostan classes. [S3I4MD]

On the other hand, Fatou Diallo and Dembaye (who participated in the programme) said:

Omar's mother changed; she used to be ... when someone talked to her the slightest bit she would get very upset and usually would run off into the woods. Now if you talk to her in any one way or the other she won't get mad, she will tell you that you violated the human rights rules and then she laughs. [S3I11FD]

> Human rights are good because [. . .] It's about respect, it's about helping each other and it's because of human rights now we are talking about building schools and health posts. It's also why [*a long list of changes follows*]. Everything we learnt in class about human rights we go home, talk to others and practise it. [S3I1DS]

The clean village and the human rights mantra are similarly observable changes; however, they differ in who can observe those changes. The first (the cleanliness) was observed by visitors coming to the village from neighbouring communities; as such, community members could see themselves changed through the eyes of the outsiders. They could see change happening and could see others seeing change happening. The second (the mantra) offered an opportunity to non-participating members to investigate the content of those words and, very importantly, echoed across all households witnessing that new things were happening in the village, and possibly contributed to making real the possibility of other changes. The village changed in a way that could be observed by outsiders and insiders. The perception of change widened the space for other changes to happen and for the invisible power dynamics to begin to be challenged.

GENDER ROLES AND RELATIONS: INVISIBLE POWER

Gender roles and relations in Galle Toubaaco were shaped by unequal access to key resources, but access to resources is not likely to be an observable change soon. Gender distribution of labour in itself would not be a primary concern in human rights and human development terms anyway. In Galle Toubaaco, equal respect and dignity was the first big step that emerged from informants' narratives. Other extremely important liberating gender challenges could follow, those that Kevane (2004) properly emphasised: that is, challenging unequal inheritance, unequal rules of marriage formation and dissolution, rules against working outside the home without permission, rules about mobility and travel, and maternal health, for instance. Flexibility around gender labour could not change quickly: labour distribution contributed to defining what being a man or woman meant in Galle Toubaaco. Identity was built on labour-related characteristics: women did not want men to do their work and vice versa. Also, community members had invested considerable capital in that distribution of labour. Tostan's indirect approach offered participants the opportunity to conceptualise new understandings of men's and women's capabilities and a dignity that they inscribed within familiar roles and relations.

The Now-Women

In the interviews conducted before the classes, informants were asked to describe how their village could become a better place in the future. Their des-criptions are rich with concrete changes that the village should go through to become a better place to live in: a health post, a shop, a school. In their narrative, there was not a single spontaneous mention of the need for a better collaboration or for different relations between men and women. Then, when I asked them to imagine how the relations between men and women could be different, still not many could. Some, for instance, did not understand the social status as unequal or unfair at all. Dembaye, in her first interview, for instance, said:

> We all want good things for our village, for our village to evolve for the better so it doesn't matter if a woman or a man speaks for us [...] This [the men taking decisions for the women] is not a problem and it won't change, this is the way we have done things for many years and it works for us. [S1I1DS]

Other informants were specifically asked if they foresaw the women contributing to future decisions taken at home or in village meetings. The intention in asking this question was to explore informants' capacity to visualise an alternative role for the women, one of talker, based on equal respect. Few responded by admitting the possibility of such a change. As seen earlier, Kardiata did so by falling into the unequal mechanism of the current social structure: 'Change is very hard in our culture but we will try. We will ask the men to work hard and allow everyone to have a voice, allow men and women to work together and make decisions together' [S1I7KS]. Others, rather (like Ami and Dembaye below), set their expectations for change on the Tostan programme:

> I think eventually as women get educated it will change and women will start speaking in meetings. [S1I6AS]

> I think with the education they will be getting in this Tostan class [... it] will help a lot. [S1I5DS]

As the classes proceeded, women and men had opportunities to discuss their own and others' perspectives and came to include respect and dignity within the attributes applicable to every human being:

> Another skit: A man [the husband/father] wants his children to leave the school. The children show disagreement. The patriarch threatens them with the use of force. A woman [the wife] enters on the scene. She says she will find someone else to work in the field and help the family but children should stay at home and study. There is a long discussion at the end of which the children don't go to work. [Diary, 08.05.2010]

The class offered participants an opportunity to practise new gender roles, based on equal respect and dignity, in front of others. In class, people discussed their equal rights and the implications of them for their daily life: '[The most interesting thing] I learnt [is] that women and men have the same right to work' [S3I10ABY].

At the end of the programme, informants linked equality and collaboration to their chances of transforming the village into a better place as part of a cause–effect relationship. Dembaye (participant) and Mas (non-participant) respectively said:

> To me everyone should be equal and we should not discriminate between genders. Because a man and a woman live in a house. If you want to help the village, you should do something that will benefit everyone, it would not be right to do something for the women and leave out the men. We live as a community and share everything and our village is better off if we treat each other as equals and don't discriminate against one another. [S3I1DS]

> What Tostan has brought between men and women here is for them to respect each other, work together and help each other. Two is always better than one. We should involve everyone in the work we are doing: men, women and children. [S3I4MD]

Since they had experienced the concrete advantage of collaboration (e.g. in cleaning the village, building the latrines or setting up a micro-credit project), at the end of the programme their idea of equality and respect was not only based on their common human nature, but on their equal contribution to the well-being of the village and the family:

> *You told me a man and a woman should be considered equal; can you tell me why?*
> They are equal because in the village they both strive to provide for the family. The men work all day to support the family and the women work hard daily to take care and support the family.
> *I am not from this village, should you and I be considered equal?*
> Yes, because we both play a part in taking care of our families. [S3I2PS]

Summing up what I said earlier, participants' understanding of equality shifted in the programme and was closely linked with their idea of collaboration. First, the imagination of a better village and the importance of collaboration to achieve it was primed in the class. Then, participants discovered equality as the recognition of mutual respect and dignity. However, still, equality was an abstract concept. Then, equality became understood as part of the social technology necessary to respond better to the daily challenges that life in Galle Toubaaco presented: 'We are all human and it doesn't matter if someone is a male or female. Anything a man can do a woman can do too' [S3I10ABY].

After the programme, informants could look at themselves and see a shift in what they were doing and what they could do; that is, in their possible freedoms and capabilities before and after the classes. In their narrative a new understanding of self emerged. While in the first set of interviews informants spoke about 'women', in the last set of interviews the term *now-women* emerged in their description of them, compared with *before-women*. Rather than being a category adopted for data analysis, the term is a semantic idiom that all informants used in the last set of interviews. Informants listed all the different capabilities and freedoms that the widening field of possibilities of the now-women began to include. Aisata, for instance, said:

> It made me proud to learn that everyone had equal rights and it doesn't matter if you are a woman or a man. Before women were not considered much, they were just supposed to get married, raise kids and take care of the home. Now we know women can

do pretty much anything a man can do. [. . .] It doesn't matter that you are a white man and I am a black woman, I can do anything you can do, the difference is in the access to education. If we both get the same education we will have equal opportunities at being whatever we want to be. [S3I3AIB]

What stands out from the passage quoted above is the change in Aisata's understanding of herself. She knew the way women were being looked at changed from *before* to *now*. Also, when she continued, 'It doesn't matter that you are a white man and I am a black woman,' she made clear that she believed herself to be part of the logic group of the now-women that knew to deserve equal respect. She developed the necessary self-awareness to see herself and the other women as changed and to compare them with the before-women. New relationships came to exist linking the world and now-women, relationships of actions and possibilities. Self-awareness is important in understanding the self as protagonist of change. In Nussbaum's and Sen's (Nussbaum 2000, 2011; Sen 1995) analyses of women who were the subject of human development programmes, what stood out to them was the fact that women saw themselves as capable of choosing different paths of action in their life (e.g. women who unveiled themselves and then went back to the veiling practice while fighting for women's right to drop it: Nussbaum 2000). Actions and identity are closely linked in that the former contribute to constructing the second. The way in which Aisata responded to the interview showed a strong sense of self as dignified equal: she looked at me in the eyes, sat at the same level with me and underlined our equality in the words she chose to answer my questions.

Informants' understanding of self, based on their concrete freedoms and capabilities, signifies a change in what they thought should be included in their toolkit of acceptable social actions. The widening field of capabilities challenged women's place in the community; women's identity grounded in their actions challenged behavioural norms regulating women's roles in the community; self-awareness challenged invisible power dynamics. The now-women narrative was more than a semantic reflection on their field of possibilities. It channelled the existence of a new understanding of self built on new freedoms and capabilities: from having understood themselves as women, they saw themselves as now-women. Female informants talked of themselves as having been before-women and having become now-women.

Now-women could access a new set of actions. Also, now-women were equal bearers of rights that could access an exciting new set of capabilities and freedoms: they could go to school, look for a job and access health services. Now-women knew that they deserved respect and non-discrimination. The category emerged in almost every female informant's narrative as if it had some liberating potential; Penda, Aisata, Dembaye, Hawa, and both the 'old' and 'young' Fatou:

> Now women are a lot more together, they go together to baptisms, weddings, they take their kids to the hospital, if they are pregnant they go for regular check-ups and they also clean up the streets together. [S3I2PS]

> Now women can go to school and get an education and we can work just like men do. [S3I3AIB]

> Human rights are good because [. . .] now women are able to go to school and get an education. [S3I1DS]

> There is much more cohesion between women now, they get along, they don't fight or argue and they do lots of things with one another. [S3I9HB]

> Now women know their rights and have a lot more influence in the decision-making of the family. [S3I11FD]

> *Why do you say the women are smarter than the men in the village?*
> The men may have been a little smarter before, but with the Tostan classes now women have gotten smart too. Now women are much smarter and work together better and there is much more solidarity between them. [S3I8FDY]

All male informants could also appreciate now-women's actions, although their perception was much more related to what men could observe about now-women in the public moments of community life, that is, village meetings or village cleanings:

> Before, many women were too shy to speak in public. Now women have gained confidence with Tostan classes and they are able to speak their minds and that made me very happy [. . .] Now women have formed an association and they clean the streets together and they put money together to invest. [S3I5DS]

> Before women were shy and afraid to come to meetings but now women attend meetings and are not afraid to speak. [S3I6SD]

Before women, when there was a meeting, would not attend but now women in my village come to meetings. [S3I13AB]

Now women see themselves very differently. Now they know that their job is not to just stay home and do housework, they can go out and work just like the men do, they need to share the household expenses with their husband. [S3I7OB]

Now women know how to behave and speak in public, they get along with each other and do many things together. [. . .] Now women have gained confidence and have realised they have a right to speak in these meetings and it's in all our interest for men and women to speak. [S3I10ABY]

Yes, now anyone who wants to say something in the meetings can do so, it doesn't matter if you are a man or a woman. Before women were afraid to speak in public but now with the Tostan classes it has changed: now women talk in meetings. [S3I4MD]

Expressions of feelings like Djombo's happiness, or like men's general enthusiastic celebration or acceptance of now-women's role, are in line with the outcomes of a liberating process through problem-posing education. Women's 'liberation' should not necessarily result in the generation of male resistance. In understanding together the relations of oppression, participants collaborate for the liberation of both subjugated and subjugators. It matters little whether that oppression is conscious or not. As Freire (1970) analysed, however, there is a risk that men and women in Galle Toubaaco faced in the process of their liberation. When oppression emerges from the oppressed people's mouths to the oppressors' ears, it results in oppressors' oppression and this might result in tension and might give rise to conflict. The problem-posing HRE, however, channelled that tension into a positive collaboration for the liberation of both. Interestingly, a now-men category also emerged in informants' narrative. Although much less present in the interviews than the now-women category, it nonetheless evidenced the collaboration between now-women and *now-men* in their mutual liberation. Omar and Penda, in particular, said:

Now men let the women go and take the Tostan classes, they give them freedom to do work outside of the home. Before men would not let women get out of the house but now women are free to get out when they choose [S3I7OB].

> Now men respect the women a lot more, they take care of their
> women and don't demand so much from them like they used to.
> They realise all the work women do. [S3I2PS]

Now-women gained a capability that before-women did not have:
speaking. Before-women recall Belenky et al.'s (1986) silent women. In
their research, silent women also attained liberation by understanding
their silenced-self in discovering their personal authority within educational processes; problem-posing educational processes, in particular,
were able to generate women's talking, eliciting their speaking capability. In Freire's (1970) libertarian education terms, the now-women
came to feel like masters of themselves and their thoughts because
they succeed in discussing their views of the world. Nussbaum (2000)
analysed a very similar case; in an Indian village that lacked a reliable
clean water supply and whose women were malnourished, the women
showed no feelings of anger or protest about the situation: since they
knew no other way. Following a consciousness-raising programme,
they could see themselves as changed: 'asked what was the biggest
change the government programme had brought to their lives, they
immediately said, as if in chorus,'We are cleaner now' (Nussbaum 2000:
114). The government programme analysed by Nussbaum challenged
entrenched satisfaction by allowing participants to widen their idea of
good human functioning. Nussbaum explains this shift in those wom-
en's understanding of their potential by implicitly pointing in the direction of Gaventa's (2006) invisible power dynamics: Nussbaum's Indian
women were unable to critically recognise the ways in which the background conditions distorted their wishes and choices. In the same way,
the women in Galle Toubaaco could not recognise the invisible power
dynamics that shaped their adaptive preferences, by subjugating their
capacity to aspire to a mere reproduction of their conditions. Through
the programme, women learnt to challenge the role they had before,
to challenge what they could accept and what actions were available
to them.

In acquiring new freedoms and capabilities, now-women did not
take over the roles and responsibilities of men. Daily roles and duties
remained unchanged; through the HRE programme, participants did
not necessarily change their opinion on what women and men did in
their daily routine. Daily jobs and tasks were based on a functional distribution of duties that responded to daily challenges and might as well
persist. Also, people invested a great amount of human capital in the

gendered division of labour, and it would be naïve (as said earlier) to imagine the women going to the market to sell the cows and the men staying at home pounding the millet. However, now-women experienced a different awareness of those tasks, what Nussbaum (2000) referred to as people's capacity to choose freely their actions following an informed-desire and Sen (1995) called the process through which people challenge lifelong habituations that shaped what they consider normal. Structural impediments might, for instance, be an obstacle to a renegotiation of gender roles. Personal choice is also important: identity was deeply woven into daily tasks; women would not easily give up their tasks to men and vice versa. So, after the three months of the HRE programme, women might still be the ones who 'take care of the family, wipe the house, fetch the water, cook' [S3I3AIB] and men those who 'respect and take care of the parents, work hard, build a house, start a family and take care of the family' [S3I6SD]. However, men's and women's understanding of now-women's capabilities and rights changed; that is, the awareness of their potential increased, to include more freedoms and awareness of self as a dignified member of the community:

Men are the ones who go out and work, the women don't have the means to go out and work but now we do know our rights. [S3I11FD]

I would not [agree with someone telling me that men and women have different rights] because there are some things that my husband may like but I would not like and there are things I like my husband doesn't like, so everyone has a right and should be able to choose what they want. The Tostan classes taught me this. [S3I3AIB]

In substance, gender roles probably did not change (yet, at least) in terms of what men and women did to help their families and community, and it would be naïve to expect them to do so. This, however, does not represent an issue in human development terms: Nussbaum's (2000) women chose to return from non-veiling to veiling while at the same time campaigning for women's freedom to give up the practice. She was not concerned about their decision, as long as it was fully free and informed. Thus, what is relevant in Galle Toubaaco is that a new way of interpreting gender relations widened up the possible ways in which those roles could be interpreted, including new capabilities and freedoms, as in the example provided by Fatou above.

At the individual level, the schemata regulating members' under-standing of gender roles and responsibilities were being stretched by experience. Seeing women behaving differently compared with before the programme and not being humiliated publicly for doing so cre-ated new clues for integrating those behaviours within what is socially accepted as normal. Strauss and Quinn (1997) argued that in similar cases, two things can happen at the cognitive level. First, people may adjust the schema, revising their understanding of the world, following the new experience they are having; however, this rarely happens after a short schema-inconsistent experience. Second, and more frequently, the schema lies dormant and can be awakened later, when people observe the same instances of cross-gender behaviours and maybe remind themselves of having observed similar behaviours before. In Galle Toubaaco, gender roles were physically instantiated; they could be changed in a short time. However, the different experience of the reality challenged the way members made sense of that reality. After the programme, informants could include in their horizon of possibili-ties the idea that women and men stood on an egalitarian basis and enjoyed the same rights.

In Freirian terms, what was a set of behaviours 'written in stone' (as Freire 1970 calls them) broke up and generated the ability to see the oppressed people's potential. Informants experienced increasingly that liberating potential throughout the programme. They began in the first class to see what they could achieve in their village and then discovered more concretely what freedoms and capabilities they could attain as human beings in their community. The potential Freire wrote about is very similar to Appadurai's (Appadurai 2004) capacity to aspire. Community members' capacity to aspire was generated by challeng-ing invisible power relations that hindered the development of certain capabilities. Having unveiled those invisible power dynamics in class, participants could challenge them in the village, impacting on women's access to overt decision-making and covert agenda-setting.

POLITICAL STRUCTURE AND DECISION-MAKING: VISIBLE AND HIDDEN POWER

Gender Factors in Decision-Making

Before the programme, women's participation in decision-making was limited. Invisible power dynamics shaped the norm of female silence:

Men tend to make most of the decisions because women are too shy and don't speak up and sometimes they are afraid to speak because they are women; [. . .] I don't recall any meeting where a man said something and a woman changed or contested the decision. [S1I5DS]

Then, the Tostan programme began. Certain key components of the HRE programme (in terms of content and pedagogy) elicited women's speaking in class. The human rights curriculum allowed participants to draft a local understanding of their right to speak based on their equality and their need to collaborate with others for achieving a better community. Women exercised that right to speak in class, first. Also, in class, they experienced their right and their capacity to contribute to decision-making, their potential as talkers and decision-makers. As Penda, interviewed half-way through the programme, said:

Before women didn't get together because of all of their work but with the class, we see each other every day and we talk to each other and have more confidence. So when there is a meeting and we are all there, we are not afraid to speak, because [in class] we have learnt how to speak and how to be listened to. [S2I4PS]

Every time, for instance, participants had to elect representatives, take decisions concerning the progress of the classes or organise a skit, women could experience that new role for themselves. Then, they took their learning back home, and exercised the newly acquired public speaking skill at home by teaching others. They were now-women: teachers and talkers. It is possibly then that they began to challenge old power relations in the household: 'before [women] had to get permission from their husband to go to meetings but now they are free to go' [S3I13AB].

Finally, they exercised the new public speaking skills and their right to speak in village meetings:

Before the women wouldn't say anything [in the meetings] but since the Tostan classes started they have been getting involved more and more. I think they are learning a lot from the classes and are gaining more confidence in themselves and they feel like they know more. [S2I15SD]

The women talk much more [in village meetings] than before, for example now when I have something to say in meetings I get up and say what I have to say where before I could not do that. [S3I3AIB]

In the meetings, they would see other community members listening to them; they would see themselves seen by others as changed, as now-women. On the other hand, community members would appreciate the capabilities that now-women developed; in the words of a male participant:

In our last interview you said – let me read it out loud – 'women and men have different roles and a woman's role doesn't include making decisions'. Do you think this is still the case?
No. Now women have gained a lot more influence in the decision-making within the family and the men understand it's important for the women to speak out loud and to work too because they can work just like the men can. [S3I7OB]

The quote above draws on a shift in the social norm regulating roles of talkers and listeners. In using the generic plural 'men', Omar made clear he believed a shift in a general belief had happened: 'men understand it's important for the women to speak out loud'. While before-women traditionally played a peripheral role in the decision-making process, now-women became active participants in village meetings. Male participating and non-participating informants described now-women's participation in the meeting as follows:

[In the meetings now] everyone speaks, women used to be too shy [. . .] but now that's not the case. Our meetings before went well but with the Tostan classes now meetings are great, they are much more lively; everybody seems to speak a lot more, express themselves better, especially the women. Everyone is much more friendly and people respect each other. [S3I13AB]

It must be because of the Tostan classes that people are more open, they express themselves much better than they used to. For example when there was a meeting before the Tostan classes people couldn't express themselves well and most women would not go to meetings and those who went to the meetings wouldn't say anything. But now when there is a meeting most of the men and women of the village attend and everyone speaks at the meetings, especially the women. The women have gained much more confidence; they are not as shy or afraid to speak in front of people any more. Everyone knows they have a right to speak and they do now. [S3I6SD]

If there is a meeting here do you think the women or the men would speak more?

At first the men spoke more and the women were shy but now the women talk just as much as the men, they are not shy any more. [S2I10AIB]

'Being shy' was how community members understood women; that is, their essence: the category that invisible power dynamics assigned to all women by shaping social norms of silence and subjugation. Their actions (e.g. active talking, suggestions or complaints) in community meetings challenged that essence with the historical power of their existence. The traditional cognitive schema that relegated women to a silent/reproductive role was challenged by the capabilities gained by now-women. New experiential clues were offered to community members that revealed the inconsistency of their belief: shy-women versus talking-women. The inconsistency required a rationalisation of the process: schemata written in stone are activated automatically and contribute to shaping people's essence; their experiential inconsistency instead requires a rational reconceptualisation of what experience is showing (Strauss and Quinn 1997).

Men in the village were possibly used to seeing one or two women speaking: the oldest ones. As Meillassoux (1991) argued, since older women have lost their fertility potential, they can be treated differently by members of the community, often in a way similar to the way male members are treated. It was the experience of seeing many women, old and young, contributing to the meeting, though, that challenged the way men understood women's roles in decision-making. Amadou and Abdoulaye recognised women's new capabilities by saying:

They [women] have changed a lot, they didn't know much, and they didn't know how to speak in public or how to behave in public. They were not clean as they are now, now they know how to behave and speak in public, they get along with each other and do many things together. [S3I10ABY]

What can you tell me about village meetings, are they run as usual?

No, it has changed a lot, before the women that attended the meetings would sit there and say nothing the whole time. Now they have gained confidence and have realised they have a right to speak in these meetings and it's in all our interest for men and women to speak [. . .] they [women] say very interesting things. [S3I13AB]

I did not find, in either the interviews or my observation, any resistance to now-women's role in the village. Possible explanations for the lack of resistance observed have been offered earlier in the book and are recalled by the quotes above. Abdoulaye's understanding of women changed to include their public speaking within the social skills they possessed. Tostan's indirect approach focused participants' efforts towards a better community for everyone, as described by participants themselves. Freire (1970) argued that when the oppressed seek liberation from oppression, the process can lead to conflict with the oppressors, unless (as in Galle Toubaaco's HRE classes) it is guided by mutual understanding and compassion. In the classes observed, and according to informants' narrative, the public unveiling of an unequal social status quo did not generate revolutionary or counter-normative violent actions. The reason seems to be that the traditional value of collaboration, primed by the goal of a better village for everyone, positively influenced the process of acceptance for now-women's social roles. In the quote cited above, Abdoulaye said that 'women say very interesting things'. Later, he and other men observed that they were satisfied that now-women, thanks to the knowledge received, were able to access and manage funds for a microfinance project. Now-women gained skills and attitudes that influenced the entire village for the better. Resistance would possibly be understood as counter-productive for the self, the family and the village as a whole. A more equally shared access to visible power processes, that is, women's capacity to speak in the village assemblies, resulted in greater benefits for both men and women. Women's access to visible power increased. Observational data show that their access to hidden power also increased:

Today I fell asleep due to the excessive heat and woke up at 8 p.m. I left my hut and I saw in the village chief's court a village meeting. I asked my interpreter what the meeting was about. She told me it was the women who summoned the meeting. They asked the village chief to summon a meeting to talk about the way in which the families contribute to the microfinance project. I asked her to investigate if this is a common practice [there would be no time to investigate this in more interviews]. She did so after the meeting. She came back after about an hour. My interpreter said:'there is a lot of discussion among the women. They are very excited because it is the first time they have summoned a meeting.' [Diary, 26.06.2010]

Power dynamics do not usually shift overnight, especially when they are embodied in traditional roles that contribute to defining members'identity. Nobody would think that now-women would take over the male elders in influencing village decisions. Possibly, such processes would be neither beneficial nor positive for the human development of Galle Toubaaco from what it was in 2010. However, now-women talked in meetings and summoned them; now-women were no longer afraid to speak in front of men. They could contribute with their ideas and concerns to the envisioning of a better community and deciding how to realise that ideal. Galle Toubaaco, at the end of the HRE programme, was in the middle of a shift in the norms regulating gender access to visible and hidden power. Diffusion from the class to the village could take time: to challenge traditional cognitive beliefs, what is exceptional must first become understood as normal at the individual level and then at the community level (Kahneman 2011; Mackie and LeJeune 2009; Strauss and Quinn 1997). The different access that different members had to similar new experiences explains the progressivity of the change. The 'young'Fatou Diallo, a young wife who was not allowed by her husband to participate in the class and had no contact with other participating women, for instance, said:

> *Why is it that the men are the ones responsible for the women and not the other way around?*
> The men are responsible for the women and for making decisions but the women also have a say in the decision-making. [. . .] For me if my husband tells me to stop doing something I will stop but at the same time I do make decisions at home too. If I make a decision I make sure my husband will accept it, because he brought me here so I have to respect him as my husband. [S3I8FDY]

Compared with other informants, the 'young' Fatou was a divergent case in terms of the amount of talking she did with participating members. 'Young' Fatoumata was only used to speaking with the wife of the village chief and (according to both) not much about the classes. Rather, they used to talk about 'our kids, cooking, and fetch wood together and we go and get water together' [S3I8FDY]. However, also in this divergent case, the experience of dialoguing with other human beings beyond functional unidirectional authoritarian communication (take the water, feed the babies, sweep the floor) led the 'young' Fatou to a reconceptualisation of self:

> The questions you ask us help us think and teach us a lot about life. For example, me, I was afraid of talking in front of people but now because of these interviews I have become more comfortable at answering questions in front of people. [S3I8FDY]

Furthermore, she could also see women's new potential and be surprised by that, possibly modelling her capabilities on theirs: 'I am surprised because I didn't know the women in our village could talk like that in front of everyone' [S3I6FDY].

There is no cognitive impairment or self-deprecation that keeps the 'young' Fatou from developing a sense of self as a talker: the interviews worked with her as the class did with others, although in a minor and shallower way. What was lacking in 'young' Fatou's experience was the constant contact with the emerging new social reality. It seems reasonable to think that community members who did not get exposed to those new experiential clues would eventually, in one way or another, experience the changing norms in the village. Possibly, their new experiences would follow the path of organised diffusion described earlier. I did not have a chance to study what happened in the village after the programme, but I did go back to Galle Toubaaco six years after; I mention what I observed then in the concluding chapter.

Age Factors in Decision-Making

As seen earlier, a traditional norm of respecting elders' authority exists in Senegal, although research showed that in urban areas this norm was being challenged in 2009 by young Senegalese seeking independence (Perry 2009). As analysed before, age in Galle Toubaaco was an important factor influencing how community members understood their and other members' access to visible and hidden power dynamics. From childhood, young people would learn to respect the elders' authority (particularly that of male elders) both in the household and in public. Tostan acknowledged traditional hierarchical relations over age and implemented two classes: one for community members below the age of 25 and one for community members over that threshold. Data show a general increase in young members' active participation in decision-making in village meetings. Amadou Ba Mbaring said:

> *Are people participating more or less compared with last year in the meetings?*
> Now everyone talks, before the young people didn't speak out in meetings but now they are free to speak and are part of the decision-making process. [S2I12ABM]

However, young members' participation was different for young men than for young women. In particular, young men seemed less active than young women (contrary to what one would expect, given the patriarchal structure of the community):

> Today one of the last meetings I will be able to observe showed a lively discussion among community members. However, I noted that, while young women would intervene individually and pas-sionately, young boys are together aside, they are talking between themselves. I even had the feeling they were conspiring. [Diary, 25.06.2010]

Boys would grow up mostly segregated by age and would be keen to respect male elders' authority. Data show that while young women became more active and critical of the status quo, young boys showed more respect and conformism with it. Chodorow (1999) suggested that similar patterns can happen in patriarchal societies because young males know that it is in their interest to comply with the status quo since they will be the ones benefiting from it as adults. Chodorow argued that human communities where children grow up in gender-segregated groups tend to overemphasise male and female identity with what is perceived as masculine or feminine, respectively. In particular, power relations reproduce themselves because boys deny their own feminine characteristics and identify power with men, while girls are left with the feminine attributes they 'need' to use to secure an economic future for themselves by finding a husband.

Freire's (1970, 2001) analysis of banking education also contributes to making sense of the reasons for a tendency towards young males' conformist or young females' anti-conformist behaviours observed in Galle Toubaaco. Banking education practices that replicate power structures and subjugate the oppressed into cycles of oppression do not only reproduce the status quo. They also protect the authorities, the bankers. In the training process to which the bankers expose the heirs, the heirs understand themselves as inheritors and, seduced by the forthcoming power, comply with the power dynamics that the banking process reproduces and reinforces. Also, the young female members of Galle Toubaaco were more used to questioning the female elders' authority because of the exogenous marriage patterns explored earlier. In Galle Toubaaco, the feeling I had of the young men conspiring during the meeting was later confirmed by some rumours: 'Last day in the village [. . .] My interpreter came and told me she heard that some young boys are planning a coup because they are not happy with the leading skills of the village chief' [Diary, 02.07.2010].

No coup (and no coup attempt) happened in Galle Toubaaco. I visited the village again in 2016, and Abdoulaye was still the village chief. However, it is significant that more young women thought of overtly collaborating with the rest of the community by talking with community members of different ages and gender, while some young men found it more natural to unite their strengths as a homogenous group based on age. The difference between young men's and women's participation was a tendency, not a standard. On other occasions, for instance, young male and female members collaborated in decision-making with the elders, helping the community. The 'young' Amadou Ba, for instance, said:

> Many decisions that are made in meetings now are made by men and women in my age range [19–25]. [For instance:] The day we had the meeting to elect the person to become treasurer of our school club, Djombo said we should appoint Fatou Diallo and we all agreed. Everyone trusted Fatou so the elders all agreed with our decision and Fatou was appointed. [S3I10ABY]

Young members' participation was also seen and acknowledged by other community members, as for instance, Fatou did in the last set of interviews:

> *What's the first thing that comes to your mind when you think about the Tostan classes?*

I used to think that it was the elders of the village who would help develop the village but now that I am taking the Tostan classes I realise it's the young people who have to work hard and develop our village. I think about that all the time now. [S3I11FD]

Following the dynamics explored earlier, young community members vernacularised an abstract knowledge (e.g. on equality or collaboration) through problem-posing education by making sense of their local reality through the emerging themes that mattered for them. One of these themes included their participation in the life of the village. They learnt about their right to speak and gained public speaking skills in class, where the facilitator built the premises for their equal and democratic participation. Before the problem-posing process, respect for the elders' authority was framed in a norm of silence and acceptance. Data show that that same social norm was reconceptualised in respecting the elders and contributing to communal decisions. The empowerment process that liberated community members from unequal norms hindering participation in visible power dynamics involved the community as a whole. The process of renegotiation of local norms included all participants and resulted in wider access to decision-making.

Data show that, following the HRE programme, participation in decision-making became wider and included segments of the community previously excluded by, or self-excluding because of, those social norms that protected the power status quo. Due to the instructional strategies put into place, the HRE programme fostered participants' capacity to speak in public and gave them an opportunity to experience contributing to decision-making.

Regarding the content, informants often referred to equality as the most interesting thing learnt in class: they widely recognised the session on non-discrimination as one of the most surprising. Discussing equality, participants came to understand gender, age, race and religion as unacceptable reasons for discrimination. On equality, participants grounded a universally shared condition of rights bearers, and in particular acknowledged theirs and others' right to participate in decision-making. In the words of the informants, equality took many names: human rights, non-discrimination or, as discussed by this female informant, democracy:

What is the most important thing you will take from the Tostan classes?
Democracy is important.

What does that mean to you?
It means equality, being able to vote for who you want. It has
taught me a lot and allowed me to think about what I was doing.
[. . .] Everyone should be treated equally, it doesn't matter if you
are a woman or a man, everyone has a right. [. . .] we have learnt
this from the class. It's best to respect the people you live with,
treat everyone equally, treat even the little kids with respect and
not discriminate because of age or gender. [S3I3AIB]

OTHER HUMAN RIGHTS-INCONSISTENT SOCIAL PRACTICES

Child and Forced Marriages

In the first set of interviews (conducted before the classes), informants
reported on the abandonment of the practice of forced marriages.
However, the analysis of those interviews showed that the invisible
power dynamics in place would be a significant structural obstacle for
those young girls in Galle Toubaaco who wanted to refuse to marry
the person chosen by their parents. I hypothesised that the pressures
of modernisation might have brought the community to act towards
the abandonment of forced marriages uncritically: transforming 'forcing' into 'asking', without conceptualising parents' influence over the
decisions of their children as a form of forced choice. Informants did
not see the practice of child marriage as problematic, and the Marxist
analysis provided earlier helped make sense of the reasons behind its
social function: forced marriages guaranteed gyneco-mobility and child
marriages maximised girls' fertility, that is, their reproductive functioning. Besides, research on the reasons behind CFM helped me understand that child marriages were practised in children's interest. Parents
married their girls sooner because they cared about them, not because
they wanted the worst for them.

The HRE class built on parents' love for their children and discussed
the inconsistency of the practice (and its implications for children) with
the value of family love. First, in class, participants started looking at
their children developmentally, as capable of taking on new roles and
responsibilities. Take, for instance, what Samba said: '[In the class] I
learnt it's better to let girls grow up and be able to make their own decisions' [S3I6SD]. This discovery opened up the space for participants to
explore alternative ways for girls to be women, possibly different from
the traditional roles of wife-only or mother-only. Then, participants

explored new possibilities for the life of girls, for instance one where they were protagonists of their lives and the choices connected to it, such as those to do with marriage. The class grounded those new possibilities (e.g. studying, becoming a nurse or getting a job) on the emerging understanding of all community members deserving equal respect and dignity. Then, from that perspective on equality, they looked at the practice of CFM:

> [In class] I learnt about human rights [. . .]. If you have a son and a daughter it's not right to put your son into school and not put your daughter in school to marry her. [S2I10AIB]

> We learnt about taking care of our health, cleaning our streets, the right to an education, and a girl being able to choose who they get married too. [. . .] I agree that it's not right to make kids do things they don't want to do and marry them when they are young. [S3I2PS]

Participants discussed the consequences of CFM; amongst these: early pregnancies, denied education and denied freedom. The conceptualisation of those consequences produced an inconsistency between their values and their actions. Recent research on value–action incoherence shows that when people reflect on the incoherence between their abstract values and their concrete actions, they tend to temporarily reorient their actions so that they become coherent with the abstract value. Prolonged reasoning or exposure to the inconsistency would result in a more permanent behavioural change (Bardi and Goodwin 2011; Torelli and Kaikati 2009). Participants explored in class the inconsistencies between a traditional, local value (loving children) and the consequences of their actions (harming children). In the interviews conducted after the programme, informants (amongst them, Fatou, Aisata and Dembaye below) referred to their intention of abandoning CFM:

> If someone comes and asks to marry my daughter I will tell them to go look for someone else because I don't want to ruin my daughter's future [. . .]. People here no longer think this is right. [S3I11FD]

> I don't want to give my daughter in marriage when she is so young. I will let her grow up first because it's not good for her, for instance she can get pregnant too soon. [S3I3AIB]

Human rights are good because [. . .] it's also why young girls are free to say no to forced marriages [. . .] I believe it's the classes that brought about this change. Now everyone knows about that. [S3I1DS]

In sum, informants reported a shifting attitude towards CFM. It can be imagined (in the absence of data due to time limitation of the research) that the practice might persist as a response to the structural challenges that contributed to its emergence. However, informants reported on a changing public understanding of it. Fatou's and Dembaye's opinions that *'everyone* knows about that' and that *'people* no longer [. . .]' manifest a change in what informants thought others (everyone; people) considered to be acceptable actions. Social norm theory explains such changes in terms of a shifting norm or a change in the way the norms are understood – which is the same (Bicchieri 2006). The class elicited discussion on the abstract human rights knowledge that participants vernacularised in their local reality. They shared their intention to abandon the practice. However, a family alone could not abandon the practice: CFM is a practice that ties different communities together. A single community exiting the practice would find itself in a dangerous and isolated position. Nevertheless, it is possible that if the community of Galle Toubaaco developed a genuine commitment to the abandonment of the practice, they could contribute to the organised diffusion of their new knowledge together with other villages participating in the programme. Participants had a genuine commitment to change the village, although in the first session they did not know how. There is a possibility that community members might have had a genuine commitment to the abandonment of CFM and needed to explore how this could happen. A wider process of abandonment should involve the network of marriageability and could follow the path of organised diffusion (described earlier in the book) that lead to the abandonment of FGC elsewhere (UNICEF 2008a). Finally, the chances are that participants might find other solutions to the problem that cannot be imagined from the current perspective of analysis.

Research on morality and decision-making has suggested that there are serious limitations on the power of cost–benefit analysis and that commitment to moral rules works as a strong motivator of human action (Bennis et al. 2010). Nobody knows what will happen to the next generation of girls in Galle Toubaaco, but there is a possibility that moral behaviour might trump current patterns of social actions and diffuse beyond the limits of the rural community, joining other communities in influencing the entire wider network of marriageability. Nobody could expect an organised abandonment of CFM in a short time span, but whatever the future impact, the significance for the current research is the informants' statements of intention to abandon the practice.

Child Labour and Child Protection Practices

The complexities of child labour were explored earlier in the book, suggesting that child labour is problematic in human development and human rights terms when it hinders children's health and access to education. Informants reported a shifting approach to child labour. According to them, the class allowed a critical analysis of children's daily life and allowed participants to discuss the idea that the work children carried out ought to be balanced with the time spent in school:

> Education is important and we should try to keep our children at school and stop asking them to work on the farms or to herd cattle so much. [S3I6SD]

> In class we learnt that it's important that we send our kids to school instead of asking them to work in the farms or to herd cattle all day. Everyone agreed with this. [S3I3AIB]

> I will work at educating my child, make sure he has all of the school supplies needed, and I will talk to my friends about getting educated and getting their kids educated, we shouldn't ask them to work all day. [S3I6SD]

Community members cared about their children: they did not learn from the classes to do so. The classes offered them an opportunity to ground the value of caring for their children in a new understanding of consequences of their daily work. Participants realised the potential of an education and the dangers related to practices that put their children's health at risk; it is because they cared about their children that they could commit to adopting different behaviours. The intention to revise their child labour practices, possibly in a way that helped them respond to daily challenges of life in rural Africa, was not the only statement of intention to adopt child protection behaviours. For instance, participants committed to behaviours that would holistically protect children's health:

> If you are sick you should go to the hospital, if you are pregnant you should get regular check-ups with the doctor. Something could happen to your child and you would never forgive yourself. [S3I2PS]

> [The most interesting thing I learnt is the] right to health [. . .] now if one of my kids gets sick I take them to the doctor. I don't rely on traditional medicine or 'go-pills' guys on the street; [. . .] Before I would buy medicine off the streets but I have learnt that the best thing to do is to take your kid straight to the doctor if they get sick. [S3I12AS]

> The kids are being taken care of much more and wear clean clothes and get regular check-ups at the doctors. [S3I4MD]

Data report various statements of intention to change behaviours related to child protection (and specifically CFM and child labour). Participants' traditional values remained untouched: participants practised CFM and child labour bearing in mind their children's good, not willing to harm them. In class, however, they came to a new understanding about the consequences of those practices and could imagine new behaviours inspired by the human rights content and the public discussion they had. In sum, participants wanted their children's good after as much as before the HRE programme. In the class they discussed, shared and committed to alternative behaviours to attain it. How those behaviours will meet the challenges that the structural configuration of their world presents to them is impossible to say; however, it is certainly possible that the changing understanding of the practices will activate different community choices in the future, allowing a different human rights-consistent response to those challenges.

POSSIBLE PITFALLS OF THE TOSTAN PROGRAMME IN GALLE TOUBAACO

Any development programme should aim at maximising benefit for the local population and minimising the danger of threatening community members' well-being. Perfection and exemplarity in similar processes are, however, difficult to achieve: pitfalls, limitations and dangers threaten the delivery of development programmes that aim at fostering social change dynamics. I identified four of those limitations and pitfalls in the work of Tostan in Galle Toubaaco, analysing the outcomes of the programme.

First, the programme might have limited impact over time. As seen in Chapter 4, structural features of members' life in Galle Toubaaco contribute in shaping the social status quo. Without a change in access to those structural resources, two future scenarios are possible. In the first, the results of the programme do not last long: access to resources would have to shift in ways that allowed women the means of production and control over their lives. The behavioural change that community members experienced after the programme then might fall back into old habits. The unsettling nature of the educational programme challenged patterns of production of the local reality that were reified by structural factors that obviously did not disappear at the end of the programme. However, another scenario exists. Community members might bargain a new power equilibrium that, although not changing access to resources for the present generation, will intertwine with external factors so as to further accelerate social change dynamics in the next generation of community members. Community members would then respond differently to external social change factors that might activate the new understandings generated in the three years of the Tostan programme.

Second, the programme did not result in a dramatic change in oppressing roles and dynamics of power. The social change that community members experienced is revolutionary if analysed from a microscopic perspective, but is almost invisible if looked at with the wrong expectations. Even with the most utopian hopes for the programme, one could not expect a change in the distribution of labour and in the way community members access the connected resources. Community members had great human capital invested in their differentiated economic roles and nobody could expect to see the men pounding the millet and the women going out to the market, one year after engagement with the programme. In similar undifferentiated economies, there are few careers open to women, or to men. What is important, then, is the spiritual, what was created and probably was still fragile: equal dignified respect for all community members. The repetition of those dynamics over the three years of the programme and beyond might consolidate the new understandings of self and others. This feature of the programme, thus, opened new possible roles and understandings stretching the boundaries of existing power relations, rather than breaking through them.

In Chapter 3, I evidenced the concern that the programme might challenge existing power dynamics in a way that would threaten the immediate well-being of the powerless, engaging them in a struggle for their liberation against the power holders. The pedagogy and the outcome of the programme highlighted a different liberating dynamic. The programme did not challenge local authorities; rather, it offered participants the opportunity to find mechanisms of collaboration between oppressors and oppressed to give voice to the latter for the benefit of both. Beyond a romanticised view of the village as unitary, what stands out is that individual informants reported on the benefits of new communal practices (e.g. village cleanliness), identifying how they would benefit self and the family. There is a risk that existing power relations, without being challenged 'revolutionarily', might in the long term resubjugate the weaker fragments of society. However, alternatively, the village might make new sense of those relations from both a cost–benefit analysis and new moral understandings of their roles and relations.

Third, as discussed in Chapter 3, development of the capacity to aspire might result in the frustration that can follow awareness of not being able to attain certain aspirations. Similar aspirations might be, for instance, a new role in village assemblies, access to education or better job prospects. There is no definitive answer to this problem if seen as a dichotomy: on the one hand, there are tacit forms of oppression that threaten the well-being of the entire community and hinder its human development. On the other, by developing capacity to aspire, members might face the impossibility of instantiating new standards for their lives to which they now aspire for themselves or their children. However, a third scenario might also rise: having developed capacity to aspire, members might actually be able to engage in changing their community and reify those aspirations into concrete actions. In situations of oppression, and without capacity to aspire, that oppression is doomed to reproduction; with capacity to aspire, there are opportunities to challenge the reproduction of the oppressive status quo or to create the aspirations that might pass from one generation to the next and accelerate social change in the future. Also, the capacity to aspire as developed through Tostan's classes is likely to gather (in class) and spread (in the village) individual sentiments of discomfort with the local situations that, possibly, were already generating similar frustrations well before the programme started.

CONCLUSION

After the HRE programme, community members developed a new understanding of how equality and collaboration could impact positively on the community's well-being. The class offered a democratic place to exercise public speaking skills and primed participants' need to collaborate for a better future that they grounded in the concept of equality. The line of successes that women experienced in the class, the triumphs over the biases created by those power relations, exponentially fostered women's self-confidence. The positive effects of women's increased self-confidence were not limited to the class: they diffused to the village. Community members experienced cognitive dissonance with respect to what experience used to tell them about gender roles. They acknowledged publicly those differences. Women reported being able to think and imagine different possibilities for themselves. The now-women category emerged in participants' description as an existential category that linked women to the factual world with which they could interact differently after the programme. New actions, new possibilities were available to now-women, challenging the traditional stereotypes that relegated women to silent roles. In the development of this self-awareness, women deconstructed invisible power dynamics that relegated them to the role of silent decision-followers. Structural access to resources shaped those invisible power dynamics. A normative forced direct change in the access to those resources, however, would not have been likely to produce a change in self-perception. The indirect problem-posing education programme, instead, challenged those invisible power dynamics and influenced women's social status. It is very unlikely, however, that women's access to resources will change overnight, following the programme. In human development terms, though, it may be important that now-women include in their field of freedoms and possibilities certain behaviours that might eventually win them access to strategic resources.

The effect of a shifting balance of invisible power relations was observed in how community members conceptualised their participation in visible and hidden power dynamics. The class, as a democratic space of discussion, gave participants an opportunity to exercise their public speaking skills and engaged them in talking about the benefits of granting everyone the right to contribute to decision-making. In class, participants stretched the boundaries of legitimate participation in decision-making. In the village, women would contribute to the meeting discussions and even summoned one with a precise political agenda. Men, in turn, reacted with little resistance to the process, perhaps by participating in women's liberation as their own and because they could see concrete advantages of women's shifting role (e.g. in a cleaner village). Young community members' participation in decision-making also increased, although the young men, possibly aware of their role as heirs, showed more conformism with the social status quo than young women.

Also, community members reified the human rights knowledge within a new understanding of human rights-inconsistent local practices. There is evidence of a shift in how participants (and, according to them, the community as a whole) understood CFM before and after the HRE programme. There is less evidence of a shift in other social practices (e.g. child labour), although some participants confirmed a change in their attitudes and behaviours. Also, there is evidence demonstrating other possible co-factors influencing participants' outlooks and behaviours related to CFM. This chapter showed that the HRE programme accelerated pre-existing social processes by bringing community members together to discuss and evaluate those social processes.

In sum, community members could restructure their visible and hidden power relations only once they challenged invisible power dynamics. Human rights provided a framework to look at the local reality and make sense of it from a new perspective. After the programme, members witnessed a shifting understanding of their community, although the effective abandonment of certain practices might take time. Also, the status quo observed at the end of the programme was certainly not completely egalitarian: in the household, women would still have to comply with their husbands' final decisions and they could not aspire to be (and perhaps not even imagine being) village leaders. However, data suggest that more debate might happen now, both within the family and in the village. New processes and understandings have entered the traditional structures of power and decision-making.

Independent evidence suggests that the results of the HRE programme in other communities are often remarkable in the long term. As an example, Diop et al. say that informants saw the effects of the

HRE programme positively in terms of 'greater control over collective hygiene, women's health, and child education; assumption of greater leadership roles; and the ability to manage a budget' (2008: 11). More recently, a random-sample mixed-method survey of direct, indirect and control villages was conducted by the CRDH (2010) to measure the effectiveness of the Tostan programme in the long term in the Senegalese regions of Tambacounda and Kolda. The study confirmed a decline in discrimination against women and girls and the abandonment of CFM and FGM in villages directly and indirectly exposed to the HRE programme. Earlier examples of positive independent evaluations of long-lasting changes included another study carried out by Diop et al. (2004) and a study commissioned by UNICEF (2008b). If past patterns continue to replicate themselves, then the community of Galle Toubaaco is likely to bring about beneficial changes. What is relevant in the data analysed in this research is the change in attitudes and behavioural intentions that have an impact in human rights terms. The advantage of the present research is that it has analysed participants' feelings and thoughts before, during and after the programme, which helped make sense of what could possibly be the beginning of a social change process. The next chapter analyses the motivators of social change in conceptual terms and links them by suggesting a dynamic of the process that motivated change in the community members' outlook and behaviours analysed in this chapter.

Part III

Helpful Development

Chapter 7

DYNAMICS OF SOCIAL CHANGE: A MODEL FOR INDIRECT DEVELOPMENT PRACTITIONERS

INTRODUCTION

This chapter looks at how human rights education contributed to social change processes in the community of Galle Toubaaco. The first section analyses how Tostan's pedagogical approach played a key role in motivating participation and challenging participants' understanding of their local social reality. I argue in particular that the pedagogy played a key role in unleashing participants' alternative understandings of their reality. The second section explores the substantive content of the programme, arguing that human rights provided an abstract knowledge that contributed in posing useful problems to participants. The third section explores how participants made sense of that knowledge together, women and men, and discusses how their interactions were particularly significant for the processes of reconceptualisation of mutual roles and relationships. The fourth section explores the cognitive processes that explain the participants' reaction to a diverging reality, and the fifth section (on the capacity to aspire) links new cognitive understandings to the capacity of imagining alternative courses of action diverging from a repetition of the past. Together with capacity to aspire, participants developed other key capabilities that fostered their community's empowerment, discussed in the following two sections in the chapter.

The next section offers an understanding of how participants shared the new knowledge with other community members, by looking at the interaction between two 'communities of practice': the class and the village. The final section argues that Tostan's 'indirect' approach to development was a catalyst for the dynamic of social change analysed in this chapter. By respecting community members' agency, the programme

helped them develop the capabilities they needed to realise their potential for leading their human development.

THE PEDAGOGICAL APPROACH OF THE HRE PROGRAMME

Tostan's Freirian pedagogy worked as a key motivator of social change
because it allowed participants to experience in class new roles, e.g.
roles of talkers and decision-makers. The Freirian approach presented
content critically to participants, leaving them the task of making sense
of the abstract knowledge in local terms. In so doing, participants' concerns emerged from the dialogue: the themes that mattered to them
became objects of discussion, rather than abstract content. Norms of
silence about certain topics were challenged and the status quo could
be looked at critically.

The HRE programme in Galle Toubaaco engaged participants in discussing and debating the human rights content in every class. The facilitator allowed the discussion to move freely over traditionally unspoken
topics and encouraged everyone to participate, breaking the traditional
social roles of talkers and listeners. HRE in Galle Toubaaco acted as
problem-posing education, asking participants to collaborate to find
solutions to what participants themselves came to understand as local
challenges (e.g. gender discrimination, access to decision-making or
village cleanliness).

Mergner (2004) further developed Freire's theories by including
an understanding of Arendt's (1994) discussion about human beings'
dignity. Mergner argued that participants need to acknowledge each
other's dignity to overcome the barriers that produce the same social
obstacles over which they are trying to prevail (i.e. to attain social
change). Without recognition of everyone's complete dignity as a
full human being, participants cannot understand ('feel') each other's oppression and then act to change the conditions creating it. In
the interviews collected at the end of the programme, informants
summoned a new understanding of community members in terms of
confidence, dignity, respect and trust:

> People have changed because they respect each other a lot more
> now. [S3I12AS]

> The women have gained much more confidence; they are no lon-
> ger shy or afraid to speak in front of people. Everyone knows
> they have a right to speak and now they do speak. Since the

Tostan classes people in the village have started spending time together every day and getting used to each other and enjoying each other's company, and, at the same time, gained trust with one another. [S3I6SD]

The class allowed participants to get to know each other more and to discover their own and others' dignity; consider Samba's quote above, where he said, 'Everyone knows [women] have a right to speak [...] people [...] gained trust with one another', adding that they 'respect each other a lot more'. As seen earlier, the discovery of equality became an overarching category that included other rights and freedoms. Participants understood equality as a necessary condition for collaboration and, on the basis of equal dignity, looked critically at certain behaviours in place in their village, by analysing their oppressive nature. In class, participants shared mutual concerns over those behaviours by collaborating towards possible solutions that would help them reify the 'better village' they visualised in the first session.

If one had to identify the most important characteristic of the Freirian pedagogy, there is little doubt that its dialogical nature should not be underestimated. Dialogue is the characteristic of problem-posing education, it is through dialogue that reciprocal love and dignity are generated; silence is instead the characteristic of banking education, silence fosters oppression and enslaves people in the process of complying uncritically with the status quo. The maieutic nature of the Freirian educational model is what Ellerman (2006) praised as its indirect feature. Rather than telling people what to do, development programmes should help people in visualising their own goals for their communities and how they can reach them. A direct approach (such as a radio message) does not flexibly integrate in the micro-context of the community and does not allow people to develop their own perspective on the issue. In such interventions, the theme is not generated by the class, it is imposed from outside. An educational programme that does not include public debating of the content cannot allow participants to explain their reasons, to understand each other. Aisata told me that:

At first they [men] refused [to agree on family planning] but after learning about it in class and seeing what having a baby every year can do to their wives they are beginning to change. A woman that has a kid every year gets sick all the time and the

children don't grow normally, they stop nursing too early and get
sick and the husband is always paying hospital bills. [S2I10AIB]

The discovery of equality in class set the preconditions for women to
be able to speak about the challenges that unwanted pregnancies put
them through. The class widened the possibilities for a shift in the way
people understood contraceptive practice because participants could
debate, discuss, challenge cultural assumptions, and together understand each other's views; that is, understand each other's conditions of
oppression (Freire 1970).

   In class, men understood women's daily life in terms of oppression
– they could 'feel' the oppression women experienced (Freire 1970).
Freirian learning strategies showed the oppressed and the oppressors
opposite views and beliefs and allowed them to work together towards
a solution, putting into practice the biggest heritage HRE owes to Freire:
the coinvestigation of generative themes (Lohrenscheit 2006; Mayo
1999). The Freirian approach allowed participants to interact freely,
challenging norms of silence and invisible power relations that traditionally assigned to women the role of listeners and to men the role of
talkers. The human rights content, then, guided participants' analysis
by offering to them a framework to understand local practices from a
different perspective.

THE SUBSTANTIVE CONTENT OF THE HRE PROGRAMME

Scholars and practitioners in the field of HRE have argued that, to
empower people at the grassroots level, participatory pedagogical
practices are key as the content of the curriculum (Bajaj 2011; Bajaj
et al. 2016; Meintjes 1997; Tibbits 2017). Ideally, participants in an
HRE programme explore human rights while investigating the conditions that shape just or unjust social practices in their local setting.
Therefore, a human rights curriculum should include culturally familiar elements; at the same time, it cannot be so bound by them that
it prevents learners from imagining more egalitarian social relationships. Merry (2006) analysed the processes through which people can
vernacularise human rights, and suggested that human rights should
be understood in local terms to be effectively used as a framework for
analysing local practices and behaviours.

   Given the existence of widely spread human rights instruments, it
is easy to see how teaching and learning about human rights could

become a one-way interaction: from teacher as authority on human rights instruments to students as passive recipients of received indisputable wisdom. Spring (2000) warned against the risks that come with applying passive approaches to human rights education. According to him, those risks are related to threatening human cultural diversity by flattening it through cultural imperialism. As seen earlier in the book, participants in Galle Toubaaco experienced the curriculum as something they could discover and remake, although this process did not come as unproblematic. Experiential learning strategies linked the abstract human rights knowledge to participants' daily practices, grounding their understanding in the familiar and the well-known, that is, concretising the new knowledge into examples they would come across in their daily life.

In the programme, participants used the abstract human rights knowledge to look critically at their local reality. They conceptually blended human rights ideas with traditional latent values analysed earlier, such as collaboration, love for the family and reciprocity. As the 'young' Amadou Ba said in his first interview: 'People here are very close, they help each other and work together and share a common goal for our village' [S1I14ABY]. The human rights knowledge was grafted by participants onto those values and showed existing inconsistencies between the values and participants' daily behaviours. Take, for instance, what Fatou said in her last interview: 'The things that I know are wrong I wouldn't do even before the classes, but the classes reinforced to me that I was doing the right thing all along' [S3I11FD]. Fatou knew what 'is wrong' (values); however, the class reinforced her idea of her 'doing the right thing', that is, the class highlighted connections and relations between values and behaviours confirming (in this case) consistency. Take what Amadou then said at the end of the classes: 'It [human rights] is doing what is right' [S3I10ABY]. 'Doing what is right' indisputably means behaving in harmony with the moral models of one's behaviours. In Amadou's narrative, human rights (the classes) were tools to analyse the need and the capacity to keep values and actions in accordance. Processes that show value/behaviour inconsistency, according to scholars of moral behaviour and social change, are likely to result in a reconsideration of those behaviours for a short time and, in case of continuing exposure to the abstract values, can result in more permanent behavioural shifts (Bardi and Goodwin 2011; Bennis et al. 2010; Torelli and Kaikati 2009).

Participants primed moral behaviours by critically analysing the human rights knowledge and grounded that knowledge in a critical understanding of them in local terms. They could dismiss them or, like Dembaye in the following quote, they could acknowledge an inherent value in the local understanding that the class had helped participants develop:'[Human rights are good for our community and] I didn't know anything about human rights, the only thing was using common sense and recognising what is right' [S3I1DS].

As seen earlier, before the HRE programme participants already shared a set of values and reciprocal behavioural expectations. The class primed those values and their importance in bringing into being a better village that participants conceptualised in the first sessions. The value of working together, key amongst existing values, was primed when discussing human rights and their applicability to all community members. The abstract human rights knowledge was then instantiated into a set of concrete behaviours: non-discrimination, family planning, child protection, to cite some. Participants grounded those behaviours in their traditional values that they came to blend or identify with human rights:

> [Human rights] means solidarity among the people in the village. [S3I2PS]

> [Human rights are important because] it's best to respect the people you live with, treat everyone equally, treat even the little kids with respect and not discriminate because of age or gender. [S3I3AIB]

> Human rights are something that everyone needs to learn, it can help you become a better person and help you live a better life. [S3I5DS]

> [Human rights are good because] it's good to get along, help each other out and treat each other with respect. [S3I11FD]

Among the examples given in this book, the one to which informants made most overwhelming reference is the case of non-discrimination and the discovery of equality. In class, participants connected the abstract human rights knowledge to their daily experience. They grounded on a shared traditional value (collaboration) their intention to adopt a human rights-consistent practice (non-discrimination). In class, participants broadened the meaning of working together and came to include non-discrimination, unity, positive reciprocity and mutual advantage in it.

In Merry's (2006) terms, participants came to their own understanding of human rights through discussion and deliberation: they translated human rights into local behaviours consistent with those same rights. By grounding international jurisprudence within local traditional values, the HRE programme offered participants an opportunity to understand the relationship between human rights-consistent behaviour and how it would benefit the community both in moral and in practical terms. In addition, the visualisation of the better village motivated their efforts, driving their following political action. Hence, as also confirmed by recent research (Bain et al. 2013), projections about the future of their community played a role in sparking attitudes and actions that supported social change.

THE PROCESS OF COINVESTIGATION BREAKING NORMS OF GENDER SEGREGATION

Freire (1970) argued that in the liberation process the oppressed and the oppressors coinvestigate the nature of the problem that the educator poses. Their collaboration, their being present for each other, is then an opportunity to develop alternative views of the status quo that avoid fatalism and resignation because it unlocks a dialogue about a reciprocal understanding of the local reality.

The class increased the dialogue amongst men and women and changed the terms of that dialogue: human rights became a new topic, unleashing new perspectives on the local reality. Chant and Gutmann offered a rationale justifying the need to include participants of both genders within development programmes: if a programme aims at empowering a community as a whole, then 'leaving men behind' (2002: 274) would generate counterforces that would eventually limit or work against women's empowerment. As informants reported, the community as a whole was empowered by the programme in terms of inter-gender relations and mutual solidarity. In Dembaye's words: 'Because of this class there is more trust between the men and the women' [S2I2DS].

The absence of men in the class would have resulted in a different – and possibly limited – impact on the community. The patriarchal structures embedded in Galle Toubaaco would have been difficult to challenge or overturn without empowering the men as much as the women in the rural community. Also, debates and discussions with men influenced women's view of themselves: in class, women had

experience of men's shifting opinions on them. The case of (or nega-
tion of) women's freedom to engage in non-domestic work (i.e. in an
income-generating job) offers a good example of the process described
above. Until the change in the 2007 Civil Law, Senegalese jurisprudence
obliged women to obtain their husbands' written permission to sign a
work contract. National law regulating the matter has been modified
in relatively recent times; logistical reasons understandably delay its
implementation in the rural areas of the country. Other than a legal
framework that changed only recently, traditional assumptions and
norms regulating gender roles represent a big challenge to women's
right to work. As seen earlier, women in Galle Toubaaco did not usually
engage in any job due to social expectations requiring them to engage
solely in domestic work.

By including participants of both genders, the HRE programme
in Galle Toubaaco gave women the opportunity to present their
requests and concerns about their right to work directly to men. As
I mentioned earlier, having to explain women's challenges to men,
women had to rationalise their experiences in detail, they had to
share with them a set of feelings, understandings and practicalities
that men most likely did not experience in their daily life. In this process, women recognised that certain issues (such as the reasons why
they need to work) deviated from men's understanding of the world
and that, therefore, their views on those issue had to be justified. In
explaining their concerns to men, the women of Galle Toubaaco came
to a deeper understanding of those concerns and recognised common
positions and views within their gender group. Men's presence in the
class represented to women a conceptual challenge: because of their
presence, women had to explain the *I* to a *non-I*, in Freirian terms. It is
in the dialogue with the *non-I* that the *I* emerges and can negotiate its
dignity with the others. According to Freire (1970), problem-posing
education unveils new perspectives on the lives of participants. In
class, women reconceptualised the self, the *I*, coming to include new
possibilities and alternatives. Women showed awareness of a change
in what they could do and be. A new existential category emerged
from the class: that of the now-women.

In a gender-segregated class, participants sharing the same gender-
related issues would not have to reconceptualise them through explanation to people alien to those challenges. Such a class would share
fewer opportunities to recognise those challenges as specific to their
gender group. Had the HRE programme included only women, men

would not have had the opportunity to listen to and understand women's concerns (on the importance of finding a job in this example) by asking, debating and experiencing (through experiential learning) their discomfort or oppression. In Galle Toubaaco, men could experience the importance for women of being able to find a job and could debate the reasons for their staying home instead.

In a women-only class, the empowerment that followed (in terms of women's knowledge of their rights and capacity to demand respect for those rights) would have been limited to the class itself. Effective social change would have required a further step, that of women challenging the status quo and the power holders defending it. In Galle Toubaaco, instead, traditional power holders participated in the classes and played a key role, by collaborating with women towards liberation and social change. As Aisata said at the end of the programme:

> We have learnt in the class together about this. Now both men and women know women can do pretty much anything a man can do. We can go to school and get an education and we can work just like men do. [S3I3AIB]

Omar, who participated in all the classes observed, made it clear during the last set of interviews: 'now the men understand it's important for the women to work too because they can work just like the men can' [S3I7OB]. In class, men and women together envisioned alternative realities, by understanding oppression and looking for liberation. As part of this process, participants learnt to aspire to alternative paths of action, they framed different social trajectories and problematised the process to put those alternatives into practice.

EXPERIENCING NEW CLUES TO MAKE SENSE OF THE WORLD

According to cognitivist theories of learning processes, the experience that human beings have of the world surrounding them influences the mental schemata through which they orient their behaviours (Strauss and Quinn 1997). The cognitivist model admits diversion from pre-existing schemata when new experiences unveil a schema-inconsistent behaviour. When this happens, those who are undergoing that experience override old schemata with new ones (Bloch 1998; Kahneman 2011; Strauss and Quinn 1997). In Galle Toubaaco, different experience of people's actions and identity challenged pre-existing individual and social explanations and understandings of community members' roles and relations.

In class, participants analysed value-incoherent practices and committed to value-consistent ones. Research on moral behaviour provided explanations of similar processes that chime with schema theory. When people discover value–behaviour inconsistencies, they tend to respond by adopting value-consistent behaviour. The more consistent the evaluative process is over time, the more likely the change is to last in the long term (Bardi and Goodwin 2011; Bennis et al. 2010; Torelli and Kaikati 2009). Human beings' equal dignity was analysed earlier as a change that stood out in Galle Toubaaco's informants' narrative about the way community members understood and committed to treating each other. The human rights classes primed the local value of collaborating for the common good. The class analysed discriminating behaviours that were inconsistent with that value and that hindered the ideal better village: people cannot work together when they discriminate among each other. Equality became a tool for the reconciliation of values and behaviours.

Bennis et al. (2010) showed that decision-making behavioural processes are often influenced by an interaction of moral rules and cost–benefit analysis (CBA) and that the former are often better suited to explain people behaviours' than the latter. I suggest that CBA intertwined with morality in influencing participants' decisions to reframe value-inconsistent behaviours to their moral understanding of those behaviours. In Galle Toubaaco, participants committed to equality as a set of behaviours because they saw the moral contribution in terms of greater collaboration. Further research should make sense of the tension between moral obligations, social norms and practical reason, exploring if CBA can intertwine with morality in fostering certain public behaviours for a greater moral gain and if over time CBA could be replaced by the integration of those behaviours within collective moral values.

Schema theory also helps explain the cognitive processes by which participants, first, and community members, thereafter, would come to understand women after the programme as, with the term analysed earlier, now-women. In class, the programme offered women the opportunity to experience new roles and to take on new responsibilities. In doing so, they developed skills and capabilities that allowed them to carry out those new tasks with higher self-confidence. Gaventa (2006) analysed people's conformity with social roles as the effect of invisible power dynamics that shape biases and prejudices. In class, women deconstructed the existent role of listeners, of silent women (Belenky et al. 1986). Female participants discovered themselves as different, as now-women capable of speaking in public, challenging invisible obstacles that would hinder their participation in village assemblies. Individually, participants had new cognitive experiences of what the women could do.

Publicly, those cognitive experiences challenged the power dynamics that shaped social behavioural expectations about women's roles. Women publicly (e.g. in the family, in the village meetings or on formal occasions) demonstrated the capacity to implement those new actions: women would act and talk differently, village members would see them doing so and (most importantly) would see other community members seeing the change. The community publicly experienced now-women as acting in ways that did not pertain to the role for women that community members were used to. The cognitive dissonance between what community members were seeing and what they knew about gender roles challenged their mental schemata used to categorise people. They responded to that experience by beginning to include new capabilities in their understanding of what a woman can do or be. Gender roles were not revolutionised overnight: gender roles were embodied into a gender distribution of labour that contributed to shaping people's identity and that responded to daily challenges. However, people's schemata regulating those roles were being stretched by the public experience of actions and capabilities that the now-women were seen to implement and possess.

The HRE classes offered participants the opportunity to widen their horizon of possibilities. In doing so, the classes exposed participants to a new knowledge and the experiences coming with it. Those experiences triggered new mental schemata by showing the schema-inconsistency of social behaviours in place (e.g. marrying young girls means they will not have a chance to go to school and might have early pregnancies – the inconsistency is exposing daughters to harm while trying to take care of them). The concrete human rights knowledge created the framework in which participants could reconsider old mental associations. A change in the context produced new 'cues and scripts' (Strauss and Quinn 1997) that reframed participants' beliefs and preferences. Participants together recognised and reasoned over their actions. The classes created the space and gave participants the tools to share their thoughts in a deliberative act that unveiled inconsistencies in their behaviours.

Deliberative acts are fundamental turning points in the understanding and reframing of social norms. Deliberative acts allow unaware norm-followers to realise the reasons for their behaviours and to change them by institutionalising new social norms (about which community members are then rationally aware) (Bicchieri 2006). In turn, then, the rationalisation of social norms impacts on social practices. Informants described this process themselves, by connecting the new knowledge, its practical implications and the shift in daily practices:

> It's because of human rights that we are now talking about build-ing schools and health posts. It's also why young girls are free to say no to forced marriages and now women are able to go to school and get an education. Because of learning about human rights now we are planting free trees all over our village. Human rights can change the mentality of people, because it teaches them how to live with one another and support each other. [S3I1DS]

In cognitive terms, participants reframed mental schemata together in class, developing capacity to aspire and expanding their capabilities and freedoms. New experiences generated new mental schemata that created the conditions for participants to discuss local social norms regulating gender relations, participation in decision-making and other social practices. The cognitive understanding of a different pres-ent unleashed a different future, where new trajectories can widen up the field of possibilities for the participants. The capacity to imagine a future that does not reproduce the past is the capacity to aspire.

DEVELOPING CAPACITY TO ASPIRE

Appadurai (2004) argued that, mainly due to poverty, the poor have a limited number of opportunities to experience alternatives to the status quo and therefore tend to comply with norms and beliefs and reinforce the social conditions in which they live. The norms to which members of Galle Toubaaco subscribed did – in Appadurai's terms – 'exacerbate their inequality, and deepen their lack of access to mate-rial goods and services' (Appadurai 2004: 66). The example of women's access to employment helps analyse the development of capacity to aspire in Galle Toubaaco. The structural circumstances of community members in Galle Toubaaco analysed earlier would carve out the future and reproduce the present based on the past, by replicating conditions of socio-economic poverty. Community members struggled to under-stand the future as realistically divergent from the present. As Ami and Amadou said:

> Here, I don't see [a woman leading the village] happening. Because I have never seen or heard of a woman chief my whole life. [S1I14ABY]

> I came here when I was 15 years old; it [the village] has been pretty much the same here and hasn't changed. [S1I6AS]

Community members made sense of the social reality as self-reproduc-ing by replicating itself over time with few changes. As Amadou said in the quote above, something that has never happened in the past will not happen in the future. Informants showed the belief that 'things will be as they have always been', that the present would fatalistically rep-licate the past.

Freire, also, referred to this limited imagination as the fatalistic res-ignation that oppressed people demonstrate in conditions of oppres-sion (Freire 1970). A relatively small number of informants argued that something had to change in their village to call an only vaguely specified 'development' into being, but what and how exactly was not yet part of their mindset:

> Between here and ten years I hope people will continue to work together [so that we will develop]. [S1I9PS]

> If everyone gets an education our village will develop and get better. [S1I14ABY]

Other informants had a more precise idea of what they wish to see in the future in their village (mainly related to what would make it easier for them to face daily challenges of rural life). However, they could not problematise the necessary steps to translate those wishes into action, that is, to break the self-repeating patterns of the past with new actions that would attain a different reality: 'We don't know if we will get a health post here but every day we wake up we pray for it. Only God knows what is going to happen but we wish for the best for our village' [S1I1DS].

At the beginning of the HRE programme, informants reported a blurry idea of how they could concretely work together to overcome the hard-ship in which they survived. Through the programme, participants learnt to conceptualise realistic and concrete expectations about what they could do and how. Freire (2002) noted that oppression limits people's capacity to imagine an alternative to the oppression they are living in. In the HRE programme, participants shared possible alternative courses of action, they discussed and visualised them: 'Now women talk about what they learned in class and about their finances and *how* they can help develop the village' [S3I3AIB]. Participants had experience of a change during the classes and started visualising that change. In other words, participants developed the capacity to aspire to a different future. In class, they problematised local issues (conceptually located in the self-reproducing present) and collaborated towards possible solutions (to be reached in the future and breaking with the status quo). Mas in his last interview evoked the entirety of Appadurai's theory in a brilliant comment:

> Now that people have started to get an education, they can talk about starting a business, think about becoming teachers, doctors or whatever you want. If you are not educated you cannot think about this kind of stuff. [. . .] [People in the village] now have an imagination and think about doing things and make decisions for themselves. [S3I4MD]

In class, participants strengthened their capacity to exercise their voice, to debate and 'oppose vital directions for collective social life as they wish[ed]' (Appadurai 2004: 66). The HRE programme gave participants the opportunity to discuss local plausible alternatives to the current cultural hegemony, engaging with local social issues and norms. Participants acquired a 'navigational' capacity, the capacity to aspire, with which they could enlarge their horizon of aspirations. In Appadurai's terms, they challenged rituals of practice and procedures (i.e. social norms) and transformed those core norms, aspiring to a future where the cyclic reproduction of the status quo could be broken. In doing this together as a community in class, participants developed a collective asset, a communal capability.

Capacity to aspire and development of capabilities are closely connected in a dialogic relation where the one fosters the other. Appadurai showed that developing concrete capabilities moves the capacity to aspire 'away from wishful thinking to thoughtful wishing' (Appadurai 2004: 82). In his terms, HRE facilitated the process by which participants in the classes in Galle Toubaaco transformed *wishes* for the future (that could be reached only by 'praying to God') into *plans* for the future to be implemented through newly acquired capabilities (managing finances, meeting with other members and talking about, as Aisata [S3I3AIB] said, 'how they can help and develop the village'). In Galle Toubaaco, developing capacity to aspire set the preconditions for developing new skills. If a future that diverged with past patterns was possible, then participants could understand themselves developmentally: as learning new skills, that is, by expanding their set of capabilities.

EXPANDING FREEDOMS AND GAINING NEW CAPABILITIES

Sen (1999) argued that a holistic approach to development should aim at enhancing the substantive freedom that one person has to choose a life he or she values. In other words, development should widen the field of alternative functioning combinations that a person can value doing or being, that is, the combinations of *functionings* that he or she can achieve. The evaluative emphasis of this approach can be either on what someone is able to do (*realised functionings*) or what real opportunities he or she has (his or her *capability set*). Data show that participants in the programme expanded their freedoms in both understandings. As seen earlier, for instance, the capability set of now-women in Galle Toubaaco expanded to include their freedom to work and their freedom to participate in decision-making.

Nussbaum (2011) collaborated with Sen on the elaboration of the capability approach and further developed it, conceptualising 10 key capabilities that are likely to play an important role in human development. Data show that, of these 10, three in particular have contributed to social change in Galle Toubaaco: affiliation, practical reason and control over the environment (recall I mentioned these three earlier on). Nussbaum (2011) defined *affiliation* as the capability to empathise with another person, and the capability to be treated as a human being worthy of respect equal to that of others. *Practical reason* is the capability to engage critically in reflection about the planning of one's life. *Control over the environment*, finally, is understood as the capability to participate effectively in political choices influencing one's life.

Affiliation was debated earlier in this research from a Freirian perspective: participants gathered together and understood other participants' views on specific social issues, guided by experiential learning. In class, participants expanded their capacity for working together; they developed new social skills and grounded them on the traditional value of solidarity:

People have changed, now people are going to school, women do things together and everyone in the village has become one. There wasn't much unity amongst the people before but the Tostan classes have changed that. [S3I6SD]

Also, participants gained the other facet of the affiliation capability: the capacity to obtain and demand dignified respect. Among the aspirations expressed before the beginning of the programme, informants included the hope of learning how to behave in public and the desire to obtain comfort within old and new roles they assumed or might assume in the future. Participants not only developed public speaking skills, they also learnt how to take on a public role and demand respect for it. For instance, before the programme, both male and female informants described women as ontologically shy. In class, women learnt how to speak out and how to 'look at other people in the eyes' [S3I12AS]. Namely, women experimented with a different role – that of talkers and politically active members – and obtained social respect for those new roles. They developed, together with other participants, affiliation in its deeper meaning: 'being able to be treated as a dignified being whose worth is equal to that of others' (Nussbaum 2011: 34). Affiliation contributed to social change as it built reciprocal respect among community members. It allowed participants to be influential in the local decision-making processes (i.e. to play a role in the *control over their environment*) and, in doing so, it made them able to export to the village level the moral choices made critically in the class (i.e. by exercising *practical reason*).

Practical reason is the capability to 'form a conception of the good and engage in critical reflections about the planning of one's life' (Nussbaum 2011: 34). As seen in the analysis of the programme, HRE classes in Galle Toubaaco triggered participants' debate about just and unjust behaviours and practices. Participants gave shape to a common understanding of what they considered morally acceptable. Most importantly, participants shared individual tenets and summoned a moral programme of actions that (as seen in the next section) became a public evaluative tool for community members' behaviours. As also seen earlier, references to this moral dimension of the HRE programme are overwhelming in the interviews:

A lot of people do something because they don't know but if they learn what they are doing is bad they will stop doing it. [S2I10AIB]

Tostan has something to do with it, people are much more aware of the world around them; they know what is right and what is wrong and you understand what you can and can't do. [...] It's like being awakened from sleep, people knew the difference between right and wrong but didn't know how to express themselves. [S3I6SD]

Many people knew what to do but didn't do it anyway but the Tostan classes helped push everyone to do what's right because it brought everyone together in one place to talk about it. [The class] made people aware that some of the things we were doing were not right and for those who already know that discrimination was wrong express themselves better and be able to speak out. [S3I7OB]

The classes gave participants the opportunity to formulate individual moral beliefs and 'speak out', share them with the rest of the class. Then, on a moral stance that became public by virtue of its public acceptance, the class reasoned together on how to change what they did not like, in other words, on how to overturn the social status quo and make it consistent with the new moral envisioning. They engaged in a critical reflection on their daily practices (e.g. child and forced marriages), shared their moral views on those practices – encouraged by the discussion on human rights (girls should not be discriminated against or married so early) – and engaged in changing those practices (deciding to abandon CFM in the class and bring up the issue at village meetings) by taking the issues that came up in the class to the political places where power could be exercised, that is, participating in decision-making or exercising control over their environment.

Control over environment has been defined by Nussbaum as 'being able to participate effectively in political choices that govern one's life' (2011: 34). Reasons explaining the relevance of this capability for social change are almost self-evident: participating in decision-making is the most direct opportunity people have to reform and influence the social status quo. The previous chapter analysed a shift in how community members reframed their participation in decision-making during and after the HRE programme. Participants took part in decision-making in class, experimenting with roles they did not have the opportunity to experience before.

In this process, women were particularly important for initiating social change. The human development approach builds on feminist development literature – from Boserup's work (1970) to more recent authors (e.g. Kuiper and Sap 1995) – identifying women as dynamic agents for change that can positively influence both men's and women's lives. For instance, women's political action can impact on the life of the community in terms of child survival and reducing fertility rates (Sen 1990, 1999). Women in Galle Toubaaco contributed to the decision-making process and to control over the environment by talking and taking positions in village meetings and assemblies. From Sen's perspective, women's participation in decision-making processes is to be understood as a step forward towards a leadership shared by both genders that would foster social change and contribute to community members' human development.

THE INTERACTIVE PROCESS BETWEEN TWO COMMUNITIES OF PRACTICE

The process of interaction between the class and the village is one of diffusion of the new knowledge and the new understanding of the community developed in the class. Participants brought that new knowledge into the village by sharing it with non-participants:

> It's nice because I am not participating in the class but I am learning from them. Sometimes after class they all get together and talk about what they learned and exchange ideas. [S2I1SB]

> Sometimes when my friends who are taking the class talk about what they learned I get into the conversation and ask questions. [S2I12ABM]

> They [participants] told me about things they learned in class and how things can change, they didn't talk about this kind of stuff before, all this started after the Tostan classes came here. [S3I4MD]

> When I get home from class every day I sit down with friends and family talk about what I learned that day. [S3I7OB]

> Once I get home I talk a lot about the class. [S2I10AIB]

> The classes changed everyone. Every time people come to class and learn something new, after getting home they share what they learned with their family and friends. So even if you weren't in class, you were still learning something from the people who are taking the classes whether it's a family member or a friend. [S3I1DS]

It [discrimination] has been talked about in class and it has been talked about in the village and now everyone knows about it [. . .] Anyone who wanted to take the class but wasn't able to, I will talk to them and teach them things I learned. [S2I9AB]

The post-structuralist analysis of learning offered by Lave and Wenger (1991) suggests that learning processes cannot be separated from the context in which they are situated. Communities of practices exist everywhere there are human beings and learning processes. The rural community of Galle Toubaaco can be understood as a CoP as a whole, where adults would be the old members (situated in various positions of centrality) and children the newcomers moving from the periphery to the centre as they show adherence to social practices and behaviours in place. The class, as seen in Chapter 6, also became a CoP.

Social interaction in class broke the traditional social schemata (and processes of gaining legitimacy) that participants experienced in the CoP-village. The facilitator and the curriculum (exposed through key instructional strategies) restructured membership relations within the CoP-class. Participants legitimated their full membership reciprocally, they reframed together their conditions as newcomers with the facilitator being the unique old member of the CoP-class, and encouraging participants to move from peripheral to more central positions. Participants broke social structures inherited from the external CoP-village and experienced being part of the new CoP-class. Here, they legitimised their old membership in the process of understanding their potential to do so: learning to speak, to listen, to represent others and to take decisions. In other words, participants became full members of a brand new community by self-legitimising their membership.

The relationship between the CoP-class and the CoP-village played an important role in the social change process. Every day, after the class, participants re-entered the CoP-village to take their social role into that CoP. The class, however, opened the horizon of social possibilities to alternative courses of action. Participants, strong in the new role acquired in the CoP-class and recreating that CoP in the CoP-village ('they all get together and talk': [S2I1SB]), could challenge membership legitimation in the CoP-village. Traditionally, in the CoP-village old members granted full membership only to those complying with the status quo in place, and thus replicated that status quo.

Participants reframed that status quo in class and challenged membership dynamics in the community by a process of diffusion of the new dynamics of the CoP-class to the CoP-village. Lave and Wenger's (1991) theory on situated learning can help understand relational dynamics influencing social change. Expanding on their theory, data seem to suggest that not only is learning situated in a context, but that different forms of learning can intertwine with non-formal learning processes in place and hence influence that context, creating the conditions for a change in the status quo. According to what the data from my research suggest, learning is indeed situated in a context that reproduces learning dynamics and processes of membership. However, diverging learning experiences seem to challenge that context so that traditional forms of legitimation are deconstructed and new dynamics enter the relationship between members. Looking at social change from a legitimate peripheral participation theory perspective, I showed that two CoPs interacted in Galle Toubaaco, reframing the dynamics regulating roles (forms of membership) and access to them within the learning context. In this process, the shift in participants' understanding of self and of others, as analysed in the research, played a key role. Participants' outlooks were influenced by the attitudes that the widening of their horizon of alternatives and capabilities fostered.

A PEOPLE-CENTRED INDIRECT APPROACH TO HUMAN DEVELOPMENT

Sen (1999) argued that established traditions can be followed without an express deliberative act. His analysis of 'human development as freedom' requires, as a basic condition, people's freedom to participate actively in the democratic processes of a given community. Tradition, though, can enforce social practices limiting people's participation in those processes and – as a consequence – restrict their freedoms; that is, limiting their human development (Sen 1999). While people should be allowed to decide what tradition they wish to follow, that decision should be free and rational, the risk being that tradition might become a source of *unfreedom*. In social norms terms, community members' participation in decision-making can be limited by persistent social norms upheld by shared mental schemata that, in turn, are caused by the self-reproducing daily experience of the life of that given community.

In Galle Toubaaco, certain sectors of the society had experience of a traditional limited participation in decision-making. The status quo reproduced itself by limiting community members' opportunities to unveil invisible power dynamics by creating experiences that diverged from the current status quo and developing the capacity to visualise a different future. Community members lacked the capabilities necessary to problematise the complexities of the process through which to instantiate that future into a series of actions.

HRE engaged participants in imagining a better future for their community, motivating them to learn how to realise those aspirations. In the learning process, participants experienced an alternative reality and different courses of action. The classes evoked traditional values through which participants examined social practices and elaborated possible alternatives. Participants broadened their capacity to aspire, thinking developmentally about themselves, their family and the village. The human rights curriculum framed their values in a concrete series of examples, through which participants made sense of human rights in their context, vernacularising them. In class, they discussed the pros and cons of the alternative reality triggered by human rights through nonformal learning strategies that showed relationships of power and oppression. Schema-inconsistent behaviours were made public, and local values were brought into coherence with one another and with international human rights. Social practices were publicly redrafted, consistent with new mental schemata and the new human rights knowledge.

Then, participants took that knowledge out, beyond the class: they learnt to take on a public role and to teach others by example. They participated in decision-making and became ambassadors of a new CoP (that of participants in the class) within their original rural community. They diffused the new knowledge by talking with others and by behaving according to the new understanding of themselves and the world developed in class. Participants, then, challenged invisible power dynamics that prevented some of them from accessing visible and hidden powers by challenging the source of unfreedom that limited their participation in public decision-making. In other words, they became protagonists of the human development of their community. Human rights education helped participants in overcoming social obstacles to the empowerment of their community and fostered their human development.

This approach to development showed consistency with indirect autonomy-respecting assistance. Rather than supplying motivation to participants, the HRE programme started with their existing motivations and supplied assistance to the development of their own capabilities and freedoms, in the direction that they deemed useful and necessary. The problem-posing approach to education implemented by Tostan used what Ellerman (2006) defined as an indirect form of development assistance from three perspectives.

First, it started from where community members were: rather than trying to transform the current 'retrograde' or 'evil' institutions, the class gave participants knowledge and experience to improve the status quo where they deemed its flaws lay. Freire argued that problem-posing education is organised by the students' understanding of their world 'where their own generative themes are found' (1970: 101).

Second, it saw the world through the eyes of participants: rather than applying a one-size-fits-all banking education, suggesting to students the right answers, the programme offered guidance on how answers could be generated and on the processes that would assist the emergence of themes that mattered in participants' world. The dialogical education implemented gave participants the opportunity to see the status quo as problematic and helped them conceptualise local challenges in human rights terms. Freire argued that an educator cannot think for others or without them. The thematic investigation can only happen as a coinvestigation that includes the educator and the participant or learner (Freire 1970). Dewey, also, encouraged teachers to provide the conditions to stimulate thinking by taking a sympathetic attitude towards the activities of the learner where the roles of teacher and learners are inverted, with the teacher learning and the student teaching (Dewey [1916] 1966).

Third, the programme respected community members' autonomy. In line with Freirian–Deweyan approaches to education and with Sen–Nussbaum approaches to development, this research suggests that transformation cannot be externally imposed. To Freire, authentic liberation is a praxis, such as community members' action and reflection on the world to transform it. Banking methods of domination cannot be used in the name of liberation, since liberation cannot be implemented by depositing it inside people as money is deposited in the bank (Freire 1970). Dewey also argued that pupils must have a genuine experience of their world, developing genuine problems and solving them using the information they are given and by testing their ideas through application (Dewey [1916] 1966). Sen (1999) and Nussbaum (2011) argued that human development is people-driven and people-centred, that its protagonists should also be the actors of the necessary social change.

Due to their funding needs, international development bodies are interested in having quantitative results quickly. I suggest that in 'indirect human development' terms, this is not possible: real, effective development takes time to change local practices. People's attitudes and motivations need to be sparked first. Then communities need to publicly acknowledge those changes, to develop the capacity to aspire to a different future, and to foster freedoms and capabilities necessary to identify problems that might prevent their aspirations from happening. Knowledge-based autonomy-respecting development programmes substitute external incentives with the generation of internal motivations that can drive change led by the protagonists of that change. Indirect approaches like the one analysed in this book are likely to show quantitatively measurable results over time, but are much more likely to foster people's human development in its real meaning than externally imposed programmes.

CONCLUSION

A process of social change took place in Galle Toubaaco. The problem-posing pedagogical approach ignited participation and fostered the emergence of the themes that mattered to participants. The human rights content guided that emergence, by suggesting different perspectives for looking critically at the social status quo. New experiences in the class (such as the women gaining public speaking skills) challenged old cognitive understandings of the status quo and allowed individuals to reframe new views of what being a community member means. Now-women emerged, for instance, as a new understanding of self and others that challenged norms of silence and subjugation. The new cognitive understanding moved from an individual process to the public sphere of the village. The interaction between two CoPs clashing about rules of membership resulted in a new understanding of invisible power relations at the public level. Community members together had experience of the change happening (a cleaner village, women talking, a microfinance project, people talking about human rights) and also, most importantly, saw others seeing that change. New social norms stretched members' roles and relationships shaped by invisible power relations. Because invisible power dynamics were challenged, community members could also challenge visible and hidden power dynamics, widening participation in decision-making and the setting of the political agenda. The human rights programme offered participants the opportunity to gently redirect self-reproducing dynamics so that they included new possible historical trajectories.

The conclusions of the research, offered in the next, last chapter of the book, suggest that research should address how HRE can challenge how people make sense of self, others and their social reality by integrating theories of invisible power dynamics, anthropological cognitivism, theories of problem-posing education that challenge cultural hegemonies, social norm theories and human development.

Chapter 8

CONCLUSION

You might be asking yourself: what changes followed the Tostan pro-gramme in Galle Toubaaco in the longer term? Long-term changes have been reported elsewhere (Cislaghi et al. 2016; Diop et al. 2008); I did not remain long enough in Galle Toubaaco to observe the longer-term changes that might have followed the Tostan programme there. I did visit Galle Toubaaco at a later point, though. It was January 2016, almost six years after the beginning of the HRE classes. We had been driving across the dunes for a few hours and, having got lost a couple of times, we had decided to ask for directions from a man, who jumped in the car and took us to the village. By the time we made it there, night had fallen. As I got out of the car, I thought we had arrived in the wrong place; right in front of me was a big concrete building that I had never seen before. I was getting back in the car when my adoptive son, Alpha, came running to greet us, with his entire family after him. It was a night of tea, chatting and laughing. They told me that, when the CEP finished, they wanted to have more education, so they lobbied the government to have a school. Many children were studying there; Alpha could now speak a good deal of French, and I could see in the eyes of his mother and father how proud they were.

I do not have evidence that would help understand the extent to which the Tostan programme had contributed to that change – nor I can engage in the complex task of debating whether it is right to ask traditionally nomadic populations to settle in the same place for their children to go to school or not. However, if the data and anecdotes collected by Tostan's internal evaluation team are representative (e.g. Cisse et al. 2016), it is likely that the CEP somehow did contribute to that change.

SOCIAL CHANGE IN GALLE TOUBAACO: GENDER RELATIONS,
POWER BALANCE AND HARMFUL PRACTICES

This book has revealed how a human rights education programme engaged participants so that they became aware of the way in which they made sense of the world. Problematic themes emerged from critical dialogue, and tacit basic assumptions about their roles and relations in the community were challenged by the programme. In particular, this book studied an HRE programme carried out in Galle Toubaaco, a rural West African community. It did so to understand its potential contribution to community members' processes of reconsideration of the local social reality. This research explored three aspects of the rural community: gender roles and relations, access to decision-making, and two harmful practices (child and forced marriages, and child labour). This book has demonstrated that human rights education had an impact on the daily life of a rural community in Senegal in terms of relational dynamics, understanding of self and others, and active participation in decision-making processes.

The first question that guided my research asked how participants in an HRE programme understood gender roles and relations in their community before and after that programme. Before the programme, gender roles and relations impacted negatively on the lives of community members – and especially on women's lives – in human rights and human development terms. A gendered distribution of labour and different marriage patterns influenced access to key resources, identified as labour resources (income, knowledge and services) and marriage resources (land and relational networks). Labour and marriage resources granted men economic and social power and hindered women's capacity to conceptualise alternative courses of action by structuring invisible power dynamics and social norms regulating members' ability to understand them as such and to change them. Dialectically, access to those resources impacted on participants' understanding of gender roles and relations, circularly reproducing patterns of gender inequality. Women in the household learnt to respect the patriarchal authority (the father's first and then the husband's) as absolute and unquestionable.

During the programme, women and men coinvestigated possible different roles by looking at their social reality from a human rights perspective. The problem-posing approach motivated the emergence of critical understandings of existing social patterns regulating gender roles and relations. Also, through participative pedagogy, women realised their public speaking potential and experience; what Gaventa (2003) called a series of growing successes against the existing biases and prejudices. Women's growing confidence in their public speaking skills allowed them to contribute to village meetings.

In Chapter 6 I showed that, in informants' understandings of women, a new semantic category emerged, that of the now-women. Now-women could access a new set of freedoms and capabilities. Community members acknowledged the ontological category of the now-women and saw the concrete benefit of its emergence for the entire village: a cleaner village, microfinance projects and wider contributions to the meetings, among others. People's awareness about women's possible actions and capabilities changed. Gender roles in the family with the related division of labour remained mostly untouched. A different awareness of what women could do for the village changed the relationship between community members and stretched the horizon of possibilities, which in the future might result in further change with members addressing other gender inequalities.

In human development terms, the realisation of an expansion in people's freedoms and capabilities represents the key challenge of communities' empowerment. Nussbaum (2000) argued in particular that unequal conditions for men and women to enhance their level of capabilities is a problem of justice because it hinders the choice of central human functionings. Giving women a voice to help improve their lives (and the life of their community, as in the case of Galle Toubaaco) should be the priority of all development programmes, since it addresses global problems of gender inequality and social injustice. Women's agency is critical in human development theory because it impacts on rural communities as a whole. Sen (1999) argued that women are key agents of social change, especially in promoting child survival and reducing fertility rates; and Nussbaum (2011) suggested that seeking women's justice through the development of their capabilities goes together with the more general approach of taking each person as an end, impacting on more just and dignified living conditions.

The second question that this book answered, on how the classes challenged the public decision-making processes, required exploring who had access to and participated in the decision-making process of a given community before and after an HRE programme. At the various levels of Galle Toubaaco's political structure, the male elders controlled visible and hidden power by deciding what could come under discussion in the village and doing most of the talking in village meetings. This unequal distribution of power was seen as unproblematic by those who were disadvantaged by it.

The confidence that women gained in the classes combined with the public speaking skills developed during the HRE programme. Also in class, participants were engaged in small tasks that required exercising democratic decision-making. All participants had the opportunity to become responsible for small assignments and could influence their final outcomes (e.g. a sketch, reporting on what a small group said or organising other participants to carry out a piece of classwork). After the programme, the political organisation was untouched: male elders still occupied key political roles; however, women's participation in public decision-making increased and young community members were seen by informants as having become more politically active.

Not all women and youths demonstrated the same capacity to access visible and hidden power after the programme. In addition, male and female young community members demonstrated different understandings of the ways in which they could contribute to the public political life of the community, with the young men showing more conformism with the social status quo. In Freirian terms, this difference could be motivated by young men understanding their role as one of heirs to power, and thus seeing how convenient it was for them to conform with the social and political reality. However, in the data there was evidence of general wider public speaking and decision-making skills of community members who were previously at the margin of the public political sphere. Participation in the political life of the community is key in human rights and human development terms. Human rights law protects that participation and regards it as a standard of dignified life. Human development theory argues that human beings must be given the opportunity to frame and give direction to their local reality (Nussbaum 2011; Sen 1999). Democratic participation in the decision-making processes is thus a fundamental feature of communities' empowerment.

The third question asked what other human rights-relevant social practices participants in an HRE programme came to understand as harmful, and how they promoted their change. Evidence showed that two social practices harmed community members' life from a human rights perspective and hindered their human development: child and forced marriages, and child labour. Child and forced marriage impacts on girls' health, freedoms and capabilities. Before the programme, informants described child marriages as not being forced. However, invisible household power dynamics hindered young girls' capacity to refuse the husband that their parents had chosen for them. Child labour was instead seen as problematic because it hindered children's health and schooling opportunities.

In the HRE programme, participants looked critically at those two social practices. Informants said they intended to abandon CFMs in the future. It can be speculated that if the intention diffuses to the entire marriage network, the practice will be effectively abandoned in the next generation. Child labour practices were in place because they helped families cope with their daily challenges. There was only a little evidence of the intention to drop the practice, although there was wider evidence of the emergence of other child-protecting practices. Contrary to CFM, child labour does not bind rural communities together and is not upheld by relations in the social network, but has a tight link with the way in which families respond to the daily challenges that life in a rural area of West Africa presents to them. Informants' statements evidence the value they gave to education and their desire to send their children to school. The economic benefits coming from a new role for the women might in the future reduce the need to employ as many children in pastoral and agricultural work.

How did people achieve these individual and collective changes? Social norm theory argues that certain public behaviours are in place because their renegotiation requires collective action. People follow self-harming public behaviours because the individual withdrawal from a practice results in greater loss than compliance with it. Alternatively, individuals might comply with self-harming practices and behaviours because they do not see them as such. Human development theory argues, for instance, that traditions can be followed without express deliberative acts and that human development instead requires a deliberate and free process of coscientisation resulting in people's informed actions (Sen 1999). Problem-posing pedagogy offered participants the tools to start that process of coscientisation: the dialogic nature of problem-posing education engaged participants in a critical understanding of their local practices and helped them problematise the world. New themes emerged in the classes that impacted on participants' understanding of their local reality (e.g. the village emerged as dirty). In the human rights classes, participants looked at their local reality from a human rights perspective and used the abstract human rights knowledge to examine their daily practices.

In Galle Toubaaco, participants were exposed to experiences that were new to them: women gained self-confidence and spoke in class, participation was democratic and decision-making was shared, women would address the men directly, and common dignity and equality were cited as new behavioural standards. The women discovered a new role, as talkers and decision-makers. The men acknowledged that role, reinforcing women's new understanding of self. Participants' capacity to aspire expanded: they envisioned a different future for themselves and others, and understood collaboration and equality as fundamental to reach that future. The new knowledge and understanding diffused from the class to the village. The concrete visible changes (e.g. the cleanliness of the village and the human rights mantra I mentioned earlier) contributed to fostering the idea that the community and its members were also changing. Female participants, in particular, both saw themselves and were seen as different. Their new capabilities and public actions broke some diffused stereotypes (such as 'women are shy') and unlocked new possible ways of being: the now-women.

Galle Toubaaco is obviously not isolated from the rest of the world: a process of social change was already in motion, in the world around (and within) the village, due to several global, material and structural factors (such as the emerging global human rights ideology, world modernisation, women's empowerment processes happening in the country, and the industrialisation and diffusion of the means of communication). The HRE programme, though, accelerated certain dynamics of social change and helped participants engage meaningfully and actively with the changing world around them. Let me draw an unusual comparison. Existential philosopher Arendt (1994, 2003) exhorted human beings to take on their personal responsibility under dictatorship. In her work, Arendt found a solution to the problem of telling right from wrong when the majority of the environment has 'prejudged the issue' (2003: 50). People – Arendt said – do not usually oppose dictatorship because human beings are ontologically scared of taking on the responsibility of judging power as wrong, as doing that might expose them to mockery and derision. I suggest that in Galle Toubaaco, participants have together overcome that fear, unveiling and then opposing themselves to the dictatorship of certain social norms. They could challenge what they thought was the morality of the majority because they built in the classroom a new moral thought, taking on new moral responsibilities together, as a group. Participants dismissed what Arendt (2003) called 'superior orders' by understanding, naming and shaming 'dictators' (using Arendt's words metaphorically) they had stopped listening to: unhealthy social norms and unjust invisible power dynamics. In doing this, they gained self-confidence and pride, they gained 'the honour of man: not perhaps of mankind, but of the status of being human' (Arendt 2003: 65).

A THEORY OF CHANGE FOR THE CEP: THREE STEPS FOR SOCIAL CHANGE

A comprehensive theory of change for the Tostan programme has been described elsewhere (Cislaghi et al. 2016, 2017; Gillespie and Melching 2010). Here, I provide a shorter and simpler version of that theory, drawing on both my own findings and those of Cislaghi et al. (2016).

First Step: Motivation

Through the HRE classes, the Tostan programme offers participants a critical curriculum they can use to problematise the status quo and uncover socio-political problems in their community that matter to them. After the HRE classes, the CEP also presents participants with information on a variety of topics like, just to cite a few: health, hygiene, project management, literacy, numeracy and democracy. These new classes equip participants with the knowledge they need to continue effectively the process of problematisation that begins in the HRE classes. With new knowledge about health, for instance, lack of vaccination or poor handwashing become issues calling for urgent action.

Next, participants' discussions about the future they envision for their community help them reconcile individual and collective aspirations; individual (old and new) hopes and desires find expression in the future participants envision together. Not only do participants identify existing problems and challenges to address, they also share a vision of how that could be done and where doing so would take them. That vision is already motivational in itself, but it also increases motivation as participants' self- and collective efficacies expand and they come to believe they can actually achieve it. Recall that self- and collective efficacies are one's beliefs that one is capable of putting in place the necessary actions to achieve a certain outcome alone (individually) and with others as a group (collectively) (Bandura 1995). As participants begin to enact change in their own lives and in the community at large (e.g. by cleaning up the village), the idea that they are indeed capable as both individuals and as a group to make change happen motivates them towards doing more to achieve further change: seeing is believing (Cislaghi et al. 2016).

Second Step: Deliberation

The classes that help participants uncover and recognise collective motivations for change also offer participants a space where they can deliberate on what they should do to achieve that change. The Tostan programme equips participants with the skills they need to conduct effective democratic deliberations, public speaking being the most important for that purpose. Also important are the project management skills that participants use to realise their aspirations: Tostan trains participants in creating and implementing collaborative action plans to achieve the change they have envisioned. As they do so, then, norms within the class begin to shift: norms on who takes decisions, on who leads and participates in the public discussions, and on who covers leadership and management roles, for instance.

As the programme progresses, participants begin to deliberate outside of the classroom, both privately and publicly, with other non-participating community members as well: men, women, youths, leaders, and other key influencers or community workers. As they do so, effectively applying the public speaking skills rehearsed in class, more people become motivated to enact the actions requested to achieve positive change.

Third Step: Action

As the group of motivated agents of change expands and integrates community members who did not participate in the classes, they begin to carry out the actions they agreed on to achieve both individual and collective change (e.g. child vaccination, lobbying the government or public cleaning). As they do so, not only do people recognise that life conditions in the village are improving, they also see themselves as different, both as they themselves reflect on their new achievements and through the eyes of the outsiders who visit the changing village. Visitors become mirrors for community members to reflect on the change happening within themselves, as well as in their community. As change agents recognise the positive outcomes of their work, their and observers' motivation grows more; the group expands further to incorporate new community members. New positive social norms emerge that are sealed by public events, some formal (e.g. a public declaration of abandonment of child marriage) and others informal (e.g. women speaking in public and nobody daring to tell them to shush). Since, as seen earlier, norms often exert influence through negative sanctions for non-compliers, when people witness everyone abiding by the new norm, most do not have an interest in diverging from the new acceptable behaviour.

COMPARING THE TOSTAN MODEL: THREE CASE STUDIES

The literature on community-led development is vast, and its review goes beyond the purpose of this book. Many NGOs use community conversations for facilitating social change, but very few of them implement an integrated programme that unfolds over three or more years, and that helps communities achieve their own vision by increasing collective well-being (as Tostan does). In this book, we have also seen that the Tostan programme has some critical limitations, the most important being its limited applicability. It is not known how the CEP would work on a large scale or in urban contexts, and other models seem just as promising. Interestingly, some of these promising models embody in different ways the three steps described above (motivation, deliberation and action for change). Here, I examine three promising programmes (some of which operate in contexts similar to Tostan's), looking at what can be learnt as they are compared with the CEP. The three programmes I look at (Abriendo Oportunidades, SASA! and VAMP) work to achieve greater gender equality in three different continents (South America, Africa and Asia, respectively).

Abriendo Oportunidades

The Abriendo Oportunidades programme, implemented in Guatemala by a group of community-based organisations coordinated by Population Council, aims to improve the life of Mayan girls aged 8–18 living in Guatemala's rural and poorest communities. In the country, the quasi-totality of the Mayan population has limited access to basic services: water, health and schooling. Most Mayan girls also experience child marriage and (unsurprisingly, as the two are often related) school drop-out, which makes them Guatemala's most vulnerable population (Catino et al. 2012; Rogow et al. 2013).

Key in the programme are the girls-only clubs, one for girls aged 8–12 and one for girls aged 13–18 in each community. The clubs meet weekly and are mentored by local women (aged 18–25) trained by the implementing NGOs. The activities follow a set curriculum; each month, the first two weeks provide important information and knowledge to girls (e.g. on their rights and health), the third week is recreational and the last aims to build girls' life skills (Rogow et al. 2013). The programme has gone through many revisions. In its last iteration, practitioners have included an envisioning activity at the beginning of the curriculum. Girls are asked to imagine what rights they would grant to all if they were establishing a new community (Rogow et al. 2013). The envisioning process, reminiscent of Tostan's, proved itself to be effective:

> The girls identified the right to shoes. We thus realized that by being more concrete, this approach did not assume that the girls' priorities were necessarily the same things that facilitators and programme managers were thinking. By allowing the girls to start where they were, it opened a door for them to think critically and discuss their needs. (Rogow et al. 2013: 162)

The meetings that follow the envisioning process aim to increase girls' self-esteem, expand their aspirations, strengthen relations amongst them, provide them with critical life skills, and equip them with knowledge on sexual and reproductive health. Girls graduating from the programme become mentors, and establish regional and national networks. The programme is currently being evaluated through a randomised controlled trial run by Population Council, but preliminary internal evaluations (conducted in 2007 and 2011) suggest that the programme is helping participating girls remain longer at school, achieve better grades, find paid employment, delay age of marriage and first child, and have higher self-efficacy and self-esteem than non-participating girls (Population Council 2009).

As this promising programme expands and evolves, it might benefit from looking at Tostan's approach to community engagement. Even though Abriendo Oportunidades does work with community leaders, establishing contracts with them to commit to supporting girls in the programme, it falls short of working with the community at large. That might be critical for its sustainable success; talking about the successes of the programme, one staff member recognised that the programme was not achieving as much in influencing girls' contraceptive practices: 'Adolescents don't do those things because it still involves a lot of influence from our parents, friends, or even our boyfriends when we can't negotiate with them' (Wehr and Tum 2013: 139). Changing social expectations and norms – the 'influence' parents and boyfriends are said to have in the previous quote – requires working with the entire network of people sustaining those expectations. Programmes that work to strengthen girls' knowledge and skills to resist community expectations, but do not work with the rest of the community to change those expectations, might increase conflict and harm, instead of reducing them. Abriendo Oportunidades does strengthen girls' peer networks, creating a space where girls' individual aspirations can become collective plans in the peer group. But the programme could achieve more by expanding aspirations further so that they become aspirations and action priorities for boys, parents and other community stakeholders, too.

SASA!

SASA! is a community mobilisation approach designed by the NGO Raising Voices to prevent violence against women and HIV, freely available to any organisation willing to implement it. SASA! means 'now' in Kishwahili, but the name of the programme is also an acronym for its four phases: Start, Awareness, Support, Action. The programme was initially created to be implemented in the city of Kampala, Uganda, but since 2008 it has been implemented in over 25 countries (Heilman and Stich 2016; Raising Voices et al. 2015).

While Tostan uses human rights to frame community discussions on health and well-being, SASA! invites participants to have conversations around power and power balances. In the first phase, Start, an organisation planning to implement the SASA! programme trains its staff on power and gender equality. Staff members then select community and institutional activists that receive similar training. The training is motivational, similarly to what happens in the first step of the Tostan model described above. In the second phase, Awareness, activists reach out to others in their communities and institutions to share their new understanding of power balance and gender relations. As that happens, new people join the movement for change and begin to deliberate on the strategies required to achieve that change, similarly to what happens in Tostan's organised diffusion process. The third phase, Support, strengthens community members' skills and networks, encouraging them to support the change taking place in their settings. In the last phase, Action, community members try out together new behaviours and publicly celebrate change (similarly to what Tostan does with public declarations) (Kyegombe et al. 2014). The actions undertaken by community members and change activists do not follow a specific NGO-directed curriculum; they vary across settings, allowing people to respond to the characteristics of the contexts where they are carrying out their efforts (Heilman and Stich 2016).

A recent evaluation suggested that a three-year implementation of the SASA! programme was successful in engaging both communities and government services, and, in turn, in shifting social norms sustaining violence against women (Abramsky et al. 2016). The SASA! programme generated much interest among scholars, donors and practitioners as it is one of the few approaches that have been proven to be working in the urban setting to reduce violence against women (Abramsky et al. 2014).

Men and women participate together in SASA! activities, as happens in the Tostan classes. Similar to what myself and others have found for the CEP, SASA! practitioners found that the mixed-gender learning increased both reciprocal understanding between men and women, as well as the diffusion of ideas among other men and women living in the intervention settings (Cislaghi et al. 2016; RaisingVoices et al. 2015). Even though the mixed-gender approach seemed revolutionary when Tostan and others began to implement it in the early 1990s, today there is common agreement that it is a prerequisite to achieving effective change in community norms (Jewkes et al. 2015). Further, SASA!, as Tostan also does, includes a variety of methods to engage different community actors; just to cite a few: community conversations, door-to-door discussions and radio programmes.

Two features of SASA! are different from Tostan. The first difference is in the approach to community work: SASA! integrates community engagement activities in its methods, while Tostan's CEP embeds features of full community leadership. SASA!'s community engagement methods serve a defined strategic objective (to reduce rates of violence against women and HIV) chosen by the NGO in the first place. Tostan, instead, leaves communities free to decide where they should focus their actions. In other words, while SASA! communities are engaged to act on a specific issue, Tostan's communities lead their own development trajectories. The second difference between SASA! and Tostan is in the scope of their work. While SASA! focuses on violence and HIV, Tostan invites participants to find strategies to achieve community well-being acting across several domains of community life and against the many challenges they face: economic, political, relational, and so on. Future interventions could study the SASA! method to understand whether its approach – that seems to be effective in the urban context, where Tostan as well as many other community-led NGOs have not yet worked as much – could be expanded to address a wider range of people-chosen aims through people-led actions.

VAMP

VAMP (Veshya Anyay Mukti Parishad) is an Indian sex-worker collective founded in 1995 by 50 members; in 2011, it already counted more than 5,000 members and had given origin to another four similar collectives (Ratman 2015; VAMP/SANGRAM 2011). In the late 1980s, Meena Seshu, a former social worker and one of the VAMP founders, had been growing despondent with conventional approaches to helping sex workers. Most of the challenges that sex workers faced were not known to or addressed by local social services. Three of the most pressing, and yet mostly overlooked, were maltreatment by the police, risk of contracting HIV and discrimination in the community (Cornwall 2016; Seshu and Pai 2014).

Seshu began by facilitating group meetings where sex workers could look critically at their own life conditions and identify common challenges (similarly to what happens in the first months of the CEP). Even though they focused largely on HIV/AIDS, their concerns included other social, psychological and economic issues affecting their lives (VAMP/SANGRAM 2011). Sex workers deliberated together on what they could do to address those challenges, and enacted a threefold strategy to ameliorate their conditions: (1) *persuading* other community members; for instance, they would discuss with vegetable sellers, who previously discriminated against them, how sex workers are an important source of revenue for them, and discriminating against them does not benefit either the seller or the sex worker; (2) *protesting* at police stations and government offices and to politicians: marches of large numbers of sex workers were episodic but very effective, to the point that VAMP would exercise influence over decision-makers even by just threatening to carry out a protest; and (3) *exchanging favours* with politicians, local social organisations and the police to gain leverage over key stakeholders (Cornish et al. 2010).

The results of VAMP's work are outstanding: they eradicated under-age sex work in their communities, increased availability and quality of condoms for sex workers, established a safe hostel where they can continue their studies, reduced police abuse and violence, strengthened relationships of solidarity among community members, increased sex workers' confidence to call for help, and dramatically reduced community discrimination against them (Cornwall 2016). Cornwall (2016) identified three steps that led to VAMP's success, that resonate with the three steps I identified above in the CEP: (1) developing critical consciousness of their situations, which motivated them to act; (2) building trust and capacities to collaborate effectively, taking strategic decisions on the actions to pursue; and (3) enacting change in collaboration with key community stakeholders.

VAMP is a genuinely people-led initiative; their slogan – 'Save us from the Saviours' – embodies Ellerman's important message: empowerment only comes from within and cannot be given by others (Ahmed and Seshu 2012; Cornwall 2016; Ellerman 2006). VAMP and Tostan are very different in their methods and activities, but they both try to help people identify common problems and collaborate to enact effective change strategies they have agreed upon together. VAMP seems to be a very promising model to facilitate the work of those groups that are homogenous for gender, class or other social conditions. In other contexts, self-organised community-based organisations might benefit from integrating discussions on human rights and democracy (as in Tostan's HRE classes) at the start of their work. In heterogeneous groups, strong power imbalances can infiltrate group dynamics and capture the democratic spirit of the process. Without critical discussions about non-discrimination, equality and democratic decision-making, for instance, the power-holding elites could hijack the discourse and make sure that all decisions benefit them in the first place, perpetuating the same conditions of inequality that in turn generate the challenges that the group is trying to address.

VAMP's is a truly inspiring model of indirect development. With their work, the VAMP collective is telling the world that not all sex workers need or want to be rescued, and that many of them are capable of advocating for their own rights and acting for their own well-being – an important message to those working to achieve global justice.

FOUR CONTRIBUTIONS TO THEORY AND PRACTICE OF INTERNATIONAL DEVELOPMENT

Findings from this research will be helpful to scholars and practitioners looking for models to enact indirect development theory that result in positive social improvement and higher gender equality. Here are four key messages that emerged from this research and that will help them in their work.

Indirect Development Can Be Enacted through Freirian Education

Human development theory can be used for an indirect approach to development that empowers people with the agency they need to change their social reality. Rather than nannying people's choices, development programmes should create conditions for people to take informed, responsible decisions through which they can direct their private and public life (Nussbaum 2011; Sen 1999). In this process, education is critical because it enables access to other freedoms and capabilities: 'a person may benefit from education [. . .] in being able to choose in a more informed way, in being taken more seriously by others and so on' (Sen 1999: 194). Even though Sen understood the importance of education for human development, he did not acknowledge the specific potential of problem-posing education as a tool to spark new critical understanding of the local reality and help people lead the social change process.

Ellerman (2006) pushed Sen's approach further, looking at similar people-led programmes as models of 'indirect' development, that is: programmes that do not help people but rather 'help people help themselves'. He acknowledged the importance of education as a tool for critical reflection, but his work lacks an understanding of how Freirian problem-posing education can be implemented to foster indirect human development; it lacked a model of operationalisation.

I suggest that Ellerman's model can be enacted through the Freirian problem-posing approach to nonformal participative education (1970). Problem-posing education fosters the emergence of the themes that matter for the participants (their problems), making them protagonists of their future. Freire's approach could be implemented in a human rights framework to facilitate the emergence of generative themes that matter to participants, by offering them an alternative perspective from which to read their local reality. This book contributes to these theories by offering an educational model at the grassroots level that embodies an indirect approach to human development. The model suggests that Freirian problem-posing education can help community members develop motivation to address local social injustices and work together to influence their social and political environments.

Nonformal Human Rights Education Can Facilitate Transformative Change at the Cognitive and Social Level

Nonformal approaches to human rights education are said to have behavioural change potential (Amnesty International 2011; Bajaj 2011; Bajaj et al. 2016; Flowers et al. 2000, 2007; Tibbits 2002). However, there is not much in the literature about the cognitive and social processes that can result from critical exposure to a nonformal human rights education programme. Cognitive schema theory and social norms theory were used in this research to understand the dynamics of social change that followed the human rights education programme. Participants and other community members came to develop new understandings of self and others, overriding or modifying previously existing collective schemas regulating their social roles and relationships. In enacting those new roles, they challenged existing social and gender norms, eventually achieving their renegotiation. The public enactment of new behaviours and social practices challenged individuals' schemas, both of participating and non-participating community members, forcing community members to integrate those new, initially exceptional, behaviours within their understanding of what is acceptable and 'normal'.

Fostering a Core Community of Motivated Individuals First Helps Achieve Change on a Larger Scale Later

Theorists who studied CoPs acknowledged the existence of a constellation of CoPs in the same context (Lave and Wenger 1991; Wenger et al. 2002). A rural community can host different CoPs: male adolescents, farmers, power holders, amongst many possible others. Tostan created a new community, among class participants, where rules of behaviour were renegotiated democratically. Its members were confident in each other and together enacted a strategy of change in their community, by both publicly enacting new behaviours and motivating non-participating members to join them in those new behaviours. The strategy proved effective: non-participating members joined in the movement for change and strengthened participants' new actions and confidence. Lave and Wenger's theory does not fully explain how a 'deviant' CoP hosted by or included in a wider one can influence patterns of knowledge of the wider community. My research suggests that the way members of the smaller communities renegotiate their membership and develop self-confidence can influence relations among members in the wider community, reframing behavioural rules and members' outlook on reciprocal roles and relationships.

From a more theoretical standpoint, my findings contribute to CoP theory as they offer an understanding of the role that power plays in the interaction between different CoPs. Lave and Wenger were aware that power relations can enable or hinder access to the social practices of a community (Contu and Willmott 2003; Lave and Wenger 1991). They also acknowledged that 'unequal relations of power must be included more systematically in our analysis' (Lave and Wenger 1991: 42). An analysis of those relations is instead prominent in my research. Gaventa's (2006) understanding of power was used in this research, together with social norms theory, to give an understanding of how learning and power processes intertwined in the lives of the people living in Galle Toubaaco. The work emerged as a point of departure, rather than one of arrival, and suggests future research in the same direction.

Changing Social Norms Requires Understanding Dynamics of Power and Helping People Renegotiate Them

In accessing available resources and in responding to the challenges that life in their environment presents, communities of human beings negotiate behavioural norms that regulate social roles and power relations among them. There are many potential social solutions to those challenges, each resulting in a social equilibrium of some sort and defining appropriate behaviours in each context. Human beings in a community settle, over time, in one of the many possible social equilibria. Sometimes, the social equilibrium might offer effective solutions to people's social problems, and yet grant freedoms and power unequally. For instance, responding to danger of rape, a community might have settled in a social equilibrium where women never leave the household alone, so that, over time, the women who do leave the household alone are not considered respectable – that is, there is a social norm against women leaving the household.

Norms exist that assign power to some and not to others. Norms around power might persist over time because of spontaneous processes and/or because power holders consciously enforce them. Spontaneously, norms around power might sustain the power equilibrium by excluding from the decision-making process those who could threaten the equilibrium, even when power holders are not consciously invested in maintaining the equilibrium as it is. On the other hand, power holders might also have an active interest in protecting norms that grant power to them. Changing social norms requires unlocking people's awareness of how those norms limit participation of some in the decision-making process, and helping the powerless and power holders work together for the improvement of their life conditions. As revealed in this book, in Galle Toubaaco that process was initiated by a critical human rights education programme.

FUTURE RESEARCH TRAJECTORIES

Due to its scope and very nature, my research did not fully explore the complexities of the processes that create and reproduce invisible power dynamics. However, the implications of those processes for the human development of men and women in rural communities emerged as critical and pointed at future research trajectories that could integrate this conceptual framework with other critical approaches.

This study suggests that the microanalysis of how people behave as they absorb new information and the way in which they dialogue critically about their social reality can have implications for other fields of research. In particular, this research calls for an understanding of similar issues from the point of view of those critical theorists and sociologists who are studying the lived world, the connections between human beings, and how they contribute to socially constructing it and to challenging these constructions. I suggest that further research should explore indirect approaches that can offer communities the opportunity to engage in a dialogue about what they understand as threatening the well-being of their members. Research must explore how community members can be offered the space to discuss if (and how) to address those conditions.

In HRE, the self is empowered, but in the context of the community. As individual consciousness shifts, the whole consciousness of the class shifts. From being passive recipients of social norms that have been handed down to them, people become critical observers first, and then teachers of others and politically active community members. Most of the models available do not engage with the complexity of this double-faceted empowerment; this research calls for an exploration of a new model that can make sense of community-led empowerment that breaks the reproduction of an unjust status quo. As the people living in Galle Toubaaco demonstrated, human rights education offers a pedagogical model that addresses the worries of both those concerned with the relative nature of human rights and those that rightfully want to address local issues of social justice. We should now use these insights to inform interventions on a larger scale and, as we do so, increase our understanding of how we can best achieve greater justice for women and men globally.

NOTES

1. An exclusive interview with Barbie Savior can be found at ≤https://culture-stories.co/meet-africas-barbie-savior/> (last accessed 12 June 2017) and *The Guardian* newspaper online hosts 11 of the best aid parodies at ≤http://www.theguardian.com/global-development-professionals-network/2014/dec/19/11-of-the-best-aid-parodies> (last accessed 12 June 2017).
2. In the word 'Fulɓe', the hooked b represents a labial implosive stop b.
3. The government of Macky Sall effectively abolished the Senate in September 2012 (Allison 2012).
4. Identifiers for participants' quotes include: (1) the moment of the interview (S1: before the HRE classes; S2: during the HRE classes; and S3: at the end of the HRE classes); the number of the interview for that set; and participants' initials. Note that names have been changed to protect participants' anonymity.
5. Around £26.
6. The Wolof word used in Senegal for the Muslim holiday *Eid al-Adha*.
7. See Chapter 4.
8. See Box 4.2 for an overview of the Kobi 1.

REFERENCES

Abrams, M. H. (1971), *The Mirror and the Lamp: Romantic Theory and the Critical Tradition*, Oxford: Oxford University Press.

Abramsky, T., K. Devries, L. Kiss, J. Nakuti, N. Kyegombe, E. Starmann, B. Cundill, L. Francisco, D. Kaye, T. Musuya, L. Michau and C. Watts (2014), 'Findings from the SASA! Study: A Cluster Randomized Controlled Trial to Assess the Impact of a Community Mobilization Intervention to Prevent Violence against Women and Reduce HIV Risk in Kampala, Uganda', *BMC Medicine*, 12(122), 1–17.

Abramsky, T., K. M. Devries, L. Michau, J. Nakuti, T. Musuya, N. Kyegombe and C. Watts (2016), 'The Impact of SASA!, a Community Mobilisation Intervention, on Women's Experiences of Intimate Partner Violence: Secondary Findings from a Cluster Randomised Trial in Kampala, Uganda', *Journal of Epidemiology and Community Health*, 70(8), 818–25.

Abu-Lughod, L. (1991), 'Writing against Culture', in R. Fox (ed.), *Recapturing Anthropology*, Albuquerque: SAR Press, pp. 137–62.

AFDB (2010), *Republic of Senegal: Country Strategy Paper 2010–2015*, Dakar: African Development Bank.

Agarwal, B. (1995), 'Gender, Property, and Land Rights', in E. Kuiper and J. Sap (eds), *Out of the Margin: Feminist Perspectives on Economics*, New York: Routledge, pp. 192–213.

Ahmed, A. and M. Seshu (2012), '"We Have the Right Not to Be 'Rescued'. . .": When Anti-trafficking Programmes Undermine the Health and Well-being of Sex Workers', Northeastern Public Law and Theory Faculty Research Papers Series, 2012(103), *Anti-Trafficking Review*, 1, 149–68.

Allen, C. (1995), 'Understanding African Politics', *Review of African Political Economy*, 22(65), 301–20.

Allen, C., C. Baylies and M. Szeftel (1992), 'Surviving Democracy?', *Review of African Political Economy*, 19(54), 3–10.

Allen, G. (1992), 'Active Citizenship: A Rationale for the Education of Citizens?', in G. Allen and I. S. Martin (eds), *Education and Community: The Politics of Practice*, London: Cassell, pp. 130–44.

257

Allison, S. (2012), 'Senegal Abolishes Senate – Selfless Gesture or Selfish Politicking?', *Daily Maverick*, 21 September, <http://allafrica.com/stories/201209210625.html> (last accessed 12 June 2017).

Amanor, K. S. (2007), 'Conflict and the Reinterpretation of Customary Tenure in Ghana', in B. Derman, R. Odgaard and E. Sjaastad (eds), *Conflicts over Land and Water in Africa*, Oxford: James Currey, pp. 33–59.

Amanor-Wilks, D.-E. (2009), 'Land, Labour and Gendered Livelihoods in a "Peasant" and a "Settler" Economy', *Feminist Africa*, 12, 31–50.

American Anthropological Association (1947), 'Statement on Human Rights', *American Anthropologist*, 49(4), 539–43, <http://direitosehumanos.files.wordpress.com/2008/03/satement-45.pdf> (last accessed 12 June 2017).

Amnesty International (1996), *First Steps: A Manual for Starting Human Rights Education*, London: Amnesty International.

Amnesty International (2011), 'What Is Human Rights Education?', <http://www.amnesty.org/en/human-rights-education> (last accessed 12 June 2017).

Amnesty International (2012), *Senegal: The Human Rights Situation*, London: Amnesty International.

Appadurai, A. (1986), 'Theory in Anthropology: Center and Periphery', *Comparative Studies in Society and History*, 28(2), 356–61.

Appadurai, A. (2004), 'The Capacity to Aspire: Culture and the Terms of Recognition', in V. Rao and M. Walton (eds), *Culture and Public Action*, Stanford: Stanford University Press, pp. 59–84.

Arab Institute for Human Rights (2002), *Workshop on HRE Issues in Human Rights NGOs: Good Practices in Human Rights Education and Training; Guidelines, Indicators and Evaluation*, Marrakesh: Arab Institute for Human Rights.

Arendt, H. (1994), *Eichmann in Jerusalem: A Report on the Banality of Evil*, New York: Penguin.

Arendt, H. (2003), *Responsibility and Judgement*, ed. J. Kohn, New York: Shocken.

Arslan, Z. (1999), 'Taking Rights Less Seriously: Postmodernism and Human Rights', *Res Publica*, 5(2), 195–215.

Awogbade, M. (1983), *Fulani Pastoralism: Jos Case Study*, Zaria: Ahmadu Bello University Press.

Azarya, Y., A. Breedveld, M. De Bruijn and H. Van Dijk (eds) (1999), *Pastoralists under Pressure? Fulbe Societies Confronting Change in West Africa*, Leiden: Brill.

Azarya, Y. and P. K. Eguchi (eds) (1993), *Unity and Diversity of a People: The Search for Fulbe Identity*, Osaka: MINPAKU.

Aziz, N. (1999), 'The Human Rights Debate in an Era of Globalization', in P. Van Ness (ed.), *Debating Human Rights: Critical Essays from the United States and Asia*, London: Routledge, pp. 32–55.

Bachrach, P. and M. S. Baratz (1962), 'Two Faces of Power', *The American Political Science Review*, 56(4), 947–52.

Bacquelaine, M. and E. Raymaekers (1987), *Non-formal Education in Developing Countries: Information File Number 10*, Geneva: International Bureau of Education.

Bain, P. G., M. J. Hornsey, R. Bongiorno, Y. Kashima and D. Crimston (2013), 'Collective Futures: How Projections about the Future of Society Are Related to Actions and Attitudes Supporting Social Change', *Personality and Social Psychology Bulletin*, 39(4), 523–39.

Bajaj, M. (2011), 'Human Rights Education: Ideology, Location, and Approaches', *Human Rights Quarterly*, 33(2), 481–508.

Bajaj, M., B. Cislaghi and G. Mackie (2016), 'Advancing Transformative Human Rights Education', in G. Brown (ed.), *The Universal Declaration of Human Rights in the 21st Century*, Cambridge: Open Book Publishers.

Bandura, A. (1995), *Self-Efficacy in Changing Societies*, Cambridge: Cambridge University Press.

Banerjee, A. V. and E. Duflo (2011), *Poor Economics*, Philadelphia: Public Affairs.

Bardi, A. and R. Goodwin (2011), 'The Dual Route to Value Change: Individual Processes and Cultural Moderators', *Journal of Cross-Cultural Psychology*, 42(2), 271–87.

Basu, K. (1998), *Child Labor, Cause, Consequence, and Cure, with Remarks on International Labor Standards*, Washington DC: World Bank.

Basu, K. B. and P. Hoang Van (1998), 'The Economics of Child Labor', *The American Economic Review*, 88(3), 412–27.

Baxi, U. (1998), 'Voices of Suffering and the Future of Human Rights', *Translational Law & Contemporary Problems*, 8(125), 125–69.

BBC (2012a), 'Abolish Senegal Senate to Fund Flood Relief, Says Sall', *BBC News, Africa*, 29 August, <http://www.bbc.co.uk/news/world-africa-19407427> (last accessed 12 June 2017).

BBC (2012b), 'How Abdoulaye Wade's Star Has Faded', *BBC News, Africa*, 31 January, <http://www.bbc.co.uk/news/world-africa-16815521> (last accessed 12 June 2017).

BBC (2012c), 'US Secretary of State Clinton Hails Senegal Democracy, *BBC News, Africa*, 1 August, <http://www.bbc.co.uk/news/world-africa-19073601> (last accessed 12 June 2017).

BBC (2017), 'Senegal Profile', *BBC News, Africa*, 19 January, <http://www.bbc.co.uk/news/world-africa-14093674> (last accessed 12 June 2017).

Beckett, D. and P. Hager (2002), *Life, Work and Learning: Practice in Postmodernity*, London: Routledge.

Bednar, J., A. Bramson, A. Jones-Rooy and S. Page (2010), 'Emergent Cultural Signatures and Persistent Diversity: A Model of Conformity and Consistency', *Rationality and Society*, 22(4), 407–44.

Bednar, J. and S. Page (2007), 'Can Game(s) Theory Explain Culture?: The Emergence of Cultural Behavior within Multiple Games', *Rationality and Society*, 19(1), 65–97.

Beitz, C. R. (2009), *The Idea of Human Rights*, Oxford: Oxford University Press.

Belenky, M. F., B. M. Clinchy, N. R. Goldberger and J. M. Tarule (1986), *Women's Way of Knowing: The Development of Self, Voice, and Mind*, New York: Basic Books.

Benerìa, L. (1979), 'Reproduction, Production and the Sexual Division of Labour', *Cambridge Journal of Economics*, 3(3), 203–25.

Benerìa, L. (2003), *Gender, Development and Globalization: Economics as if All People Mattered*, London: Routledge.

Benerìa, L. and G. Sen (1981), 'Accumulation, Reproduction, and "Women's Role in Economic Development": Boserup Revisited', *Journal of Women in Culture and Society*, 7(2), 279–98.

Bennis, W. M., D. L. Medin and D. M. Bartels (2010), 'The Costs and Benefits of Calculation and Moral Rules', *Perspectives on Psychological Science*, 5(2), 187–200.

Benoit, M. (1975), *Le chemin du Peul du Boobola*, Bondy: ORSTOM.

Benoit, M. (1988), 'Les Bowébés du Kantoora (Sénégal): À propos de l'état pastoral', *Cahiers de sciences humaines*, 24(3), 379–88.

Benson, C. (2004), 'The Importance of Mother Tongue-Based Schooling for Educational Quality', , paper commissioned for the *EFA Global Monitoring Report 2005, The Quality Imperative*, <http://unesdoc.unesco.org/images/0014/001466/146632e.pdf> (last accessed 12 June 2017).

Best, F. (2002), 'Les droits de l'homme et l'éducation', *International Review of Education*, 48(3–4), 229–38.

Besteman, C. (1995), 'Polygyny, Women's Land Tenure, and the "Mother–Son Partnership" in Southern Somalia', *Journal of Anthropological Research*, 51(3), 193–213.

Bicchieri, C. (2006), *The Grammar of Society*, Cambridge: Cambridge University Press.

Bierkester, T. J. and C. Weber (eds) (1996), *State Sovereignty as Social Construct*, Cambridge: Cambridge University Press.

Bierschenk, T. (1999), 'Structures spatiales et pratiques sociales chez les Peuls du nord du Bénin', in R. Botte, J. Boutrais and J. Schmitz (eds), *Figures Peules*, Paris: Karthala.

Bigelow, B. and B. Peterson (eds) (2002), *Rethinking Globalization: Teaching for Justice in an Unjust World*, Milwaukee: Rethinking Schools.

Bloch, M. E. F. (1998), *How We Think They Think*, Oxford: Westview Press.

Boal, A. (1979), *Theatre of the Oppressed*, London: Pluto Press.

Boal, A. (1995), *The Rainbow of Desire: The Boal Method of Theatre and Therapy*, London: Routledge.

Boccanfuso, D. and L. Savard (2008), *The Food Crisis and Its Impacts on Poverty in Senegal and Mali: Crossed Destinies*, Sherbrooke: University of Sherbrooke.

Bond, P. (2006), *Looting Africa*, London: Zed Books.

Boserup, E. (1970), *Women's Role in Economic Development*, London: Allen & Unwin.

Botte, R. (1999),'Un Peul peut en cacher un autre', in R. Botte, J. Boutrais and J. Schmitz (eds), *Figures Peules*, Paris: Karthala, pp. 7–18.

Botte, R., J. Boutrais and J. Schmitz (eds) (1999), *Figures Peules*, Paris: Karthala.

Bourdieu, P. (1977), *Outline of a Theory of Practice*, Cambridge: Cambridge University Press.

Boutrais, J. (1994), 'Remapping the Fulani', *Cahiers d'études africaines*, 34(133–5), 137–46.

Breedveld, A. and M. De Bruijn (1996),'L'image des Fulbe. Analyse critique de la construction du concept de pulaaku', *Cahiers d'études africaines*, 36(144), 791–821.

Brown, R. H. and L. Bjawi-Levine (2002), 'Cultural Relativism and Universal Human Rights: Contributions from Social Science of the Middle East', *The Anthropologist*, Special Issue 1, 163–74.

Buhl, S. (1999),'Milk, Millett and Mannerisms: Gendered Production among Fulbe Pastoral and Agropastoral Households in Northern Burkina Faso', PhD thesis, University College London.

Burnham, P. (1999), 'Understanding Social Change in Fulbe Society', in Y. Azarya, A. Breedveld, M. De Bruijn and H. Van Dijk (eds), *Pastoralists under Pressure? Fulbe Societies Confronting Change in West Africa*, Leiden: Brill, pp. 269–84.

Cardenas, S. (2005),'Constructing Rights? Human Rights Education and the State', *International Political Science Review*, 26(4), 363–79.

Catino, J., A. Colom and A. D.Valle (2012),'Abriendo Oportunidades in Guatemala', in J. Sewall-Menon, J. Bruce, K. Austrian, R. Brown, J. Catino, A. Colom, A. D. Valle, H. Demele, A. Erulkar, K. Hallman, E. Roca and N. Zibani (eds), *The Cost of Reaching the Most Disadvantaged Girls: Programmatic Evidence from Egypt, Ethiopia, Guatemala, Kenya, South Africa, and Uganda*, NewYork: Population Council.

CERD (2012), *Consideration of Reports, Comments and Information Submitted by States Parties under Article 9 of the Convention: Sixteenth to Eighteenth Periodic Reports of Senegal*, Geneva: United Nations, <http://www.bayefsky.com/ summary/senegal_cerd_c_sr2180_2012.doc> (last accessed 12 June 2017).

Chabal, P. and J.-P. Daloz (1999), *Africa Works: Disorder as Political Instrument*, Oxford: James Currey.

Chanda, A. (1999), *Non-formal Education for Human Rights in Zambia*, Oxford: African Books Collective.

Chant, S. and M. C. Gutmann (2002),'"Men-Streaming" Gender? Questions for Gender and Development Policy in the Twenty-First Century', *Progress in Development Studies*, 2(4), 269–82.

Chodorow, N. J. (1999), *The Reproduction of Mothering: Psychoanalysis and the Sociology of Gender*, updated edn, Berkeley: University of California Press.

Chong, D. (2000), *Rational Lives: Norms and Values in Politics and Society*, Chicago: University of Chicago Press.

Cislaghi, B. (2016), 'Why Do People's Values Matter in International Development?', in T. Fouquet (ed.), *Transition humanitaire au Sénégal*, Paris: Karthala, pp. 191–205.

Cislaghi, B., D. Gillespie and G. Mackie (2016), *Values Deliberation and Collective Action: Community Empowerment in Rural Senegal*, New York: Palgrave Macmillan.

Cislaghi, B., D. Gillespie and G. Mackie (2017), 'Expanding the Aspirational Map: Interactive Learning and Human Rights in Tostan's Community Empowerment Program', in M. Bajaj (ed.), *Human Rights Education: Theory, Research, Praxis*, Philadelphia: University of Pennsylvania Press, pp. 251–66.

Cisse, M., N. S. Diouf, P. Gueye, V. Manel and E. Larson (2016), *A Community-Led Approach to Community Empowerment in Mali, Mauritania, Guinea, and Guinea-Bissau: Midline Evaluation Brief*, Dakar: Tostan.

Clark, A. F. (1997), 'Fulbe/Fulani/Peul: Origins', in K. Shillington (ed.), *Encyclopedia of African History*, vol. 1, London: Fitzroy Dearborn, pp. 534–5.

Claude, R. P. (1999), *Enhancing Participatory Non-formal Education among Cambodian Human Rights NGOs: A Report with Recommendations for The Asia Foundation*, <http://erc.hrea.org/Library/research/TAFreport.html> (last accessed 1 February 2015).

Claude, R. P. (2000), *Popular Education for Human Rights: 24 Participatory Exercises for Facilitators and Teachers*, Amsterdam and Cambridge, MA: Human Rights Education Associates, <http://www.populareducation.co.za/sites/default/files/hr_education.pdf> (last accessed 12 June 2017).

Claude, R. P. and G. J. Andreopoulos (1997), *Human Rights Education for the Twenty-First Century*, Philadelphia: University of Philadelphia Press.

Clegg, S. R. (1989), *Frameworks of Power*, London: Sage.

Cliff, T. (1984), *Class Struggle and Women's Liberation*, London: Blackwell.

Coburn, K. (1968), *Inquiring Spirit: A Coleridge Reader*, New York: Minerva Press.

Colley, H., P. Hodkinson and J. Malcom (2002), *Non-formal Learning: Mapping the Conceptual Terrain. A Consultation Report*, <http://www.infed.org/archives/e-texts/colley_informal_learning.htm> (last accessed 12 June 2017).

Constitute (2012), *Senegal's Constitution of 2001 with Amendments through 2009*, trans. Jefri J. Ruchti, Hein Online, <https://www.constituteproject.org/constitution/Senegal_2009.pdf?lang=en> (last accessed 21 June 2017).

Contu, A. and H. Willmott (2003), 'Re-embedding Situatedness: The Importance of Power Relations in Learning Theory', *Organization Science*, 14(3), 283–96.

Cornish, F., A. Shukla and R. Banerji (2010), 'Persuading, Protesting and Exchanging Favours: Strategies Used by Indian Sex Workers to Win Local

Support for Their HIV Prevention Programmes', *AIDS Care*, 22(Suppl. 2), 1670–8.

Cornwall, A. (2016), 'Women's Empowerment: What Works?', *Journal of International Development*, 28(3), 342–359.

Council of Europe (2007), *Mini-Compendium on Non-formal Education*, Strasbourg: Council of Europe.

Council of Europe (2009), DJS/EYCB/HRE Forum/2009/025 – Forum on Human Rights Education, Strasbourg: Council of Europe.

CRDH (2010), *Évaluation de l'impact du Programme de Renforcement des Capacités des Communautés mis en œuvre par Tostan en milieu rural sénégalais dans les régions de Tambacounda et de Kolda, en 2009*, Dakar: Centre de Recherche pour le Développement Humain.

Creevey, L. (1996),'Islam, Women and the Role of the State in Senegal', *Journal of Religion in Africa*, 26(3), 268–307.

Dahl, R. A. (1961), *Who Governs? Democracy and Power in an American City*, New Haven, CT: Yale University Press.

Dahl, R. A. (1971), *Polyarchy: Participation and Opposition*, New Haven, CT: Yale University Press.

Dalacoura, K. (1998), *Islam, Liberalism and Human Rights: Implications for International Relations*, London: I. B. Tauris.

Davidheiser, M. and A. M. Luna (2008),'From Complementarity to Conflict: A Historical Analysis of Farmer–Fulbe Relations in West Africa', *African Journal on Conflict Resolution*, 8(1), 77–103.

de Beauvoir, S. (1973), *The Second Sex*, New York: Vintage Books.

De Bruijn, M. and H. Van Dijk (1994),'Drought and Coping Strategies in Fulbe Society in the Haayre (Central Mali)', *Cahiers d'études africaines*, 34(133–4), 85–108.

d'Engelbronner-Kolff, M. (1998), *The Provision of Non-formal Education for Human Rights in Zimbabwe*, Oxford: African Books Collective.

Der Thiam, I. and M. Gueye (2000), *Sénégal*, Paris: Jeune Afrique.

Dewey, J. [1916] (1966), *Democracy and Education*, New York: Free Press.

Dewey, J. and J. Tufts (1908), *Ethics*, New York: Henry Holt.

Diop, C. A. (1989), *The Cultural Unity of Black Africa: The Domains of Patriarchy and of Matriarchy in Classical Antiquity*, London: Karnak House.

Diop, N. J., M. M. Faye, A. Moreau, J. Cabral, H. Benga, F. Cissé, B. Mané, I. Baumgarten and M. Melching (2004), *The TOSTAN Program: Evaluation of a Community Based Education Program in Senegal*, Dakar: Population Council, GTZ and Tostan.

Diop, N. J., A. Moreau and H. Benga (2008), *Evaluation of the Long-Term Impact of the TOSTAN Programme on the Abandonment of FGM/C and Early Marriage: Results from a Qualitative Study in Senegal*, Washington DC: Population Council.

Diouf, M. (1992), 'State Formation and Legitimation Crisis in Senegal', *Review of African Political Economy*, 19(54), 117–25.

Djedje, J. C. (2008), *Fiddling in West Africa: Touching the Spirit in Fulbe, Hausa, and Dagbamba Cultures*, Bloomington: Indiana University Press.

Donnelly, J. (1984), 'Cultural Relativism and Universal Human-Rights', *Human Rights Quarterly*, 6(4), 400–19.

Donnelly, J. (2000), 'Human Rights and the Dialogue among Civilizations', unpublished paper, University of Denver.

Donnelly, J. (2003), *Universal Human Rights in Theory and Practice*, 2nd edn, New York: Cornell University Press.

Dupire, M. (1996), 'Reflexions sur l'ethnicité peul', in *Itinérances en pays peul et ailleurs, mélanges à la mémoire de P. F. Lacroix*, vol. 2, Paris: Société des africanistes, pp. 167–81.

Easterly, W. (2006), *The White Man's Burden*, Oxford: Oxford University Press.

Easton, P., K. Monkman and R. Miles (2003), 'Social Policy from the Bottom Up: Abandoning FGC in Sub-Saharan Africa', *Development in Practice*, 13(5), 445–58.

Easton, P., K. Monkman and R. Miles (2009), 'Breaking Out of the Egg', in J. Mezirow and E. W. Taylor (eds), *Transformative Learning in Practice: Insights from Community, Workplace, and Higher Education*, San Francisco: Jossey-Bass.

Ellerman, D. (2006), *Helping People Help Themselves*, Ann Arbor: University of Michigan Press.

Elster, J. (2007), *Explaining Social Behaviour: More Nuts and Bolts for the Social Sciences*, Cambridge: Cambridge University Press.

Engels, F. (1902), *The Origins of the Family, Private Property and the State*, Chicago: Kerr.

Englebert, P. (2009), *Africa: Unity, Sovereignty and Sorrow*, London: Lynne Rienner.

Eraut, M. (2000), 'Non-formal Learning, Implicit Learning and Tacit Knowledge in Professional Work', in F. Coffield (ed.), *The Necessity of Informal Learning*, Bristol: Policy Press, pp. 12–31.

Espskamp, K. (2006), *Theatre for Development: An Introduction to Context, Applications and Training*, London: Zed Books.

Fatton, R. (1987), *The Making of a Liberal Democracy: Senegal's Passive Revolution, 1975–1985*, Boulder, CO: Lynne Rienner.

Fausto-Sterling, A. (1985), *Myths of Gender*, 2nd edn, New York: Basic Books.

Fausto-Sterling, A. (1987), 'Society Writes Biology/Biology Constructs Gender', *Daedalus*, 116(4), 61–76.

Faye, J. (2008), *Land and Decentralisation in Senegal*, Nottingham: Russel Press.

Ferguson, J. (2005), 'Decomposing Modernity: History and Hierarchy after Development', in A. Loomba, K. Suvir, M. Bunzi, A. Burton and J. Esty (eds), *Postcolonial Studies and Beyond*, Durham, NC: Duke University Press, pp. 166–81.

Ferguson, J. (2006), *Global Shadows: Africa in the Neoliberal World Order*, Durham, NC and London: Duke University Press.

Flowers, N., M. Bernbaum, K. Rudelius-Palmer and J. Tolman (2000), *The Human Rights Education Handbook: Effective Practices for Learning, Action and Change*, Minneapolis: University of Minnesota Press.

Flowers, N., M. E. Brederode Santos, Z. Szelényi and D. Nagy (2007), *Compasito: Manual on Human Rights Education for Children*, Brussels: Council of Europe.

Folbre, N. (1982),'Exploitation Comes Home: A Critique of the Marxian Theory of Family Labour', *Cambridge Journal of Economics*, 6(4), 317–29.

Folbre, N. (1986), 'Hearts and Spades: Paradigms of Household Economics', *World Development*, 14(2), 245–55.

Fordham, P. E. (1993), 'Informal, Non-formal and Formal Education Programmes', in YMCA George Williams College, *YMCA George Williams College ICE301 Lifelong Learning Unit 2*, London: YMCA George Williams College.

Foucault, M. (1991), *Discipline and Punish: The Birth of a Prison*, London: Penguin.

Franck, T. M. (2001), 'Are Human Rights Universal?', *Foreign Affairs*, 80(1), 191–204.

Freeman, M. (2002), *Human Rights: An Interdisciplinary Approach*, Cambridge: Polity Press.

Freire, P. (1970), *Pedagogy of the Oppressed*, Harmondsworth: Penguin.

Freire, P. (1973), *Education for Critical Consciousness*, London: Continuum.

Freire, P. (1995), *Pedagogy of Hope: Reliving Pedagogy of the Oppressed*, New York: Continuum.

Freire, P. (1998), *Teachers as Cultural Workers: Letters to Those Who Dare Teach*, Boulder, CO: Westview Press.

Freire, P. (2001), *Pedagogy of Freedom: Ethics, Democracy, and Civic Courage*, Oxford: Rowman & Littlefield.

Freire, P. (2002), *Pedagogy of the Oppressed*, 30th anniversary edn, New York: Continuum.

Freire, P. and D. P. Macedo (1995),'A Dialogue: Culture, Language and Race', *Harvard Educational Review*, 65(3), 377–402.

Fulu, E. and S. Miedema (2015), 'Violence against Women: Globalizing the Integrated Ecological Model', *Violence against Women*, 21(12), 1431–55.

Gaventa, J. (1980), *Power and Powerlessness: Quiescence and Rebellion in an Appalachian Valley*, Urbana: University of Illinois Press.

Gaventa, J. (2003), *Power after Lukes: An Overview of Theories of Power since Lukes and Their Application to Development*, Brighton: Institute of Development Studies.

Gaventa, J. (2006), 'Finding the Spaces for Change: A Power Analysis', *IDS Bulletin*, 37(6), 23–33.

Gellar, S. (1995), *Senegal: An Africa Nation between Islam and the West*, Boulder, CO: Westview Press.

Gellar, S. (2005), *Democracy in Senegal*, New York: Palgrave.

Gerber, P. (2011), 'Education about Human Rights: Strengths and Weaknesses of the UN Declaration on Human Rights Education and Training', *Alternative Law Journal*, 36(4), 245–9.

Gillespie, D. and M. Melching (2010), 'The Transformative Power of Democracy and Human Rights in Nonformal Education: The Case of Tostan', *Adult Education Quarterly*, 60(5), 477–98.

Goodhart, M. (2003), 'Origins and Universality in the Human Rights Debate: Cultural Essentialism and the Challenge of Globalisation', *Human Rights Quarterly*, 25, 935–64.

Gramsci, A. (1972), *Selection from the Prison Notebooks*, New York: International Publishers.

Gueye, M., L. Gambi and F. Bonatesta (1995), *I Wolof del Senegal*, Turin: L'Harmattan.

Haffanden, W. J. R. (1930), *The Red Men of Nigeria*, London: Seeley, Service.

Harvey, D. (2005), *The New Imperialism*, Oxford: Oxford University Press.

Hayward, C. R. (2000), *De-facing Power*, Cambridge: Cambridge University Press.

Heilman, B. and S. Stich (2016), *Revising the Script: Taking Community Mobilization to Scale for Gender Equality*, Washington DC: International Center for Research on Women.

Hesseling, G. (1985), *Histoire politique du Sénégal. Institutions, droit et société*, Paris: Karthala.

Heyns, C. H. and F. Viljoen (2001), 'The Impact of the United Nations Human Rights Treaties on the Domestic Level', *Human Rights Quarterly*, 23(3), 483–535.

Hoffman, B. D. and C. C. Gibson (2005), 'Fiscal Governance and Public Services: Evidence from Tanzania and Zambia', paper presented at the WGAPE, Santa Clara University, <http://www.sscnet.ucla.edu/polisci/wgape/papers/9_GibsonHoffman.pdf> (last accessed 21 June 2017).

Hofstede, G. (2001), *Culture's Consequences: Comparing Values, Behaviors, Institutions, and Organizations across Nations*, Thousand Oaks, CA: Sage.

Hornberg, S. (2002), 'Human Rights Education as an Integral Part of General Education', *International Review of Education*, 48(3–4), 187–98.

Houtsma, M. T., A. J. Wensick, H. A. R. Gibb, W. Heffening and E. Lévi-Provençal (eds) (1993), *Brill's First Encyclopaedia of Islam, 1913–1936*, vol. 3, Leiden: Brill.

Hrbek, I. (1992), *General History of Africa*, abridged edn, vol. 3: *Africa from the Seventh to the Eleventh Century*, Berkeley: University of California Press.

Hudeki, M. (2008), 'Non-formal Education for Sustainable Development in Turkey', *Adult Education and Development*, 70(1), 169–78.

Human Rights Watch (2010), *'Off the Backs of Children': Forced Begging and Other Abuses against Talibés in Senegal*, New York: Human Rights Watch, <https://www.hrw.org/sites/default/files/reports/senegal0410webwcover.pdf> (last accessed 12 June 2017).

Human Rights Watch (2012), 'Senegal: Human Rights Priorities', <http://www.unhcr.org/refworld/docid/4f82e60a2.html> (last accessed 12 June 2017).

Huth, A. G., S. Nishimoto, A. T. Vu and J. L. Gallant (2012), 'A Continuous Semantic Space Describes the Representation of Thousands of Object and Action Categories across the Human Brain', *Neuron*, 76(6), 1210–24.

ICRW and Instituto Promundo (2007), *Engaging Men and Boys to Achieve Gender Equality: How Can We Build on What We Have Learned?*, <https://www.icrw.org/wp-content/uploads/2016/10/Engaging-Men-and-Boys-to-Achieve-Gender-Equality-How-Can-We-Build-on-What-We-Have-Learned.pdf> (last accessed 12 June 2017).

IPEC (2011), *Children in Hazardous Work: What We Know, What We Need to Do*, Geneva: International Labour Organization.

Issa, A. and R. Labatut (1974), *Sagesse de Peuls nomads*, Yaounde: Editions CLE.

Jennings, M. K. and R. G. Niemi (1981), *Generations and Politics*, Princeton, NJ: Princeton University Press.

Jewkes, R., M. Flood and J. Lang (2015), 'From Work with Men and Boys to Changes of Social Norms and Reduction of Inequities in Gender Relations: A Conceptual Shift in Prevention of Violence against Women and Girls', *The Lancet*, 385(9977), 1580–9.

Johnson, N. K. (2003), 'The Role of NGO in Senegal: Reconciling Human Rights Policies with Health and Developmental Strategies', paper presented at the American Political Science Association, Philadelphia.

Ka, S. (2001), 'Senegal', in J. Krieger (ed.), *The Oxford Companion to the Politics of the World*, 2nd edn, Oxford: Oxford University Press, pp. 761–2.

Kahneman, D. (2011), *Thinking, Fast and Slow*, New York: Farrar, Straus and Giroux.

Kardam, N. (2009), *Women's Human Rights Training Program 1995–2003: Evaluation Report*, <http://www.kadininsanhaklari.org/static/yayin/makale-rapor/eval_report.pdf> (last accessed 12 June 2017).

Kashima, Y., J. Shi, K. Tsuchiya, E. S. Kashima, S.Y.Y. Cheng, M. M. Chao and S. Shin (2011), 'Globalization and Folk Theory of Social Change: How Globalization Relates to Societal Perceptions about the Past and Future', *Journal of Social Issues*, 67, 696–715.

Kassé, A. F. (2003), 'Women in Politics in Senegal', paper presented at the IDEA, EISA and SADC Parliamentary Forum Conference on Implementation of Quotas: African Experiences, Pretoria, South Africa.

Keizer, K., S. Lindenberg and L. Steg (2013), 'The Importance of Demonstratively Restoring Order', *PLoS One*, 8(6), e65137.

Keown, D. (1995), 'Are There "Human Rights" in Buddhism?', *Journal of Buddhist Ethics*, 2, 3–27.

Kevane, M. (2004), *Women and Development in Africa*, London: Lynne Rienner.

Kevane, M. and L. Gray (1999), 'Diminished Access, Diverted Exclusion: Women and Land Tenure in Sub-Saharan Africa', *African Studies Review*, 42(2), 15–39.

Koenig, S. (2001), 'Human Rights Education for Social Transformation: Innovative Grassroots Programs on Economic, Social and Cultural Rights', in D. Barnhizer (ed.), *Effective Strategies for Protecting Human Rights: Prevention and Intervention, Trade and Education*, Aldershot: Ashgate.

Krause, G. A. (1883), 'Die Fulen (Ful-be) in Afrika und ihr Ursprung, das Ausland', *Wochenschrift für Länder-und Völkerkunde*, 56, 181–9.

Kuiper, E. and J. Sap (1995), *Out of the Margin: Feminist Perspectives on Economics*, New York: Routledge.

Kuschel, K. J. and H. Küng (eds) (1993), *A Global Ethic: The Declaration of the Parliament of the World's Religions*, London: SCM Press.

Kyegombe, N., E. Starmann, K. M. Devries, L. Michau, J. Nakuti, T. Musuya, C. Watts and L. Heise (2014), 'SASA! is the medicine that treats violence': Qualitative Findings on How a Community Mobilisation Intervention to Prevent Violence against Women Created Change in Kampala, Uganda', *Global Health Action*, 7, 25082.

Lamberts, K. and D. Shanks (eds) (1997), *Knowledge, Concepts, and Categories*, Hove: Psychology Press.

Lave, J. and E. Wenger (1991), *Situated Learning*, Cambridge: Cambridge University Press.

Leblon, A. (2006), *Le puulaku. Bilan critique des études de l'identité peule en Afrique de l'Ouest*, Aix-en-Provence: CEMAF.

Leymarie, I. (1978), 'The Role and Function of the Griots among the Wolof of Senegal', PhD dissertation, Columbia University.

Lohrenscheit, C. (2002), 'International Approaches in Human Rights Education', *International Review of Education*, 48(3–4), 173–285.

Lohrenscheit, C. (2006), 'Dialogue and Dignity – Linking Human Rights Education with Paulo Freire's "Education for Liberation"', *Journal of Social Sciences Education*, 5(1), 126–34.

Loomis, N. (2012), 'Police, Protesters Clash as Senegal Vote Nears', *CNN*, 17 February, <http://edition.cnn.com/2012/02/17/world/africa/senegal-violence> (last accessed 12 June 2017).

Lukes, S. (1974), *Power: A Radical View*, 2nd edn, New York: Macmillan.

Maccoby, E. E. (1995), 'The Two Sexes and Their Social Systems', in P. Moen, G. H. Elder and K. Lüscher (eds), *Examining Lives in Context: Perspectives on the Ecology of Human Development*, Washington DC: American Psychological Association, pp. 347–64.

McCowan, T. (2011), 'Human Rights, Capabilities and the Normative Basis of "Education for All"', *Theory and Research in Education*, 9(3), 283–98.

McFarland, S. (2008), 'A Tribute to the Architects: Eleanor Roosevelt, Charles Malik, Peng-chun Chang, John Humphrey, and René Cassin', paper presented at the ISPP 31st Annual Scientific Meeting, Sciences Po, Paris, <http://www.allacademic.com/meta/p261353_index.html> (last accessed 12 June 2017).

Mackie, G. (2000), 'Female Genital Cutting: The Beginning of the End', in B. Shell-Duncan and Y. Hernlund (eds), *Female Circumcision in Africa: Culture, Controversy and Change*, Boulder, CO: Lynne Rienner, pp. 253–81.

Mackie, G. and J. LeJeune (2009), *Social Dynamics of Abandonment of Harmful Practices: A New Look at the Theory*, vol. 2009-06, Florence: Innocenti Research Centre.

McLaughlin, F. (1995), 'Haalpulaar Identity as a Response to Wolofization', *African Languages and Culture*, 8(2), 153–68.

McQuoid-Mason, D., E. L. O'Brien and E. Green (1991), *Human Rights for All: Education Towards a Rights Culture*, Claremont: David Philip Publishers.

Mahabal, K. B. (2005), 'Reframing Human Rights', paper presented at the Third Berlin Roundtables on Transnationality (Reframing Human Rights I), 3–7 October 2005, <http://www.irmgard-coninx-stiftung.de/fileadmin/user_upload/pdf/archive/138Bali-Mahabal.pdf> (last accessed 1 January 2016).

Mahruf, C., M. Shohel and A. J. Howes (2006), 'Nonformal Education for Sustainable Development: A Bangladeshi Perspective', paper presented at the 10th APED International Conference on Education, Bangkok.

Manglapus, R. S. (1978), 'Human Rights Are Not a Western Discovery', *Worldview*, 4, 2, <http://worldview.cceia.org/archive/worldview/1978/10/3101.html/_res/id=sa_File1/v21_i010_a001.pdf> (last accessed 12 June 2017).

Mann, M. (1986), *The Sources of Social Power*, Cambridge: Cambridge University Press.

Marks, S. (1983), 'Peace, Development, Disarmament and Human-Rights Education: The Dilemma between the Status-Quo and Curriculum Overload', *International Review of Education*, 29(3), 289–310.

Mayo, P. (1999), *Gramsci, Freire and Adult Education: Possibilities for Transformative Action*, London: Zed Books.

Mbaye, A. (2007), *Outcomes and Impact of Adult Literacy Programs in Senegal: Two Case Studies*, College Park: University of Maryland.

Mbow, P. (2008), 'Senegal: The Return of Personalism', *Journal of Democracy*, 19(1), 156–69.

Mbow, P. (2009), 'Evolving Role for Senegalese Women in Religion', *Common Ground News Service*, 10 March, <http://www.commongroundnews.org/article.php?id=25012&lan=en&sid=1&sp=1&isNew=0> (last accessed 12 June 2017).

Mehta, C. and J. Strough (2010), 'Gender Segregation and Gender-Typing in Adolescence', *Sex Roles*, 63(3–4), 251–63.

Meillassoux, C. (1960), 'Essai d'interprétation du phénomène économique dans les sociétés traditionnelles d'autosubsistance', *Cahiers d'études africaines*, 4, 38–67.

Meillassoux, C. (1973), 'The Social Organisation of the Peasantry: The Economic Basis of Kinship', *Journal of Peasant Studies*, 1(1), 81–90.

Meillassoux, C. (1991), *Femmes, greniers et capitaux*, 2nd edn, Paris: L'Harmattan.

Meintjes, G. (1997), 'Human Rights Education as Empowerment: Reflections on Pedagogy', in R. P. Claude and G. J. Andreopoulos (eds), *Human Rights Education for the Twenty-First Century*, Philadelphia: University of Philadelphia Press, pp. 64–80.

Meisek, S. (2004), 'Which Catharsis Do They Mean? Aristotle, Moreno, Boal and Organization Theatre', *Organization Studies*, 25(5), 797–816.

Mergner, G. (2004), 'Paulo Freire, algunas ideas sobre la razón en la soldaridad', in A. M. Araújo Freire (ed.), *La pedagogía de la liberació en Paulo Freire*, Barcelona: Grao, pp. 71–94.

Merry, S. E. (2006), *Human Rights and Gender Violence: Translating International Law into Local Justice*, Chicago: University of Chicago Press.

Messer, E. (1993), 'Anthropology and Human Rights', *Annual Review of Anthropology*, 22, 221–49.

Mill, J. S. [1869] (2008), *The Subjection of Women*, Philadelphia: University of Pennsylvania Press.

Ministère de l'Intérieur (2008), *Decret n° 2008-747 du 10 juillet 2008 portant création de départements et d'arrondissements*, Dakar: Secrétariat Général du Gouvernement, <http://www.jo.gouv.sn/spip.php?article7212> (last accessed 12 June 2017).

Monteil, C. (1950), 'Réflexions sur le problème des Peul', *Journal de la Société des Africanistes*, 20(2), 153–92.

Morsink, J. (1999), *The Universal Declaration of Human Rights: Origins, Drafting and Intent*, Philadelphia: University of Pennsylvania Press.

Moyo, D. (2009), *Dead Aid*, New York: Penguin Books.

Mukhopadhyay, M. (1995), 'Gender Relations, Development Practice and "Culture"', *Gender and Development*, 3(1), 13–18.

Murithi, T. (2007), 'A Local Response to the Global Human Rights Standard: The Ubuntu Perspective on Human Dignity', *Globalisation, Societies and Education*, 5(3), 277–86.

Mutua, M. (1996), 'The Ideology of Human Rights', *Virginia International Law Journal*, 36(Spring), 589–657.

Mutua, M. (2007), 'Standard Setting in Human Rights: Critique and Prognosis', *Human Rights Quarterly*, 29(3), 547–630.

Nash, J. (1952), 'Non-Cooperative Games', *The Annals of Mathematics*, 54(2), 286–95.

Nieuwenhuys, O. (1996), 'The Paradox of Child Labor and Anthropology', *Annual Review of Anthropology*, 25, 237–51.

Nisbett, R. E., K. Peng, I. Choi and A. Norenzayan (2001), 'Culture and Systems of Thought: Holistic Versus Analytic Cognition', *Psychological Review*, 108(2), 291–310.

Nussbaum, M. (1997), *Cultivating Humanity: A Classical Defence of Reform in Liberal Education*, Cambridge, MA: Harvard University Press.

Nussbaum, M. (1999), 'In Defense of Universal Values', *Occasional Paper Series*, Notre Dame: The Joan B. Kroc Institute for International Peace Studies at the University of Notre Dame, <http://philosophy.uchicago.edu/faculty/files/nussbaum/In Defense of Universal Values.pdf> (last accessed 12 June 2017).

Nussbaum, M. (2000), *Women and Human Development: The Capabilities Approach*, New York: Cambridge University Press.

Nussbaum, M. (2011), *Creating Capabilities*, London: Harvard University Press.

Ogawa, R. (1993), 'Ethnic Identity and Social Interaction: A Reflection on Fulbe Identity', in Y. Azarya and P. K. Eguchi (eds), *Unity and Diversity of a People: The Search for Fulbe Identity*, Osaka: MINPAKU, pp. 37–69.

Ogawa, R. (1994), 'Gaabgol et Kuumeen: Cohésion sociale et disparités économiques', *Cahiers d'études africaines*, 34(133–5), 281–93.

OHCHR (1998), *United Nations Decade for Human Rights Education 1995–2004: Lessons for Life*, HR/PUB/DECADE/1998/1, New York: United Nations.

OHCHR (2003), 'Summary of National Initiatives Undertaken within the Decade for Human Rights Education (1995–2004)', <http://www.ohchr.org/EN/Issues/Education/Training/Pages/Initiatives.aspx> (last accessed 12 June 2017).

OHCHR (2006), *Plan of Action for the World Programme for Human Rights Education*, New York: United Nations.

OHCHR (2011), *United Nations Declaration on Human Rights Education and Training*, A/HRC/RES/16/1, Geneva: United Nations.

Osborne, M. (2000), *An Introduction to Game Theory*, Oxford: Oxford University Press.

Osler, A. and H. Starkey (1996), *Teacher Education and Human Rights*, London: David Fulton.

Ouattara, M., P. Sen and M. Thomson (1998), 'Forced Marriage, Forced Sex', *Gender and Development*, 6(3), 27–33.

Pearson, R. and C. Sweetman (eds) (2011), *Gender and the Economic Crisis*, London: Oxfam.

Perry, D. (2009), 'Fathers, Sons, and the State', *Cultural Anthropology*, 24(1), 33–67.

Phillipson, R. (1996), 'Linguistic Imperialism', *English Language Teaching*, 50(6), 160–7.

Pollis, A. and P. Schwab (1979), *Human Rights: Cultural and Ideological Perspectives*, New York: Praeger.

Population Council (2009), 'Abriendo Oportunidades ("Opening Opportunities")', <http://www.popcouncil.org/research/abriendo-oportunidades-opening-opportunities> (last accessed 12 June 2017).

Preis, A.-B. (1996), 'Human Rights as Cultural Practice: An Anthropological Critique', *Human Rights Quarterly*, 18(2), 286–315.

Print, M., C. Ugarte, C. Naval and A. Mihr (2008), 'Moral and Human Rights Education: The Contribution of the United Nations', *Journal of Moral Education*, 37(1), 115–32.

Putnam, R. D. (1973), *The Beliefs of Politicians: Ideology, Conflict, and Democracy in Britain and Italy*, New Haven, CT: Yale University Press.

Quartz, S. R. and T. J. Sejnowski (2002), *Liars, Lovers, and Heroes: What the New Brain Science Reveals about How We Become Who We Are*, New York: W. B. Morrow.

Rahman, A. and N. Toubia (2000), *Female Genital Mutilation: A Guide to Laws and Policies Worldwide*, New York: Zed Books.

Raising Voices, LSHTM and CEDOVIP (2015), *Is Violence against Women Preventable? Findings from the SASA! Study Summarized for General Audiences*, Kampala: Raising Voices.

Ralph, M. (2015), *Forensics of Capital*, Chicago: University of Chicago Press.

Ramcharan, B. G. (2000), 'Human Rights: Universality and Cultural Diversity', in F. Coomans (ed.), *Rendering Justice to the Vulnerable*, The Hague: Kluwer Law International, pp. 239–58.

Ratman, D. (2015), 'Dignity to Sex Work', *Live Mint*, 7 November, <http://www.livemint.com/Leisure/pNfD4rrJwCji3JVwtzDmYP/Dignity-to-sex-work.html> (last accessed 12 June 2017).

Ray, D. (ed.) (1994), *Education for Human Rights: An International Perspective*, Paris: International Bureau of Education.

République du Sénégal (1996), *Decret n° 96-228 du 22 mars 1996 modifiant le décret n° 72-636 du 29 mai 1972 relatif aux attributions des chefs de circonscription administrative et des chefs de village*, Dakar: République du Sénégal, <http://www.jo.gouv.sn/spip.php?article7746> (last accessed 12 June 2017).

Riesman, P. (1992), *First Find Your Child a Good Mother*, New Brunswick, NJ: Rutgers University Press.

Risse, T., S. C. Ropp and K. Sikkink (eds) (1999), *The Power of Human Rights: International Norms and Domestic Change*, 7th edn, Cambridge: Cambridge University Press.

Rodin, A. M. (2012), *The Contribution of Human Rights Education to Building Peaceful Coexistence in Schools Based on Democracy and Solidarity*, Washington DC: Office of Education and Culture, Organization of American States, <http://portal.oas.org/LinkClick.aspx?fileticket=oEfUgsWxpUM=&tabid=1232> (last accessed 12 June 2017).

Rogow, D., N. Haberland, A. Del Valle, N. Lee, G. Osakue, Z. Sa and M. Skaer (2013), 'Integrating Gender and Rights into Sexuality Education:

Field Reports on Using It's All One', *Reproductive Health Matters*, 21(41), 154–66.

Rousseau, J.-J. [1762] (1979), *Emile, or on Education*, New York: Basic Books.

Sachs, J. (2005), *The End of Poverty: Economic Possibilities for Our Time*, New York: Penguin Press.

Sako, P. S. (1998), *Senegal*, Bologna: Pendragon.

Salamone, F. A. (1985), 'Colonialism and the Emergence of Fulani Identity', *Journal of Asian and African Studies*, 20(3–4), 194–202.

Salamone, F. A. (1997), 'Fulbe/Fulani/Peul: Cattle Pastoralism, Migration, Seventeenth and Eighteenth Centuries', in K. Shillington (ed.), *Encyclopedia of African History*, vol. 1, London: Fitzroy Dearborn, pp. 534–5.

Sall, I.-A. (1999), 'Crise identitaire ou stratégie de positionnement politique en Mauritanie: le cas des Fulɓe Aynaaɓe', in A. Bourgeot (ed.), *Horizons nomades en Afrique sahélienne. Sociétés, développement et démocratie*, Paris: Karthala, pp. 79–98.

Saltzman Chafetz, J. (2006), *Sociology of Gender*, New York: Springer.

Salzman, P. (1980), 'Processes of Sedentarization as Adaptation and Response', in P. Salzman (ed.), *When Nomads Settle*, New York: Praeger.

Santoir, C. (1994), 'Décadence et résistance du pastoralisme. Les Peuls de la vallée du fleuve Sénégal', *Cahiers d'études africaines*, 34(133–5), 231–63.

Schattschneider, E. E. (1960), *The Semisovereign People: A Realist's View of Democracy in America*, New York: Holt, Rinehart and Winston.

Seck, P. (2007), *The Rural Energy Challenge in Senegal: A Mission Report*, Geneva: World Health Organization.

Sen, A. (1990), 'Gender and Cooperative Conflicts', in I. Tinker (ed.), *Persistent Inequalities: Women and World Development*, New York: Oxford University Press, pp. 123–49.

Sen, A. (1995), 'Gender Inequalities and Theories of Justice', in M. Nussbaum and J. Glover (eds), *Culture, Women and Development*, New York: Oxford University Press, pp. 259–74.

Sen, A. (1999), *Development as Freedom*, Oxford: Oxford University Press.

Sen, A. (2007), *Identity and Violence: The Illusion of Destiny*, London: Penguin.

Sen, G. and C. Grown (1987), *Development, Crises and Alternative Visions*, New York: Monthly Review.

Seshu, M. S. and A. Pai (2014), 'Sex Work Undresses Patriarchy with Every Trick!', *IDS Bulletin*, 45(1), 46–52.

Sfard, A. (1998), 'On Two Metaphors for Learning and the Dangers of Choosing Just One', *Educational Researcher*, 27(2), 4–13.

Shell-Duncan, B. (2008), 'From Health to Human Rights: Female Genital Cutting and the Politics of Intervention', *American Anthropologist*, 110(2), 225–36.

Shor, I. and P. Freire (1987), 'What Is the Dialogical Method of Teaching?', *Journal of Education*, 169(3), 11–31.

Skutnabb-Kangas, T. (2000), *Linguistic Genocide in Education or Worldwide Diversity and Human Rights?*, Mahwah, NJ: Lawrence Erlbaum Associates.

Sow, F. (2003), 'Fundamentalisms, Globalisation and Women's Human Rights in Senegal', *Gender and Development*, 11(1), 69–76.

Spring, J. (2000), *The Universal Right to Education: Justification, Definition, and Guidelines*, Mahwah, NJ: Lawrence Erlbaum Associates.

Starkey, H. (ed.) (1991a), *The Challenge of Human Rights Education*, London: Cassell for Council of Europe.

Starkey, H. (ed.) (1991b), *Socialisation of School Children and Their Education for Democratic Values and Human Rights: Report of the Colloquy of Directors of Educational Research Institutions*, Strasbourg: Council of Europe.

Stenning, D. J. (1959), *Savanna Nomads*, London: Oxford University Press.

Stockman, L. and C. Barnes (1997), 'Minority Children of Somalia', in M. S. Hamus, S. Chakma, K. Hedlund Thulin and A. S. Monzòn (eds), *War: The Impact on Minority and Indigenous Children*, London: Minority Rights Group International, pp. 111–32.

Strauss, C. and N. Quinn (1997), *A Cognitive Theory of Cultural Meaning*, Cambridge: Cambridge University Press.

Stroud, C. (2003), 'Postmodernist Perspectives on Local Languages: African Mother-Tongue Education in Times of Globalisation', *International Journal of Bilingual Education and Bilingualism*, 6(1), 17–36.

Suárez, D. (2007), 'Education Professionals and the Construction of Human Rights Education', *Comparative Education Review*, 51(1), 48–70.

Suárez, D. and F. Ramirez (2004), 'Human Rights and Citizenship: The Emergence of Human Rights Education', *CDDRL Working Papers*, 12, <http://cddrl.fsi.stanford.edu/sites/default/files/ramirez_suarez_6.25.2004.pdf> (last accessed 12 June 2017).

Sweetman, C. (1995), 'Editorial', *Gender and Development*, 3(1), 1–6.

Szeftel, M. (2000), 'Clientelism, Corruption & Catastrophe', *Review of African Political Economy*, 27(85), 427–41.

Talla, R. (1999), 'Participation des femmes aux instances de décision au Sénégal. Des chiffres qui parlent [Participation of Women in Decision-Making in Senegal. The Numbers That Speak]', *Pop Sahel: bulletin d'information sur la population et le développement*, 28, 38–41.

Tibbits, F. (2002), 'Understanding What We Do: Emerging Models of Human Rights Education', *International Review of Education*, 48(3–4), 159–71.

Tibbits, F. (2017), 'Evolution of Human Rights Education Models', in M. Bajaj (ed.), *Human Rights Education: Theory, Research, Praxis*, Philadelphia: University of Pennsylvania Press, pp. 69–95.

Tomaševski, K. (2001), *Human Rights in Education as a Prerequisite for Human Rights Education*, Gothenburg: Raoul Wallenberg Institute.

Torelli, C. J. and A. M. Kaikati (2009), 'Values as Predictors of Judgments and Behaviors: The Role of Abstract and Concrete Mindsets', *Journal of Personality and Social Psychology*, 96(1), 231–47.

Tostan (2009a), *Kobi I – Manual of the Facilitator*, English edn, Dakar: Tostan.

Tostan (2009b), *Tostan: Creating Community-Led Development through Participatory Education*, Dakar: Tostan.

Tostan (2009c), *Tostan: Community-Led Development*, Washington DC: Tostan.

Toulmin, C. (2007), 'Negotiating Accesss to Land in West Africa', in B. Derman, R. Odgaard and E. Sjaastad (eds), *Conflicts over Land and Water in Africa*, Oxford: James Currey.

Tsikata, D. (2009), 'Gender, Land and Labour Relations and Livelihoods in Sub-Saharan Africa in the Era of Economic Liberalisation', *Feminist Africa*, 12, 11–30.

UN (2011), 'Praising Senegal's Progress on Human Rights, UN Official Says More Work Is Needed', *UN News Service*, 18 March <http://www.unhcr.org/refworld/docid/4d884f88d.html> (last accessed 12 June 2017).

UNDP (2010), *Human Development Report 2010*, New York: Palgrave Macmillan.

UNDP (2016), *Human Development Report 2016*, New York: United Nations Development Programme.

UNECA (2013), *Economic Report on Africa*, Addis Ababa: United Nations Economic Commission for Africa.

UNESCO (1974), *Recommendation Concerning Education for International Understanding, Co-operation and Peace and Education Relating to Human Rights and Fundamental Freedoms*, Paris: United Nations Educational, Scientific and Cultural Organization.

UNESCO (2001), *Le développement de l'éducation. Rapport national du Sénégal*, Paris: United Nations Educational, Scientific and Cultural Organization.

UNESCO (2003), *UNESCO and Human Rights Education*, Paris: United Nations Educational, Scientific and Cultural Organization.

UNESCO (2006), *Guidebook for Planning Education in Emergency and Reconstruction*, Paris: United Nations Educational, Scientific and Cultural Organization.

UNICEF (2001), *Early Marriage and Child Spouses*, Florence: Innocenti Research Centre.

UNICEF (2005), *Female Genital Mutilation/Cutting: A Statistical Exploration*, New York: United Nations Children's Fund.

UNICEF (2008a), *Coordinated Strategy to Abandon Female Genital Mutilation/Cutting in One Generation*, New York: United Nations Children's Fund.

UNICEF (2008b), *Long-Term Evaluation of the Tostan Programme in Senegal: Kolda, Thiès and Fatick Regions*, New York: United Nations Children's Fund.

UNICEF (2009a), *Rapport de l'enquête sur les objectifs de la fin de décennie sur l'enfance*, Dakar: Government of Senegal and United Nations Children's Fund.

UNICEF (2009b), *State of the World's Children*, New York: United Nations Children's Fund.

United Nations (1948), *The Universal Declaration of Human Rights*, <http://www.un.org/en/universal-declaration-human-rights/index.html> (last accessed 12 June 2017).

United Nations (1966), *International Covenant on Economic, Social and Cultural Rights*, <http://www.ohchr.org/EN/ProfessionalInterest/Pages/CESCR.aspx> (last accessed 12 June 2017).

United Nations (1979), *Convention on the Elimination of All Forms of Discrimination against Women*, <https://www.un.org/womenwatch/daw/cedaw/> (last accessed 12 June 2017).

United Nations (1989), *Convention on the Rights of the Child*, <http://www.unicef.org/crc/> (last accessed 12 June 2017).

United Nations (1999), *Convention Concerning the Prohibition and Immediate Action for the Elimination of the Worst Forms of Child Labour*, <http://www.ilo.org/dyn/normlex/en/f?p=1000:12100:0::NO::P12100_INSTRUMENT_ID:312327> (last accessed 12 June 2017).

United Nations (2008), 'Drafting of the Universal Declaration of Human Rights: A Historical Record of the Drafting Process', <http://research.un.org/en/undhr> (last accessed 12 June 2017).

United Nations (2011a), *Core Document Forming Part of the Reports of States Parties: Senegal*, Geneva: United Nations, <http://www2.ohchr.org/english/bodies/cerd/docs/coredocs/HRI.CORE.SEN.2011.pdf> (last accessed 12 June 2017).

United Nations (2011b), *Resolution Adopted by the Human Rights Council 16/1: United Nations Declaration on Human Rights Education and Training*, A/HRC/RES/16/1, New York: United Nations, <https://documents-dds-ny.un.org/doc/RESOLUTION/GEN/G11/124/78/PDF/G1112478.pdf?OpenElement> (last accessed 12 June 2017).

VAMP/SANGRAM (2011), 'The VAMP/SANGRAM Sex Worker's Movement in India's Southwest', in S. Batliwala (ed.), *Changing Their World*, 2nd edn, Toronto: Association for Women's Rights in Development, pp. 33–5.

Van Dyken, J. (1990), 'The Role of Languages of Minority Groups for Literacy and Education in Africa', *African Studies Review*, 33(3), 39–52.

Walker, M. and E. Unterhalter (2010), *Amartya Sen's Capability Approach and Social Justice in Education*, New York: Palgrave Macmillan.

Waltz, S. (2001), 'Universalizing Human Rights: The Role of Small States in the Construction of the Universal Declaration of Human Rights', *Human Rights Quarterly*, 23(1), 44–72.

Weber, M. (1968), *Economy and Society*, New York: Bedminster Press.

Weber, M., A. M. Henderson and T. Parsons (1947), *The Theory of Social and Economic Organization*, Oxford: Oxford University Press.

Wehr, H. and S. E. Tum (2013), 'When a Girl's Decision Involves the Community: The Realities of Adolescent Maya Girls' Lives in Rural Indigenous Guatemala,' *Reproductive Health Matters*, 21(41), 136–42.

Weinbrenner, P. and K. P. Fritzsche (1993), *Teaching Human Rights: Suggestions for Teaching Guidelines*, Berlin: German Commission for UNESCO.

Weiss, Y. (1997), 'The Formation and Dissolution of Families: Why Marry? Who Marries Whom? And What Happens upon Divorce?', in M. R. Rosenzweig and O. Stark (eds), *Handbook of Population and Family Economics*, Amsterdam: Elsevier Science, pp. 82–123.

Welch, C. E. J. (1995), *Protecting Human Rights in Africa: Strategies and Roles of Nongovernmental Organizations*, Philadelphia: University of Pennsylvania Press.

Wenger, E. (1998), *Communities of Practice*, Cambridge: Cambridge University Press.

Wenger, E., R. McDermott and W. M. Snyder (2002), *Cultivating Communities of Practice*, Boston: Harvard Business School Press.

White, J. (2000), 'Rural Transition: Agricultural Development and Tenure Rights', paper, Washington DC: Johns Hopkins University.

World Bank (2013), 'Senegal', World Development Indicators, <http://data.worldbank.org/country/senegal> (last accessed 12 June 2017).

Zechenter, E. M. (1997), 'In the Name of Culture: Cultural Relativism and the Abuse of the Individual', *Journal of Anthropological Research*, 53(3), 319–47.

Zounmenou, D. (2008), 'Senegal's Democracy: Has Wade Lost His Edge?', *African Security Review*, 17(3), 75–9.

INDEX

EU representative:
Easy Access System Europe
Mustamäe tee 50, 10621 Tallinn, Estonia
Gpsr.requests@easproject.com

www.ingramcontent.com/pod-product-compliance
Lightning Source LLC
Chambersburg PA
CBHW050631280326
41932CB00015B/2599